# YOU WON'T BELIEVE THIS!

## UNDERSTANDING AND MANAGING THE HABITS OF

# GOSSIP

**Arthur Dykstra, Timothy Williams,
Elaine Porterfield**

 High Tide Press

Published by High Tide Press, Inc.

301 Veterans Parkway, New Lenox, IL  60451

www.cherryhillhightide.com

You won't believe this! Understanding and managing the habits of gossip,
Arthur Dykstra, Timothy Williams and Elaine Porterfield

ISBN: 978-1-892696-47-9

Interior illustrations by Brian B. Oyster

Printed in the United States of America

# TABLE OF CONTENTS

# ACKNOWLEDGMENTS

A good editor is an invaluable ally and resource when writing a book. The authors of this book owe a deep debt of gratitude to our editor at High Tide Press, Mary Rundell-Holmes. She was tireless in keeping us on track, ensuring the quality of writing and making sure that all footnotes and endnotes were included and properly formatted. We are also deeply grateful to the other staff at High Tide, including Anne Ward who read and critiqued an original draft of the book. Her work, along with that of Catrina Harris on design and graphics, is much appreciated. Bob Sandidge deserves a word of thanks as well for reviewing the book, taking on the little jobs that moved the project towards completion and his substantial efforts developing promotional material.

The authors also owe a debt of gratitude to persons who provided valuable input on content. Blaine Sampson of Blue Ocean Consulting provided a lengthy interview useful for the chapter on high-tech gossip. Jamal Rahman, a Muslim Sufi minister, gave freely of his time to provide insight into what Islam has to say about gossip. Rabbi Ted Falcon provided extensive discussion and source material on Judaism and gossip. Others who shared specific examples and concerns about gossip include Joan Hallinan, Nate Cohen and Judy Lensen. Thanks also to Jim and Elaine Nelson for their encouragement.

Valuable administrative support came from Patti Marcellus and Debra Lynn Raimondi. In addition, we appreciate the help of Mike Mecozzi, Sherry Ladislas and Thane Dykstra, who read early drafts of the work and offered their input.

The authors are further indebted to the boards of Trinity Services and Trinity Foundation for their encouragement and support. Trinity Services Board of Directors: Raymond McShane, Ken Stromsland, Barbara Hall, Jan Agazzi, Scott Creech, Bob Libman, Barbara McGoldrick and Rolf Troha. Trinity Foundation Board of Directors: George Troha, Mike Sieling, John Slack, Robert Borgstrom, Klint DeGeus and Charley Smith.

This work is the creation of three authors who shared in the origination of thought, the research behind the ideas and the work of putting thought and research on paper. They are grateful to each other for the open discussion of ideas, the collaborative spirit in which work was completed and the support to the project that each provided. The process took longer than expected, but it always proceeded with positive energy.

And, finally, a special thanks to Charley Smith who finally let Art drive.

# INTRODUCTION

## The most powerful force in the universe is gossip.
### 16TH CENTURY POET

T he voicemail to the human resource director came anonymously, "Check out the relationship between a certain female manager and a recently hired young man that she supervises. The pair is secretly dating," the caller stated before hanging up. Gossip? Maybe. Should it simply be ignored? Probably not.

Many managers can be forgiven for thinking of gossip as unworthy of their attention since they consider it idle chitchat for nosey workers who should be engaged in more productive activities. Certainly, the tendency through the years has been to dismiss it as a pastime for the less educated or the lower ranks. Check out any MBA syllabus, and you almost certainly won't find a course on gossip, though you'll find plenty on organizational efficiencies or on teaming and collaborative strategies.

But is gossip trivial? Is it really unworthy of a manager's attention?

We strongly believe that the answer is no. The truth is that gossip can have a major destructive impact on an organization, so it is clearly worth your attention. Gossip, all too often, represents the destructive side of human communication. Through it, people express anger, concern, fear, disappointment, anxiety and even superiority. It's a predictable aspect of human interactions, and undoubtedly has been around as long as humans have communicated with one another.

Gossip is about enforcing social norms and morality, often in a destructive manner. It's about rebelling in repressive environments. It's a way to pull down a fellow worker seen as uppity. It's often a red flag that something is amiss in a workplace, long before a brave or smart worker approaches a manager to discuss a problem openly.

Does any of this sound familiar? It should. Many managers (and, frankly, anyone else working in an organization) have likely encountered or will encounter a situation like the one that follows, in that favorite newspaper personal advice column, "Dear Abby." Smile at the venue, if you will, but this letter makes clear the psychic toll gossip can take on any workforce.

> Dear Abby,
>
> After I dated an older man, I gained a bad reputation among some lower-level, gossipy co-workers at my job, even though I tried to keep it quiet and denied it.
>
> Now I've started a friendship with an older man at the company where I work. Although we are just friends, these co-workers think there is something more and are spreading gossip saying that we are having an affair.
>
> This could be damaging to both my career and my friendships with the man and my co-workers. How can I stop the gossip? Or does my past behavior make me forever guilty?
>
> -Not loving it in New York[1]

During the past forty years, we've had the opportunity, from many different perspectives, to evaluate the negative impact of gossip in the workplace. As employees, as managers, a CEO and president of a major human service agency, a professor, a journalist, an arbitrator of employee disputes and even occasional gossips ourselves, we have seen and experienced the impact of gossip in the workplace. This collective experience combined with a strong interest in researching the subject and concern with what can be done about gossip in the workplace led to this book.

But don't just take our word on the importance of tending to gossip in the workplace. As we'll show you, recent public discourse on the topic is simultaneously enlightening, unnerving and fascinating.

But that discourse doesn't limit itself to the problem of gossip in the workplace. Rather, the subject is much broader, encompassing family life, churches, volunteer groups, youth sports, any professional association that we belong to and the political arena. Malicious communication is all too often an element in every aspect of our personal and professional lives. While we have restricted the scope of this book largely to the workplace, the concepts often have universal application. A church pastor may have as much interest in the information as a manager at a local car dealership, a college dean as much as a construction project manager.

We realize that categories are often artificial. This is clearly true with the concept of gossip. A review of the literature shows that the word *gossip* encompasses a variety of different types of informal communication. We're using the term in a narrow and restricted way, focusing on communication that is personally harmful, malicious and often vicious. In our definition, gossip simply doesn't occur in the presence of the person being talked about. And, if the gossiper is confronted with statements that were made, he or she will usually flatly deny it.

Furthermore, we're specifically concerned with gossip's negative impact on performance within an organizational or institutional setting. Our primary goal is to provide a thorough understanding of gossip and offer some strategies leaders can use to overcome its destructiveness. Informal communication is an essential part of organizational behavior in our view, but it doesn't have to have a malicious, corrosive element. Gossip is all too often a beast running free in the workplace, inflicting great harm. It must be tamed and controlled to minimize the damage, allowing those in a workplace to work in harmony and achieve their greatest potential.

Managers, who are concerned with the well-being of their employees and with organizational performance, must use as much sophistication when dealing with gossip as they would any other problematic area of business life. Managing gossip requires work, because when a leader or manager analyzes it, he or she must also think about concerns like the atmosphere of a workplace, whether interactions between employees tend to be more positive than negative and whether positive communication is even encouraged. It makes managers think about a workplace's corporate culture or style, something often admittedly uncomfortable. But ignore it at your own peril. If the style of your workplace is oppressive, or the overall tone or practices in the workplace seem repressive, you will inevitably find toxic gossip flourishing. In addition, it's important to remember that culture trumps policies and procedures every time.

Consider the case we started this introduction with–the anonymous accusations regarding the supervisor and the young man she supervised. The message on the answering machine was not gossip per se. (The explanation for this appears later in the book.) However, the phone message may very well have been the product of workplace gossip because, without question, personal relationships between supervisors and subordinates are a tempting venue for malicious communication.

Let's look more closely at the circumstances and their impact. Here were two good employees–one with solid tenure with her company and one who had been recently hired and already shown substantial promise. The personal relationship between them caused not one but three anonymous phone calls. Why anonymous? Did employees at the company fear retribution if they spoke on the record to upper managers about the relationship in question? Or was the subject so uncomfortable employees simply didn't want to talk openly with management about it?

Whatever the reason, the situation became so inflamed, and those involved so consumed by the gossip around it, that the supervisor handed in her resignation under some pressure from management, and the young man quit his job. That meant this company lost two employees; one new and energetic and one who had provided valuable leadership over several years. While the accusation turned out to be true, the problem of the personal relationship was easier to deal with (many organizations have specific policies to manage these situations) than the impact of the gossip on this workplace.

Our consulting experience convinces us that gossip is a critical, often volatile issue for managers, one that is at times extremely difficult to address. But with some reflection and practice, we believe that gossip can be understood, thoughtfully handled and tamed. We like the word *tamed* because it connotes refocusing negative, uncontrolled energy toward a positive, constructive outcome.

While we don't suggest that this book covers everything there is to know about gossip, we do want to help managers and leaders understand how to cope with it and demonstrate how to lead a workplace where communication is inclusive, positive and supportive. Though a reader should gain insights into his or her personal behavior, we are most concerned with how to change the culture of a team or organization for the better.

Moreover, the proliferation of ever-improving technology makes it a good time to consider gossip. E-mail, instant messaging, texts, tweets, hybrid personal digital assistants-cell phones, blogs and/or personal web pages kept by employees can make gossiping quicker, faster and perhaps even more wounding than ever. (See Chapter 3.) Without careful consideration of all forms of electronic communications, and clear workplace policies, organizational leaders can find themselves riding a tiger. One simple piece of gossip from a workplace can literally circle the globe in a flash, destroying the reputations of companies, agencies or individuals. We intend to help you control this tiger.

Finally, the sheer volume of practitioner feedback we have received regarding gossip leads us to believe this book is needed. Our hope is that you find it relevant, applicable and helpful. Most importantly, we've worked to craft a book that thoughtfully and carefully addresses the destructive effects of gossip in an organization and offers a guide to preventing the destruction.

We have divided the book into ten chapters and an Afterthought.

One simple piece of gossip from a workplace can literally circle the globe in a flash, destroying the reputations of companies, agencies or individuals.

The first five chapters explore the topic of gossip from a definitional standpoint. Chapter 1 defines and presents types of gossip, while Chapter 2 sets out the harms it causes. Chapter 3 describes the impact technology has on gossip; Chapter 4 examines perspectives on the relationship between gender and gossip; and Chapter 5 reviews what the great religions have to say about it.

The next four chapters focus on taming negative gossip in the workplace. Chapter 6 outlines methods to assess its prevalence in the workforce, and Chapter 7 suggests strategies for making organizationally appropriate changes to reduce the practice. Chapter 8 offers advice on encouraging positive interactions, and Chapter 9 suggests ways to replace gossip habits.

Chapter 10 concludes the discussion and change techniques by emphasizing the power of the positive over the negative. With that in mind, we challenge the reader to take the steps necessary to cultivate a more positive workplace. Finally, the Afterthought addresses questions that arise resulting from the tension between some academics who see a virtue in gossip and practitioners who view it as a destructive force since they deal with its impact daily.

Are we naïve to believe that gossip can be effectively eliminated? We don't think so. There is much evidence that congenial, affirming workplaces are not unattainable dreams; they do exist, and salacious, destructive communication can be erased and replaced with mutual respect when a team or organization is managed well. In addition, we show that gossip-free workplaces almost always enjoy superior performance.

However, we're not satisfied with achieving just a civil, congenial workplace. We're convinced by our own experience and by our understanding of positive psychology that it is possible not only to isolate and control the negative, we can move the cultures of our organizations to a higher plain. In her book *Positivity*, Barbara Fredrickson states boldly that:

> Whatever your current circumstances, you've got what it takes to reshape your life and the world around you for the better. You have, already within you, the active ingredient that's needed to craft a happy life that's full of growth and creativity, and to be remarkably resilient in hard times.[2]

When viewed from the perspective of constructive growth, organizations are no different from individuals. Most have what it takes to reshape themselves. What Fredrickson posits for the individual is equally true for organizations; they can become better places to work.

On the other hand, we provide no quick fixes. Instead, our goal is to share deeper insights into how to address a problem that impacts millions of people every day, insights that if implemented will have a lasting effect on the well-being of any organization. The discussion that follows will help leaders and managers isolate the problem within a workplace, provide ideas on how to coach employees to higher and better standards of behavior, and present steps to help shape an organization into a more constructive place for all to flourish. In short, we believe this book will help readers understand why gossip in its malicious, destructive form is almost uniformly negative and how to replace it with positive patterns of communication that will energize the workplace.

# GOSSIP DEFINED

Sometimes, the worse the thing you say, the more people want to believe it. And then they can't wait to repeat it.

**KIM GATLIN**

I t should have been the most light-hearted work event of the year for a vice president of a small Midwestern company. The annual holiday party was underway, and more than 600 employees and guests were enjoying good food, fun and the foxhole camaraderie of colleagues working in the healthcare field.

As his wife chatted with other partygoers, the senior manager took a female employee out for a turn around the dance floor. No smoldering glances were exchanged, no inappropriate touches given. All was just as it seemed–a simple dance at the company party. Afterwards, the supervisor went back to sit next to his wife.

A day later, an employee made an appointment to talk with the CEO. It seems that the company was abuzz with certain people talking of an "affair" between the manager and the woman he danced with. The previously unsullied reputations of both were damaged and becoming more so as time passed–but neither knew it yet.

As the gossip spread like wildfire, its effects rocked the workplace. The supervisor's authority and credibility with his employees diminished as employees wasted work time passing along the "news." And the woman involved in the non-affair felt the sting of sharp glances or "knowing looks" coming her way.

Unfortunately, sharing a juicy tale for just a second around the coffee pot, in the copy room or at the vending machines seems to be irresistible, and this is gossip at its worst. In fact, the story will likely cause harm whether it is true or false. In all cases, at least initially, the person or people being gossiped about have no idea what is happening and can do nothing to stop its spread. The calamity is that afterwards those involved will never be able to reach every person who has heard the story to explain the error and the truth. It's a bell that can't be unrung.

Gossip isn't, of course, confined to workplaces. It can wash through churches, mosques and synagogues, besmirching the reputation of leaders or congregants. It darkens the reputation of teachers or professors in the halls of learning, and can bring down public officials. It can destroy the positive efforts of the nonprofit institution, rip apart a neighborhood and undermine personal relationships. Whatever the institution or organization, gossip can have a destructive impact.

## Definition of Gossip

*The Oxford English Dictionary* provides insight into the genesis of the word gossip. It comes from Old English (as far back as 1014) and once had a benign meaning. It originally meant a godfather or godmother (god-sib), later a close friend or close relationship, so it carried a sense of intimacy. This meaning grew to include communication between close friends, intimates. Historically, the word carries a sense of trifling, idle talk, tittle-tattle with an edge of quarrelsomeness.

A survey of several references can expand our understanding of the word as it is used currently. Wikipedia, for instance, indicates that "gossip consists of casual or idle talk of any sort, sometimes (but not always) slanderous and/or devoted to discussing others."[1] In an article titled "Gossip: A Feminist Defense," Louise Collins defines gossip as "the social practice of chatting with friendly acquaintances about third parties known to us about aspects of their private lives."[2] Gail Collins, on the other hand, defines gossip in her book *Scorpion Tongues* as the dissemination of "unverified information about a person's private life that he or she might want to keep hidden."[3]

Nan DeMars emphasizes the negative in her very readable book, *You Want Me to Do What?* when she links office gossip to the violation of a person's right to privacy and to a business' need for confidentiality when she writes:

> Gossip – the indiscriminate chatter about someone else's private affairs–is probably the most common case of breakdown of confidentiality, and it merits some special attention. We all recognize it for what it is because every one is tempted to gossip. If the sins of the flesh are the world's oldest sins, the sins of the wagging tongue take second place.[4]

Patricia Meyer Spacks points out that historically gossip has included both a positive and a negative side. In her book *Gossip*, she states that:

> The moralistic castigation of private gossip over several centuries suggests continuing vivid perception of its social threat–a threat equivalent in certain respects to that of unrestrained lust. Yet gossip, like sex, embodies positive forces. Its energies, as I suggested in the last chapter and will argue more fully in the next, lend themselves simultaneously to the **destruction** and the **sustenance** of human ties.[5] [Emphasis added]

Obviously, the word gossip includes a broad spectrum of communication–everything from benign, even supportive personal chatter to insidious, sinister interactions. Therefore, dealing forthrightly with the negative requires that a distinction be made between the most destructive aspects from other dimensions of gossip. In the article noted above, Louise Collins, explains the problem as follows:

> Some would say my characterization of gossip has omitted its central feature: that all gossip is malicious. If this is intended as a stipulated truth, I will give the critic the term "gossip" and retain "guossip" as labeling a kind of discourse that is just like gossip, but not all of it is malicious.... In my view, only some gossip is malicious, and malicious gossip is parasitic on ordinary gossip, as lying is parasitic on sincere discourse.[6]

Recognizing that not everything called gossip falls into the category of malicious, we agree with Collins that perhaps we need two different words to differentiate between the positive and negative aspects. Therefore, we draw a distinction between "social" gossip and "malicious" gossip. Social gossip refers to the broad spectrum of communication that is personal in nature but can be viewed as having a positive social impact. Malicious gossip references the destructive element, a caustic aspect of interpersonal communication. When we use the word gossip in this book, we are generally referring to the negative element. We have tried to be careful, whenever necessary, to draw a distinction between the two types of gossip.

## The Four Ds of Malicious Gossip

While malicious gossip has many facets and subtleties. At its core, it almost always consists of some combination of four key elements: dishonesty, distortion, defamation and dissonance.

*Dishonesty*: Gossip based on dishonesty simply misleads the hearer. The facts of the assertions made are not true. A person might say, "Did you know that Mary and Robert had an affair?" or "I heard Jim was fired from his last job," knowing that the statement is false.

*Distortion*: Techniques of distortion in the context of malicious gossip occur when the gossip twists or creates negative meaning by altering the interpretation of events or circumstances. It can happen through exaggeration. For example, an employee's spouse telephones once or twice a day, and the gossip reports that the husband or wife is constantly interrupting the employee at work. Unfortunately, this

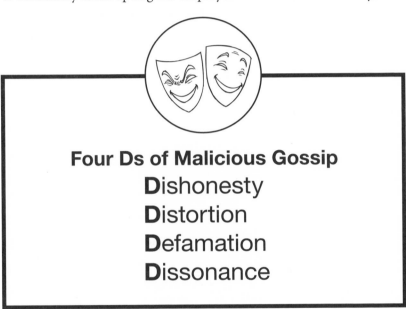

**Four Ds of Malicious Gossip**
## **D**ishonesty
## **D**istortion
## **D**efamation
## **D**issonance

message is often accompanied by another negative statement: "I hear they are having marital problems."

Malicious gossip may also occur through misdirection. In this instance, an employee might innocently share the fact that he and his buddies are going on a fishing trip together, and the gossip tells a coworker that the employee and his wife never go on a vacation together. The intent of the twisted message is apparent; the character or conduct of a fellow employee is being damaged or called into question.

*Defamation*: This type of malicious gossip, involves an attack on character. The perpetrator purposefully seeks to ruin the reputation of another employee, perhaps a competitor or rival for a promotional opportunity or some other similar benefit. Whether false or true, the reports are used as a weapon and targeted to damage the career or work of another employee.

*Dissonance*: This form of gossip occurs when negative statements are spread to inflict harm by creating discord. Matters long forgotten and no longer relevant may be brought up to generate angst. This activity is a favorite in the political arena. "When he was a college student, twenty years ago, didn't he smoke marijuana?" The point is brought up not for a constructive purpose but to undermine and sabotage. Dissonance interferes with a sense of fellowship and camaraderie.

## The Characteristics of Malicious Gossip

In our discussion of malicious gossip, we are concerned with interpersonal communication that includes some combination of the following five characteristics:

- The content of the personal communication is judgmental, demeaning, critical, disparaging or has similar negative connotations. The intent is to characterize the person gossiped about as being deficient in some unacceptable way.
- The content may include privileged or private information that the gossip is disseminating inappropriately.
- Malicious gossip never occurs in the presence of the person(s) being talked about. When people share malicious stories, they quickly change the topic when the victim approaches.
- When a victim confronts the gossip, he or she normally denies having engaged in any inappropriate behavior.
- Typically, the malicious gossiper has a hidden motive such as elevating personal importance, creating feelings of superiority, punishment or validation, taking down a rival, or similar motivations.

These five characteristics narrow the discussion about gossip in three important ways. First, informal, personal communication of a positive nature is not malicious gossip–at least from our perspective. For example, when one employee approaches another to share positive information about a third employee's child having just been admitted to a prestigious university, the interaction cannot be defined as negative gossip. For one thing, there is no reason to change the content of the conversation if the employee being discussed joins the conversation. Rather, congratulations are in order. In addition, the employee would have no reason to deny sharing this information as it affirms the person being talked about.

The five defining characteristics also narrow the focus by removing from our discussion any informal communication that can reasonably be called benign. It is not, for instance, about two people chatting idly about colleagues, family and friends even when that interaction may at times contain some negative information. Gabbing is a healthy and necessary social function.

Finally, our focus is narrowed because we do not include any communication that is a genuine effort to resolve a problem. For example, when an employee approaches a manager with an urgent request to address a personal problem that has become the focus of gossip, sharing this information does not constitute malicious gossip. Here, the motive is not ulterior but rather transparent and constructive, an effort to identify the problem with the goal of taking action to resolve it.

## Gossip as Organizational Communication

Formal organizations (i.e., a company, nonprofit, school, church, or other similar institution) by their very nature have two layers of communication–formal and informal. Formal communication follows the chain of command, uses standardized forms for everything from office supplies to request for services, and is accountable. It may assign liability, and is recorded and saved in court documents, employee handbooks, quarterly and annual reports. Formal communication includes traceable information (i.e., who signed on or off on a budget item or a decision). It's an e-mail blast. It's the CEO's state of the organization annual speech, court depositions, company web pages and the accounting department's monthly report. As you can see, formal communication is impersonal, at best, and often slow and ponderous.

In contrast, informal communication involves less "rigid" interchanges. For instance, it can include interactions such as phoning someone to ask when a report can be expected, or others like employee blogs, tweets, posts on Facebook, texting and comments in the lunchroom. It's frequently information people are reluctant to put into any kind of written form*, so statements begin with "Don't quote me but…." Often, such information is highly accurate, even if not tied to a single source or written down. Informal conversation is short, sweet or not so sweet and to the point, and usually much more transparent than the formal.

But don't make the mistake of thinking it serves a less important purpose than formal communication. It frequently forms the basis of making good decisions in a timely fashion. Any smart employee knows the wisdom of getting some informal advice. To ignore such information means decisions made in a vacuum or decisions made based only on information obtained through formal channels.

As a subset of informal communication, gossip has none of the elements of formal interactions, particularly those related to making a permanent record and holding individuals accountable. In fact, those who indulge in it don't usually want their "fingerprints" discovered. In addition, since it depends on personal relationships, word can spread with amazing speed.

The power of malicious gossip should not be underestimated since it can have a significant impact on the organizational culture,

---

*E-mails and texting are beginning to change the landscape since they are retrievable and often used for informal communication. This can result in both personal embarrassment and significant organizational problems–think Hillary Clinton's personal e-mails and Congress.

productivity and employee morale. Therefore, leaders must address it constructively. (See Chapters 6-10 for strategies.)

## Gossip vs. Rumor

Alexander Pope was an 18th-century English poet, probably best known for his satirical verse and for his translation of Homer. He is also credited for penning the following verse:

> "The flying rumors gathr'd as they roll'd,
>
> Scarce any tale was sooner heard then told;
>
> And all who told it added something new,
>
> And all who heard it made enlargements too.[7]

In the world of informal communication, we find it important to distinguish gossip from rumor[†] for a number of reasons. A review of practitioner literature indicates that a substantial number of publications mix the two, creating a lack of clarity and clouding specific issues with gossip. For example, an article titled "The Poison of Workplace Gossip" provides a bulleted list of the negative "effects of gossip." One of the bullets is the statement that "rumors are not necessarily 100% true and are often embellished to make them 'juicier.'"[8] As will be discussed below, the accuracy of organizational rumors is a whole separate study for some very important reasons. The accuracy of gossip is a concern but for an entirely different set of reasons.

Though gossip and rumor are children of a common mother, the two have some important differences. Gossip, in all its rich forms, is composed of information about people and relationships. It concerns the exchange of personal information in a manner that can be either positive or negative. On the other hand, while rumor can involve the

---

[†]The authors are aware that words have whatever meaning is ascribed. We believe that the distinctions we are making throughout this book are consistent with a more rigorous academic usage and helpful to our basic purpose.

# FORMAL COMMUNICATION

- Is written or created in storable form
- Is recorded and saved
- Can be retrieved
- Follows a chain of command
- Facilitates and clarifies responsibility
- Becomes part of an organization's history
- Is often slow
- Holds communicators accountable.

transmission of personal information, it has a broader subject matter that may include topics like pending raises or wage freezes, plant closures, business expansion–"have you heard . . .?" Rumor spreads primarily based on social relationships and, as any plant or middle manager can tell you, it can spread as quickly as gossip.

DiFonzo and Bordia provide a succinct and helpful explanation of the difference in *Rumor Psychology* when they write:

> However, rumor and gossip are not equivalent concepts; they differ in function and content. Rumor's function is to make sense of an ambiguous situation or to help people adapt to known or potential threats; gossip serves social network formation and maintenance. Put another way, rumor is intended as a hypothesis to help make sense of an unclear situation whereas gossip entertains, bonds and normatively influences group members.[9]

Rumor and its impact on an organization have often been studied, generally with a focus on two opposite concerns. The first looks at distortion in message sharing. The common focus for this approach is error–how and why messages become unreliable. From this perspec-

# INFORMAL COMMUNICATION

- Is often unwritten or not recorded in any way
- Is dependent on personal relationships–knowing someone
- Includes phone calls, e-mails, text messaging
- Involves direct interaction with those not in the chain of command
- Can be very accurate in a different way than formal communication
- Can also be very inaccurate
- Is quick and nimble
- Is difficult to hold anyone accountable for
- Can be gossip, rumor or simple conversations.

tive, rumor is best understood as a false report. The fact that rumors may be swirling throughout the organization is viewed with alarm because of the perceived inaccuracies.

Gordon Allport and Leo Postman's classic work *The Psychology of Rumor*, introduces us to the concepts of "leveling," "sharpening" and "assimilating."[10] Leveling concerns the loss of vital facts during the serial transmission of information. Sharpening is the adding of factual information consistent with the communicator's perspective. Assimilating is the process by which the story is changed to make sense to those sharing the information. We have all had the experience of finding that a story we have heard is totally distorted–in other words, leveled, sharpened and assimilated.

Much has been written about how to keep rumors from starting in an organization and how to minimize the damage from the stories that do get started. While we're skeptical of the ability to squash rumors, these studies provide substantial insight into the speed and idiosyncrasies of the informal communication process.

A second approach to the study of rumor views it as a collective sharing. From this perspective, each person who participates in the rumor is seen as adding to the transaction. The common theme of this work is accuracy. Rumor is seen as serial information gathering, a collecting or pooling of facts with each person contributing something. As a result, rumors are often startlingly correct. The participants to the rumor, therefore, serve an investigative reporter function.

In his thoughtful book *Improvised News,* sociologist Tomatsu Shibutani offers numerous examples where groups of people collecting tidbits of information by way of rumor construct an extraordinarily accurate picture of upcoming events that are supposedly privileged or classified. Many of his examples involved military situations where the scuttlebutt amongst the enlisted men was full of extremely accurate information related to troop movements and other military activities.[11]

How is it that the troops can have a very precise and correct understanding of their departure time on a military transport ship when that information is a closely guarded secret? Or how can employees know with reasonable certainty and accuracy about plant closures and layoffs even though no formal announcement has been made by company officials? The obvious answer to these questions is that the process of rumor has resulted in the collection of various tidbits of information that when pieced together provide the insight that is supposedly privileged information.

In a presentation to the American Management Association, Elaine Re claimed that "the office grapevine is at least 90 percent to 93 percent accurate."[12] While this figure obviously depends on a clear determination of what messages are in the grapevine and a specific understanding of the concept of accuracy, it does provide perspective with regard to the basic fact that organizational rumor can be highly accurate.

In our view, the differences in the two approaches to studying rumor simply highlight basic facts about the accuracy or inaccuracy of informal communication. Frequently, information transmitted through the grapevine can become highly distorted. On the other hand, when participants in the grapevine choose to pool their information on a matter of some concern, Shibutani's research clearly shows that they may be able to construct a highly accurate picture of what is occurring.

Classically, the inherent nature of rumor allows it to be used as a trial balloon. Consider the following case in which a manager was thinking about promoting a worker to foreman. The man was his number one candidate, but the manager had a sense that the union disliked him. If true, it was pointless to promote him. So the manager deliberately disseminated the rumor that the worker was going to

*This Soviet war poster conveys the message: "Don't chatter! Gossiping borders on treason" (1941). American World War II poster by Seymour R. Goff, also known as Ess-ar-gee.*

be the next foreman on the production line. The union representatives indeed went ballistic after hearing the news, and marched into the manager's office demanding to know if it was really true or just scuttlebutt (inaccurate grapevine information). There was no way they could support that promotion, they said, and trouble lay ahead if it happened. The manager, getting the information he needed, was able to sit back and deny that it was a possibility. He could then, with little loss of credibility, start finding another candidate who could be supported by both management and the union.

Unlike rumor, gossip is not used in a strategic way for constructive purposes. Gossip can hurt. Its targets get angry and upset. Gossip is personal–"Did you see how late that young Anderson guy is coming in every day? It looks like he may be out partying and drinking too much every night." (It's interesting how a more benign explanation seldom comes up. It's possible, for example, that Anderson stops by his mother's home every day on the way to work because she is recovering from surgery, and he simply doesn't feel the need to announce to his coworkers that his mother just had a hysterectomy.)

While each can contain elements of the other, gossip involves the sharing of strictly personal news–whether good or bad–between two or more individuals about a third. The person who gossips is only incidentally interested in the truthfulness of what is being talked about. He or she focuses more on sharing stories that are interesting, secretive, exciting, juicy, scandalous, spicy, salacious and sensational, regardless of truth.

While both rumor and gossip involve the informal sharing of information, primarily based on personal relationships, we see a significant difference between the two in both content and tone. The fact that rumor is often called *scuttlebutt* while malicious gossip may be referred to as *backbiting* or *slander* helps illustrate the point.

On the other hand, gossip and rumor collide when gossip spreads by way of the grapevine. In this case, gossip becomes the subject matter of rumor. A slanderous statement, for example, can be the content of the scuttlebutt. The damage the victim of malicious gossip experiences becomes magnified when it moves through an organization by way of the grapevine.

## Gossip as Conspiracy Theory

Conspiracy theories are wonderfully entertaining, full of intrigue, mystery and implied motivation. If you pick any subject and go to the Internet, you will likely find a good conspiracy theory. Take the benign subject of toll roads, for example. An online search quickly unearths some extensive conspiracy theories. It seems that toll roads are being built in America as part of a shadowy effort to implement a one-world order. One which is more current than it may seem at first glance, appeared in the December 10, 2007, issue of *Newsweek*, an informative article titled "Highway to Hell." It seems that a very well-developed conspiracy theory exists related to the building of a NAFTA superhighway secretly intended to link Canada, the U.S. and Mexico. According to the theory, some kind of unholy alliance between governments and private consortiums promotes the idea. The goal is to create an integrated North American Union complete with a new currency, a central bureaucracy and borderless travel within the union.[13]

Conspiracy theories are intriguing because they typically involve a unique mixture of rumor and gossip, and like other forms of gossip, can be quite damaging. There is, for example, an organization called the Security and Prosperity Partnership of North America (SPP), launched on March 23, 2005, through a meeting in Waco, Texas, with the support of President George W. Bush. Its mandate was to reduce the threat of terrorist activity and promote commerce between the three countries (Canada, Mexico and the USA). A visit to its website, however, uncovers a lot of defensive reaction to the superhighway conspiracy and an effort to dispel the myths created by the theorists (gossipers). It attempts to convince people that the highway project has a necessary and beneficial purpose with no intention of undermining the sovereignty of any of the three countries.[14]

Similarly, according to the article, the governor of the state of Texas had, at that time, championed the construction of a new 1,200-mile superhighway through Texas. Different from the standard freeway, the Texas superhighway was to include light rail, utilities and Internet cabling. Construction was projected to start in 2009. According to *Newsweek*, "Texas officials are still trying to convince locals that their $180 billion idea was not hatched to undermine American sovereignty." The Texas Transportation Commissioner is quoted in the article as knowing nothing at all about the North American Union or the NAFTA superhighway until he started to be "badgered" about whether the Texas superhighway was part of this conspiracy.[15]

This story draws attention to a destructive aspect of gossip that is not typically considered. Clearly, the Texas superhighway has its proponents and its opponents, along with plenty of room for constructive political debate over the merits of such a project. Unfortunately, the debate occurs in the form of Internet gossip and the authors of this book consider it gossip because the discussion tends to cast aspersions on key individuals. How can one effectively debate a point of view where fact and fantasy are so intermixed? And how does a person like the governor of Texas defend himself against shadowy arguments that he's a player in a conspiracy to undermine the sovereignty of the country?

Of course, by the time this book goes to press, the story may seem dated. Think again, and google the issue on the Internet. The shadowy discussion of the SPP rages on. Neither the denials nor time have quelled the attacks for a considerable number of years. The conspiracy debate has a life of its own not subject to rational discussion. Sounds like malicious gossip in the workplace, doesn't it?

Frankly, we thought about including conspiracy theory as a central issue in this book. The fact that it can have such an overwhelmingly negative impact on efforts of government agencies to provide public services would clearly justify its inclusion. Ultimately, however, we've chosen not to do so because our primary interest involves people and relationships within specific organizations. Conspiracy theories tend to be less about people and relationships known to the theory perpetrator and more about events and activities. We're specifically concerned about the destructive impact gossip has on the organization where people who know each other are gossiping about those known to them within the organization.

## Gossip as Social Control

Research reveals that gossip is a complicated issue, serving various purposes in human relations. David Sloan Wilson, an internationally known scholar on evolutionary biology at the State University of New York-Binghamton, has studied gossip extensively. His studies on human behavior, including the function of gossip among groups, make him a well-known resource on the topic. In an article published in the journal *Human Nature*, Wilson and coauthor Kevin M. Kniffin, a University of Wisconsin anthropologist, hypothesize that gossip can either serve as a tool to maintain the interests or common goals of a group, or as a form of social control. It can also be a self-serving way for a person to advance his or her own interests.[16]

Wilson and Kniffin, who examined a number of other studies on human communication, including some specifically about gossip, state that gossip may have started early in human evolution, as members of small bands groomed one another. Social grooming is an activity in which individuals in an animal group clean or maintain one another's body or appearance, an activity frequently discussed using monkeys.[17] Some researchers believe that grooming cements ties and hierarchies, allowing cooperative, coordinated work in the struggle to gather enough food to survive, raise children and protect the group from predators. Close living conditions among humans coupled with sophisticated verbal abilities unique in the animal world encouraged and helped maintain gossip.[18]

In their study of communication between members of a university rowing team of 50, Wilson and Kniffin found that gossip focused on the behavior of one young man, who skipped practices and was perceived as not pulling his weight. Few sports require team unity and coordination–so called "group-level" skills–quite like rowing. As a result, one negligent teammate can drag everyone down. The young man, known as "the slacker" in the journal article, became the butt of jokes and even the focus of personal threats. He skipped almost all daily practices and the rigorous pre-season practices, forcing teammates to work even harder to compensate for his lack of effort. Gossip abounded about his performance, or perceived lack of it, leading Wilson and Kniffin to believe that the behavior was a way of enforcing team norms. They also point out that at the same time the gossip about the "slacker" was occurring, positive talk about admired team members occurred in tandem, supporting a close-knit, tightly functioning team. In other words, positive talk went on that supported team goals, while negative gossip about violations of expected behavior was directed in a way that made it clear that such behavior wouldn't be tolerated.[19]

In the end, the "slacker" quit, and incidents of negative gossip plunged. So gossip within a group seems to have two purposes: reforming someone's behavior or absolute rejection of that behavior.[20]

Obviously, as previously noted, there are two different dimensions of gossip, one positive and one negative. Patricia Meyer Spacks describes the issue as follows:

> The sheer bulk of five centuries' of commentary on gossip suggests a phenomenon worth taking seriously. If gossip is merely contemptible, why have so many people said so much about it? A survey of what they have said over the past six centuries reveals mostly fierce castigation, with occasional acknowledgments of gossip's value. Almost never does the same commentator call attention to both positive and negative aspects. Those understanding gossip as fellowship typically deny its malice; those stressing its destructiveness ignore its bonding.[21]

The following story, taken from an old book on rumor and gossip, illustrates the difference between good and bad gossip in a delightful and somewhat humorous fashion.

> In 1888 the girls of North Hall, Newnham, debated the question of whether life without gossip would be worth living. The vote was unanimously negative, and Ms. Gladstone, the principal, defended this most just decision. However, she understood gossip to mean ready, informed and piquant conversation . . . "Foul whispering," a vulgar and shamelessly undressed tattling was furthest from her thought.[22]

Our study of the subject establishes that gossip can be viewed as an interaction continuum. One end of the continuum contains positive social interaction, the type of discourse that builds camaraderie and friendship. The other end is malicious and destructive. Obviously, there is a range of communication behavior that bridges the gap between the positive and the negative. For instance, an article in the September 2010 *Harvard Business Review* defends the proposition that it is not unprofessional to gossip at work. That article posits that:

> Gossip is merely the exchange of information between two people about a third, absent person. A huge amount of gossip is devoted to praise. If someone stays late to help you, you will probably tell someone else in your network about it. In fact, positive gossip is more typical than the negative kind. We found an even blend of positive and negative gossip in 72% of the gossip relationships, predominantly positive gossip in 21%, and predominantly negative gossip in only 7%.[23]

Consistent with the above point of view, Mike Noon and Rick Delbridge authored a lengthy article summarizing the constructive role of gossip in an organization. In it, they review a multitude of different journal articles and find that gossip is a "complex activity" that has "important implications for organizations." They found any conclusions concerning the harms associated with gossip to be superficial, noting that they result from a less than rigorous analysis of competent research. The authors state:

> The often facile considerations of gossip in the business literature typically concludes that it is "bad" and should be eradicated by managers, because employees who engage in the process of gossip are not working as hard as they could. Gossip in such "analysis" is perceived as a willful waste of time, and therefore the "theft" of the organization's money. At best, gossip is seen as an annoying distraction from the tasks in hand, and a drain on employees' energies and concentration.
>
> Typically, the prescriptive nature of many of the practitioner-oriented articles leads their authors to advise managers to eliminate gossip, possibly by using negative sanctions. In concluding that gossip can be eradicated, these authors merely underline the superficial nature of their analysis. Gossip plays a vital role in group formation, regulation and perpetration, so the removal of gossip from any social setting is not feasible unless there is a complete ban on all forms of communication.... It is facile to believe that gossip can be eliminated and futile for managers to attempt to do so.[24]

While we beg the reader's pardon for any perceived facile analysis, we persist in our efforts to address the harm and destructiveness of malicious gossip. We remain convinced that it is possible to facilitate a civil workplace where employees communicate in ways that support each other as opposed to tearing apart the fabric of their relationships. Therefore, employers have good reason to put up barriers to destructive gossip in employee handbooks because malicious communication is harmful to organizational performance.

Having fully reviewed the studies that conclude that gossip has a positive side, we question the conclusions that 1) malicious gossip is unavoidable and 2) that all of the benefits assigned to gossip are truly benefits. DiFonzo and Bordia illustrate this point when they present the five essential functions of gossip in the workplace.

1.  Helps individuals learn social information about other individuals in the organization (often without having to meet the other individual).
2.  Builds social networks of individuals by bonding coworkers together and affiliating people with each other.
3.  Breaks existing bonds by ostracizing individuals within an organization.
4.  Enhances one's social status/power/prestige within the organization.
5.  Informs individuals as to what is considered socially acceptable behavior within the organization.[25]

While we find the above a reasonable summation of the function of gossip in the workplace, we question whether all of the functions are desirable and/or necessary. Yes, one of the outcomes of malicious gossip is that it does tend to ostracize an individual within an organization. Ostracizing an individual, however, appears on its face to be counterproductive. How does it help an organization succeed when individuals within it are alienated from their fellow employees? Similarly, there is room to ponder the value of an activity engaged in for the purpose of enhancing one's social status/power/prestige particularly if that activity primarily consists of slander and backbiting.

A related summary of the positive contributions of gossip to organizational effectiveness follows.

> We suggest that the process of gossip contributes more than just the system-maintenance function previously considered. It can communicate rules, values and morals; it facilitates the diffusion of organizational tradition and history; and it maintains the exclusivity of the group. Information passed via the gossip process may offer an explanation of matters previously unclear to the group and may thus relieve feelings of insecurity and anxiety. Equally, gossip may be a vehicle for social change.[26]

While the authors of this book fully respect the results of the research on gossip as fellowship or as a mode of social control, from our perspective the fact that gossip in the general sense may have a positive side does not alter the basic reality that the salacious, demeaning side of gossip often tears organizations apart. Even a small percentage of malicious gossip can be heavily destructive in an organization. While we have heard CEOs, HR directors and other organizational leaders bemoan the impact of gossip in their organizations; we have never heard a comment such as: "I had a couple employees that were acting inappropriately. But, thank goodness for some great gossip, those two employees are now back on board."

Ultimately, the fact that benign, friendly, value supporting social interaction may, at times, provide positive benefits to the organization, does not change the destructiveness of negative gossip. Most importantly, we are convinced that malicious gossip can be isolated and dealt with separate from the more positive forms of social interaction.

## Reasons for Gossip

Gossip is for the most part the problem of an individual. It is, we believe, a learned behavior, mostly formed during our youngest years. It almost goes without saying that children learn by observing those closest to them–their family members. When they see a father leaning across the table and hear him pass on a tidbit about the new pastor's fancy clothes to a dinner guest, they learn that gossip is okay, even when told otherwise. When they hear their mother tell a friend how a coworker is conveniently late every other Monday, that's another lesson learned.

No one should be surprised that people naturally follow the behavior patterns modeled by those in their social environment. However, we cannot know precisely why people continue to indulge in gossip as they mature, even when they know the harm it can cause. Broadly speaking, gossip is sometimes simply nasty or mischievous, but reasons abound. The person may be envious or angry. Some people gossip because they have to be the center of attention–it's a power move on their part: "I know more than you know." In other cases, it may be someone further down the workplace hierarchy who uses gossip as a way to boost prestige or status: "Look at the valuable information I'm sharing with you. We're in this together." It can also be a calculated way to bring down a rival in an organization, or a way to settle a personal score.

In looking at the reasons why people engage in gossip, we are aware that substantial psychological and anthropological research on the topic of gossip exists. *Eufunctional,* a word coined by academics to oppose the word *dysfunctional,* is frequently found in the writing about gossip. The term generally applies to things considered inherently disruptive or undesirable but which may have a beneficial effect in certain situations. Anthropologically speaking, therefore, gossip combats certain unacceptable behaviors; it is eufunctional. But it's also dysfunctional in that it can create great harm and heartache.

This is not to say that anthropologists are not concerned, at times, with the negative impact of gossip. An article published in *Sex Roles: A Journal of Research* reports the story of how a young Arab woman was killed as an extension of village malicious gossip.[27] The article challenges the assumption that, because it supports tradition and stability, malicious gossip is eufunctional. Similarly, some philosophically raise serious questions as to whether any communication process that results in humiliation can be deemed eufunctional.

We agree. The positive culture of an organization can be maintained without the help of malicious gossip. The underlying point is that the beneficial characteristics of cohesiveness, adherence to workplace expectations and social stability can be fully supported without the negative side effects that come from malicious gossip.

## Controlling Gossip

We clearly wouldn't be writing this book if we didn't believe it possible to manage and control the destructive side of informal communication. Whatever the cause, we can change gossip behavior in the workplace by modeling expected behavior and making appropriate behavior on the job explicit. We may or may not know when we hire someone if he or she is a "gossip," because clearly, at the time of an interview, a person presents him or herself in the best light possible. However, gossips will eventually reveal themselves at every level of the organization.

Since gossiping is a learned behavior, it can be changed. Of course, understanding that different levels of gossip exist is essential. For example, strangers can certainly gossip together. Who hasn't swapped stories with an airplane seatmate about a nutty coworker or an accounting unit that just can't seem to get it together? This kind of interaction causes less harm than other forms of gossip, because it's on a much less intimate basis than, say, a team of coworkers who have worked together for five years. Remember the old philosophical question about whether a tree makes any noise when it falls in the forest and there is no one present to hear? Likewise, gossiping with a seatmate on a plane will most likely occur "where there is no one to hear the noise." Not so when people who work closely together engage in malicious gossip about a colleague; the harm and pain it causes is immediate, personal and on occasion extreme.

Obviously, gossip is part of the human condition just as much as kindness and hatred. We are, after all, social beings for whom human contact is an ingredient necessary to our well-being. We will never have the capacity to stop malicious gossip completely, but we can teach people how to deal with it–particularly its maliciousness. Workable strategies exist that can stem the toxic tide without plunging a workplace into totalitarianism. Therefore, it's a significant mistake to say "We're going to treat those around us with respect and simply ignore the gossip."

Consider the following anecdote that shows how important personal information can be shared within the work environment in an effective way that helps, rather than harms. As many organizational leaders know, one of the most challenging managerial situations is overseeing multiple sites. In such organizations, it's impossible for a manager to be every place at once, so he or she must rely on others for critical information.

In an organization spread out over an extended geographic area, an employee, who worked in a site apart from her manager, came to see her boss in his office. Obviously ill at ease, she reluctantly said that she needed to discuss another staff member. He didn't seem to get in before 10 a.m. and never seemed to stay past 4 p.m. He had a pattern, she said, of not showing up on Fridays and Mondays, or sometimes both days. She said she was worried that he might have a drinking problem. That was a big concern because the organization at which they worked had the responsibility of caring for very vulnerable people.

After an investigation and discussions with the man, it turned out that the situation did involve alcohol abuse, making intervention possible. Clearly, it was an appropriate conversation between the worried coworker and the supervisor because they behaved with integrity. If the manager's door hadn't been open, she might never have come in.

And, if the woman making those observations about her colleague had started telling others around the organization that she thought her coworker was a drunk, she would have engaged in malicious gossip that eventually might have degenerated into character assassination. To her credit, she chose to address the problem directly and constructively.

Of course, promoting this type of intelligent response to relational issues/behaviors requires that organizational leaders understand gossip, what constitutes good communication skills and how to keep malicious gossip from becoming an entrenched part of an organization's culture. The key to controlling malicious gossip is encouraging the positive rather than focusing on controlling the negative. Martin Seligman makes this point abundantly clear in his powerful book *Authentic Happiness* when he posits that removing the negatives in our lives does not bring about the richness of living we generally desire. He writes:

> Relieving the states that make life miserable, it seems, has made building the states that make life worth living less of a priority. But people want more than just to correct their weaknesses. They want lives imbued with meaning…[28]

> I do not believe that you should devote overly much effort to correcting your weaknesses. Rather, I believe that the highest success in living and the deepest emotional satisfaction comes from building and using your signature strengths.[29]

Precisely. Clearly, leaders must learn how to bring about a workplace that is supportive, nonjudgmental and affirming. While acknowledging the presence of the negative, their major focus must be on building the positive. Therefore, we hope to use our personal exposure to gossip, the similar experiences shared with us by our colleagues and the research we have undertaken to understand malicious gossip, to offer a course of action that helps leaders develop a workplace free of its debilitating impact.

## Chapter 1 Summary

Malicious gossip is hurtful to its targets. If ignored by managers, it can destroy reputations with remarkable speed, and cause work to grind to a halt in any organization. Gossip can best be understood by considering the following:

- Malicious gossip involves the sharing of personal information that is disparaging or confidential about a third person who is not present. The purveyor has an ulterior motive for telling the story and denies sharing it if confronted.
- Gossip is a subset of informal communication, communication that moves through an organization by way of personal relationships.
- Malicious gossip differs from rumor in that it involves the sharing of personal information–whether true or false–with malicious intent. Rumor, on the other hand, involves the collective sharing, pooling and relaying of information that can often be correct.
- While there is research evidence that indicates one dimension of gossip can play the positive role of social control, these positive outcomes must be shielded from the negative side effects of malicious gossip.
- Malicious gossiping is learned behavior that people practice for varied and understandable reasons.
- Hurtful interaction can and ought to be controlled. A manager must develop the tools necessary to shape a workplace culture free from malicious gossip.
- Malicious gossip can best be controlled by replacing it with positive communication and building an affirming organizational culture.

# Chapter 2

## GOSSIP'S DESTRUCTIVE IMPACT

Backbiters do kill more men with
a word than souldiers in the field
destroy with their sword.

**16TH CENTURY POET**

ossip is a worldwide problem. No ethnic group or nationality escapes the human tendency to malign others under the "right" conditions. For instance, gossip became such an issue in the Brazilian city of Cascavel that city council members banned all gossip on the job, with reprimands, sensitivity training and even job loss for those who transgressed.[1]

While this clearly draconian approach to the problem would likely be nearly unenforceable in any modern office setting, it points to the universality of the issue. Obviously, though gossip may be a universal issue, no one filling out a job application professes a desire to work in a poisonous atmosphere. Therefore, managers must be vigilant about staying on top of gossip. Though the goal is not to seek out and punish transgressors, organizational leaders should ensure that they have the emotional temperature of the workplace and can appropriately address the problems that so often accompany the spread of malicious stories.

Like any element of human communication, gossip can sometimes be a mysterious, frustrating behavior with motivations that are hard to discern. But there are a few inconvertible truths about its aftereffects. When allowed to get out of hand in an organization, the behavior can be devastating. Employees lose sight of their primary mission, causing a decrease in productivity, impaired morale, and distrust and insecurity among coworkers. It kills reputations, damages careers and leads excellent employees to seek new jobs, wasting the valuable training time invested in them and depriving the company of their experience. At times, it has even caused work to grind to a halt.

In spite of the negative outcomes, many find it easy to consider gossip unworthy of serious attention. After all, if it was that important, they would have given a course on it in business school, right? But ignoring gossip allows it to take on a life of its own, consuming and inflaming office communications. If unchecked, it can and will overwhelm all other forms of interaction, and waste considerable employee time. We have seen it turn the atmosphere of an organization toxic almost overnight.

Since organizations hire people to get work done, any sizeable company will employ loudmouths and verbal gadabouts as well as gossips. The big talkers are more characterized by their noise and self-absorption–telling off color jokes, relating the glory days of their youth, or continuously complaining about their lives, political parties or spouses. Gossips, on the other hand, are generally more motivated by mischief, intrigue and adventure and as a result have the potential to create greater harm.

## Social Acceptance of Malicious Gossip

Despite this, some people seem to think it almost quaint to tag gossiping as negative behavior. The proliferation of gossip about celebrities, ranging from sports figures and movie stars to politicians, has increased by a startling degree in the past few decades and loosened restraints on people's tongues in many areas of life.

Hundreds of thousands have heard about and passed along stories involving Kim Kardashian's marriage to and divorce from NBA basketball player Kris Humphries, followed by her relationship with, pregnancy, child and marriage to hip hop recording artist Kanye West. Politicians from both parties provide stories just as juicy. There is, for example, Florida Congressman Mark Foley, a Republican, with his sexually explicit Internet messages to under-age male pages, and New York Democratic Congressman, Anthony Weiner with his sexting exploits.

Since the people involved are generally well-known individuals often in important positions, media outlets may choose to categorize their actions as newsworthy. As a result, gossip and the news are often divided by a rather thin line. Unfortunately, the line has become so blurred that people find it increasingly difficult to make a distinction between the two. This constitutes a clear shift in the character of news. Before the 1970s, television/radio news contained less gossip, and was also less likely to grace the pages of a mainstream newspaper or magazine. Today, we are hit with gossip everywhere—from the supermarket check-out line to the nightly news and even our e-mail.

Just how quickly have these shifts in attitude occurred? If you go back quite a few years to the administration of Franklin Roosevelt, a couple of factors stand out. First, though Roosevelt used a wheelchair or heavy leg braces, made necessary by his bout with polio, the subject almost never came up in press photos or accounts of the time. While the president and his aides were certainly careful to put him in situations where they could depict him as vigorous and able-bodied, the press chose to avoid comment.

The other factor was Lucy Mercer, Eleanor Roosevelt's tall, blonde secretary who had at the very least, an emotional affair with Franklin, a relationship which, according to a number of historical accounts, continued sporadically in one fashion or another over several decades. Mercer visited with him just before his death in 1945, initially unbeknownst to Eleanor. Although the affair was hardly unknown around Washington and reported on occasionally in the media, it certainly never became the pulsating, 24-hour, seven-day-a-week news phenomenon seen in the case of President Bill Clinton and White House intern Monica Lewinsky. That relationship quickly dominated media airtime and pages, spawning endless political analysis though it had little to do with the genuine issues of the day.

It is now well known that President John F. Kennedy had numerous affairs while in the White House, including a liaison with a mob moll. But the press, many charmed by the young president and uneasy with trafficking in sordid gossip, looked the other way, protecting his reputation as a family man, even as Kennedy frolicked in the White House pool with young women.[2] That kind of tacit agreement between president and press broke with presidential candidate Gary Hart in 1988, who publicly committed political suicide by daring the press to "follow me around." The media took him up on the offer and uncovered his relationship with Donna Rice, a woman other than his wife. A compromising picture on the yacht Monkey Business published by the *National Enquirer* ended his presidential aspirations.[3]

In the book *Scorpion Tongues*, Gail Collins traces the history of gossip in American politics. She states that the rules for what the media published changed significantly during the late eighties and into the nineties and supports her assertion with substantial evidence. The private lives of politicians were now considered appropriate matter for publication. The politician simply had to live by the rules that the media dictated.[4]

Of course, social commentators have persuasively argued that womanizing or similar egregious behavior says something pretty important about a person's character. While that may or may not be true, the point here isn't the morality of cheating on one's spouse, but that repeatedly publicizing the salacious details of a politician's extramarital affairs on late night cable shows and on magazine pages hardly elevates the public discourse. It has, in fact, cheapened the media and, we contend, made it easier for us all to gossip.

Prominent presidential historian Doris Kerns Goodwin, a Pulitzer Prize winner in history, put it eloquently in a keynote lecture at Kansas State University in 1997.

> Just imagine what the modern media would have made of the Roosevelt White House. The secretary in love with her boss, a woman reporter in love with Eleanor…Prime Minister (Winston Churchill) drinking much of the day. And yet, fortunately, because there was an unwritten rule that the private lives of our public figures were relevant only if they had a direct impact on their leadership, these unconventional relationships were allowed to flourish. How I wish we could return to that standard today, for I have no doubt that many of our best people are unwilling to enter public life for fear of the unnecessary intrusion into their private lives.[5]

One of the authors' college history professors told students, 40-plus years ago, that he had proposed to his department chair that he offer a series of lectures titled, *American Presidents and Their Illegitimate Children*. He was turned down and told that "it would be an unseemly thing to do." We wonder if he would be turned down today–think John Edwards.

While the public seems to tolerate–and perhaps enjoy–the "newsworthy" gossip about high profile figures, we strongly believe that gossip's negative impact must be considered and controlled in the workplace context. Obviously, when an employee's private life impacts his or her work performance, private activities rightfully become a concern for the employer. However, the problems associated with the nexus between private acts and professional responsibilities should never be handled by way of malicious gossip. If there is a problem, leaders should confront it directly, face to face with the individual. The workplace never improves with the circulation of sordid, sensational stories.

## The Harm in Gossip

Mark Twain stated that "[i]t takes your enemy and your friend, working together, to hurt you to the heart; the one to slander you and the other to get the news to you."[6] Though Twain may not have had workplaces in mind, ugly, unfortunate things often occur on the job. For example, a state agency with multiple departments had a management exchange program in which a manager could work in another department for a short period of time to gain experience. On one occasion, a woman in a management position in one department was scheduled for a three-month medical leave, so a male manager from a different department requested and was given the opportunity to fill in for her. When the woman returned, the two managers reviewed the events of the previous three months over coffee.

Toward the end of their discussion, the conversation took a strange turn when the woman queried, "I suppose you've heard that I got promoted into this position because I sleep around?"

"I have heard some gossip but have paid no attention to it," the man responded uncomfortably.

At this point, the woman began to insist that he reveal the source of the gossip. The man resisted repeatedly but finally capitulated and gave the name of a female colleague. It so happened that the female colleague's husband worked in the same department as the newly returned manager. This fact gave some credibility to his admission.

The man later indicated that he spent a mostly sleepless night feeling guilty about revealing the identity of the person who told him the story. The first thing he did when he returned to his old job was to seek out the colleague whose name he had revealed. With great remorse, he informed her of what he had done and asked for her forgiveness. To his surprise, she responded coldly, "I never shared that information with you. I don't know where you got it, but it was not from me."

His colleague then sent a letter to the director of the state agency complaining about what the man had done and asserting that her reputation had been permanently damaged when he had identified her as the source of the gossip. To make matters worse, the topic became the subject of a staff meeting when the woman accused of the sleeping around brought up the story being circulated and complained about it.

Ultimately, a number of negative consequences occurred. First, the manager who divulged the gossip's name had a warning letter placed in his personnel file about his participation in the malicious tale. Second, he lost a great opportunity for promotion to the department in which he had substituted when the department head refused to select him because the situation had created too much turmoil. She also felt that her staff were all fully aware that he was one of the central players in the incident. In addition, the colleague who denied participation lost credibility with her fellow employees because they believed that she had been less than truthful when she denied being the source of the damaging story. They also considered the letter she sent to the director as overkill. While the state organization attempted to address the problems created by the malicious gossip, it found that fixing the problems caused was almost impossible.

Louise Collins notes that there are a set of negative factors generally attributed to gossip. She writes:

> Four complaints commonly lodged against gossip identify different characteristics as the root of its badness: that it is malicious, that it is pointless, that its subject matter is trivial, that it addresses important subject matter in an inappropriate way.[7]

We also recognize that part of the harm caused by negative gossip results because it becomes an inappropriate substitute for constructive behavior. Though not a comprehensive overview, the following nine types of harm can occur within an organization as a result of gossip.

First, malicious gossip clearly has a divisive impact on the workforce. It creates a discordant, hostile work environment characterized by anger and alienation.

Second, the unpleasant environment created by malicious gossip diminishes employee performance and hurts employees at a personal level. It reduces trust, makes decision-making more difficult and interferes with normal work activities. Furthermore, the negativity of gossip contracts a person's sense of possibilities; there is a pulling in, a pulling back. When a person is the subject of malicious gossip, the resulting personal pain cannot help being a significant psychological distraction.

# GOSSIP + MALICE =/= PROBLEM SOLUTION

Psychologist Barbara Fredrickson echoes the same idea from a different perspective. She states that "[p]ositivity doesn't just change the contents of your mind, trading bad thoughts for good ones; it also changes the scope or boundaries of your mind. It widens the span of possibilities that you see."[8] Negativity clearly does exactly the opposite; it narrows or constricts the way we think about things.

Third, malicious gossip never solves problems. Many years ago, the well-known psychologist Eric Berne described a particularly insidious activity he called "Ain't It Awful." Noted in his book *Games People Play*, this game involves having two players point out continuously how awful it is that someone else is doing what he or she happens to be engaged in at the moment. Consequently, none of the players ever undertake constructive activities to resolve a problem. They simply join in the whining session.[9] Malicious gossip has most of the same characteristics; it is judgment without progress. Worse, gossips are often not motivated to solve the problem because they "thrive" on telling others the latest destructive tidbit.

Fourth, the very nature of malicious gossip makes it easy for participants to deny their involvement in it and/or the accuracy of the story. The absence of accountability permits a higher level of recklessness and insidiousness.

Fifth, telling the absolute truth about people with malicious intent–slander–can also be used as a vehicle for destroying reputations and careers. Of course *backbiting*, gossip that is untrue, is usually doubly harmful. In either case, the harm can be devastating.

Sixth, without question, malicious gossiping takes up an inordinate amount of time, and the drama it creates can be very distracting. It is one thing for employees to interact during lunch times and at breaks, it is another for non-work-related discussion to be a continuous background event. Worse, how many mistakes do employees make because they are focusing on the latest juicy bit of "news" rather than on their work?

Seventh, there are two forms of insubordination. The first is the refusal to carry out a specific directive given by one's superior, and the second involves actions or comments intended to demean or discredit higher authority. Thus, malicious gossip about a manager or supervisor can often constitute insubordination. Sharing information that discredits a superior can obviously be damaging to the person, the position, the decision-making process and the organization.

Eighth, the personal and organizational damage caused by malicious gossip includes strained relationships, damaged reputations, interference with organizational effectiveness, and other similar results. These side effects of gossip are to a large degree irreparable.

Ninth, problem solving is the responsibility of management in any organization. In other words, managers should analyze the issue, determine the causes, create solutions and take action. Unfortunately, malicious gossip is not so easily addressed. Gossiping occurs in the shadows. How can improvement occur when no one is accountable? A problem has to be acknowledged and owned before it can be dealt with adequately, and the very nature of gossip is to deny ownership.

We next turn to what are, at times, the daunting legal harms associated with negative gossip.

## Gossip and the Law

As has been discussed, malicious gossip harms others through mechanisms of distortion, dishonesty, defamation and dissonance, with messages that range from the intimate to the incredible. This fact logically raises questions about legal redress. If one is harmed by distortion, dishonesty, defamation and dissonance, will the courts provide restitution?

Robert Post helps answer the question with a quick overview of the law related to recovering losses associated with gossip in a chapter in *Good Gossip*. He notes that the law has always drawn a significant distinction between defamation by way of slander and defamation by way of libel. Libel is the written word while slander is defined as the spoken; libel is a crime while slander is not. Post goes on to emphasize that "a plaintiff suing for libel could receive general and presumed damages not available to a plaintiff suing for slander."[10]

These differences were generally justified on the basis that slander (spoken word) was limited to the immediate present while libel (written word) had the potential to inflict harm beyond those present to hear the spoken word–it could be broadcast. E. L. Godkin, the editor of *Scribner's Magazine*, wrote:

As long as gossip was oral, it spread, as regarded any one individual, over a very small area, and was confined to the immediate circle of his acquaintances. It did not reach, or but rarely reached, those who knew nothing of him. It did not make his name, or his walk, or his conversation familiar to strangers.[11]

However, one should keep in mind that an individual engaged in acts of slander may find that there are exceptions to the general principle that oral statements cannot constitute defamation.

One should keep in mind that an individual engaged in acts of slander may find that there are exceptions to the general principle that oral statements cannot constitute defamation.

Beyond the law of defamation, there is also the law with regard to the right of privacy, often cited in the context of malicious gossip. In a case commonly referred to in this context, the California Supreme Court in 1931 succinctly stated that "the right of privacy can only be violated by printings, writings, pictures, or other permanent publications or reproductions, and not by word of mouth."[12] Similarly, the U.S. Supreme Court in 1989 found no right of privacy with regard to "backyard gossip."[13]

Employment law in the United States raises issues about gossip beyond personal defamation. Under the law, an employer is liable for the actions of its employees during work hours and, under certain conditions, for actions while off the clock. A short article titled "False Workplace Gossip Can Result in Company Liability" by Ken Hardin highlights the obvious relationship between malicious gossip in the workplace and employer liability. The article responds directly to a problem presented by a reader who was the target of malicious gossip. It suggests a course of action for the victim of the gossip and outlines the various liabilities that a company has if it fails to respond adequately to the problem. The author, a regular contributor to the online journal in which the article appeared, takes the following position:

> A few months ago, I took a little heat from some readers (that's fine, I'm used to it) when I suggested that managers should not only shun office gossip, but act to quash it when it begins circulating. Orwellian or not, I stand by my contention that even seemingly innocent gossip about coworkers is at best a foolish waste of time and, as in the situation described here, a potential source of liability for both managers and the company.[14]

In this case, the letter writer's sexual orientation was being questioned, and the gossip indicated that he was guilty of using male prostitutes. He denied both that he is gay and, more emphatically, that he used male prostitutes. Liability, however, is not significantly impacted by whether or not the statements being made about the individual are true. The fact that the gossip is creating a hostile environment is the paramount legal concern.[15]

In exploring the potential legal issues involved in the case, Hardin draws the conclusion that the employer, particularly if it chooses to do nothing about the malicious gossip, faces substantial liability. He includes in his analysis research conducted with the local office of the

EEOC that affirms his position. The author also explores other legal avenues by which the gossip victim might seek redress. He concludes by pointing to the letter writer's statement that senior management knows about the gossip and has chosen to do nothing about it. The article ends with the sentence, "Sounds like something a plaintiff's lawyer would love to hear."[16]

Does gossip, particularly malicious and hurtful statements, pose a legal liability to the employer as set forth in the above article? We know of no statute that specifically bars gossip in the workplace. However, malicious gossip is clearly a verbal attack on another person and thus the nature of malicious gossip makes it likely that it can be considered a prohibited action under statutes designed to ensure a supportive and harassment-free workplace. There are combinations of state and federal statutes prohibiting sexual harassment, bullying and mobbing.

In addition, many organizations have specific policies covering the same prohibitions; policies that provide for discipline if an employee engages in verbal harassment, bullying or mobbing. For example, one state agency we are aware of has an anti-mobbing policy that states that the agency "is committed to providing a safe, respectful work environment for all employees, free from mobbing behaviors."[17] From our perspective, malicious gossip that circulates in the workplace about a fellow employee can certainly be viewed as unsafe, disrespectful and mobbing behavior. A similar analysis is obviously possible with gossip viewed as sexual harassment and/or bullying. The employment policies of most organizations clearly express the desire to ensure a workplace free of socially aggressive behavior, whether it is called harassment, bullying or mobbing.

This brief sojourn into the legal and liability issues has the limited purpose of emphasizing one of the reasons why employers universally have a concern with malicious gossip and why they seek to control or remove it from the workplace. Malicious gossip obviously has the potential to cost the organization a lot of money.

## The Betrayal of Confidentiality

Clearly, gossip can often be harmful, but in several settings, it verges on the catastrophic for those concerned. They include medical and mental health offices, every aspect of the legal arena, and clergy-parishioner communications. In addition, human resource departments and accounting departments handle a tremendous amount of confidential information, ranging from healthcare accounts to office payrolls that require confidentiality and privacy.

Good judgment and discretion are critical to ensuring the privacy of workers in these arenas since confidentiality is a legal expectation. A patient, for instance, should be able to discuss medical matters with her healthcare provider without having the details spilled at a dinner party, or talk with her priest or pastor without fear that the congregation will know every intimate detail. In these professional environments, the distinction we have drawn between social gossip and malicious gossip has no importance. The right to privacy or confidentiality is not based on whether the gossip is malicious or simply idle social chatter.

Under State Bar Association codes of conduct as well as established case law, anyone who retains a lawyer has the right to discuss his or her situation freely, knowing that client-attorney privilege prevents the lawyer from divulging any of their conversation. Obviously, such information provides tempting opportunities for employees in these settings. For example, they could pass along enticing bits of news, such as "The mayor and his wife are going to couples' counseling!" "Guess who came in for a consultation about a face-lift!" or "Wait until you hear the details of this divorce!" This impulse to spill the beans may be more tempting because the gossip has no personal relationship with the person mentioned—making it easier to dehumanize him or her.

Of course, the clergy have a special obligation as well to ensure that what a congregant tells them remains confidential, barring suspected child abuse. But in many houses of worship, there is no training on confidentiality and gossip, or the harm it can cause. In addition, many religious organizations are so small that they offer virtually no new employee orientation or formal training, let alone employee handbooks. We'd all like to think that only people with the best of intentions work in such places, but sadly, that isn't true in a great many cases. Secretaries, administrative assistants, receptionists, even the church organist–all need to know that when someone comes to the clergy for counseling, their privacy needs to be respected–even the simple fact they visited at all, let alone why they came in.

Let's say, for example, that you're an obstetrician with a busy practice in Los Angeles, much in demand for your safe, professional practice. One day, a well-known actress comes to you with the news that she's pregnant, and wants you to deliver her baby. She asks whether you can assure her privacy. Of course, you say, it's a part of your professional ethics that you take very seriously. But you have records clerks, receptionists and others who may well be subjected to blandishments and outright bribery from the tabloids for photos and information.

You need to have had those very important discussions with your staff about the danger of gossiping about patients BEFORE they face the temptation to share private information. Most doctors do, of course. But how often do you repeat those conversations? How often do you update employee handbooks? Talk about gossip and expectations of privacy must be an ongoing, important part of your culture. This isn't just a problem in Beverly Hills, of course. The same damage to a patient's privacy and the same pain caused by gossip can happen in any small town setting if news of someone's medical treatment is passed on.

In all of these environments, gossip destroys professionalism, undermines trust and may precipitate legal action. And, obviously, it is profoundly wrong, with the potential for real human casualty. Some workplaces by their very nature demand privacy when services are provided. Employees of those agencies must have continuing instruction in confidentiality policies, well-written employee handbooks, and clear, unambiguous penalties for violating privacy rules.

## The Ultimate Harm

Most people understand that gossip has a destructive side. The previous discussion makes that point clearly when citing the negative impact on an individual's reputation, the loss of employment opportunities he or she experiences, the division and diminished morale it causes in the workforce, and other similar costs within the organization. The less obvious cost is that malicious gossip often excludes constructive alternatives. Where communication could have been positive, affirming and supportive, the employees/colleagues chose to engage in some form of personally demeaning interaction about a third person. It is not just that they chose a destructive course; they chose a destructive action over a positive, affirming one.

There are, however, powerful examples of those who consciously choose a constructive course of action even in situations that are extremely challenging. On October 2, 2006, one of the most heinous acts in the history of the United State occurred in a one-room Amish schoolhouse in the state of Pennsylvania. A man shot ten girls ages six to thirteen, five of whom died, and then took his own life.[18] One of the most astounding elements of this event was the response of the Amish to the death of their children. "We must not think evil of this man" is the message that was sent to the outside community. Within a very short period of time, the Amish offered the man's family help and comfort, including setting up a charitable fund to assist them. The man's funeral was attended almost exclusively by his Amish neighbors though neither he nor his family were members of the Amish community.[19]

While the Amish story is not about gossip per se, it is a story about how the choices we make in responding to life events either magnify the harm done or point us in the direction of healing and helpfulness. Bad things do happen. Unfortunately, all too often the negative event is made worse by damaging reactions.

Malicious gossip frequently involves bad situations. We have already noted that one of the harms associated with gossip is that it is judgment and condemnation without action or solution. Worse, the nature of the malicious interaction all too often adds fuel to the fire. Problems expand, and wounds become deeper, uglier and more painful.

These conditions create the ultimate harm of malicious gossip: The choice to gossip locks out constructive alternatives that have the profound ability to heal wounds, create community and bring joy to the workplace. It is one thing to recognize the obvious negative outcomes resulting from gossip, but a much deeper loss is exposed by considering the possible positive results that could have emerged had wiser, life-affirming choices directed the course of action. What the Amish have provided is an extraordinary example of how not to respond to evil with evil. Instead, they modeled the life-changing power of forgiveness, gentleness, helpfulness and kindness.

Is it possible to transfer the behavior of the Amish people into the workplace particularly with regard to how we communicate with each other? That's a good question. The most common responses we heard following the shooting were based on open admiration for the Amish community along with the assertion that as persons they would not have been able to follow their example. Fortunately, the typical workplace does not deal with issues as compelling and tragic as that faced by the Amish, but we can still learn from their example. Hopefully, through efforts to address the issue of malicious gossip constructively, most of us can recognize the value of not just eliminating it but replacing it with life-affirming communication.

## Chapter 2 Summary

Gossip can have a highly negative impact on an organization. This chapter explored the destructive impact of malicious gossip in a number of different ways and can best be understood by considering the following:

- The popularization of gossip through the media has not changed the fact that it harms the workplace.
- Malicious gossip is harmful both at a personal and at an organizational level
- Nine generic harms are obvious: 1) division and disunity, 2) diminished employee performance, 3) a poor substitute for solving the problem, 4) denial with its accompanying problems, 5) destruction of personal reputations–whether the gossip is true or not, 6) waste of time, 7) a form of insubordination when directed at a manager, 8) a cause of often irreparable damage, 9) a hard-to-address shadow activity.
- Gossip raises potential legal issues both with regard to the law of defamation and the employer's potential liabilities associated with the legal requirement to provide a workplace free from bullying, mobbing and sexual harassment.
- The law of defamation as it involves libel encompasses only written gossip.
- Special consideration needs to be given to the problem of gossip in those organizations where confidentiality is a prime concern. Medical establishments, law offices and religious institutions are three prime examples. The public has come to expect that personal problems brought to these forums will not be disclosed by careless employees.
- The ultimate harm is that malicious gossip displaces life-celebrating and affirming behaviors, a practice that can be changed to initiate profound, positive impact in the workplace.

# Chapter 3

## HIGH-TECH GOSSIP

### Gossip's hurtful sting
### is sharpened on Web.
#### HEADLINE, CHICAGO *TRIBUNE*

*Chicago Tribune* article titled "Gossip's hurtful sting is sharpened on Web" raised questions about the negative impact of Internet "rumor sites." Published a few years back, the article referenced the suicide of a well-known local advertising executive and speculated on the role that some harsh, demeaning criticism leveled against him on a website closely associated with gossip in the advertising industry might have played in his death. The article highlights how high-tech modes of communication multiply the potency of gossip's dark side.[1] In fact, the Internet has become a well populated habitat for what are now called "hate trolls."

As instances of the damage caused by malicious gossip on the Internet rise so has public awareness of the problem. The "blog blowback" is one of the ways some have chosen to address the issue. The term refers to criticism of the Internet critic/gossip. An example of blog blowback could be "It looks like this stupid blog can kill more than a career." The previously cited article notes that "blog blowback is an increasing online occurrence as gossip, rumor and criticism move from the water cooler to the Web."[2]

While we are primarily concerned with personal interaction between individuals in the workplace, no discussion of gossip would be complete without some reference to how technology has changed the landscape of human communication dramatically and created an extraordinary venue for gossip. Perhaps, more than any other single variable, the Internet has altered social attitudes toward the practice. While malicious gossip has historically been banned both by the great religions of the world and by cultural values and beliefs, it is now trumpeted throughout the Internet. It often appears that the nastier, more salacious the account, the greater the chance that it will find its way to a high-tech outlet. And, while there are certainly criticisms of Internet gossip, the legitimacy of gossip blogs and websites appears to be almost unquestioned. They have unfortunately become an acceptable part of our lives and culture.

Columnist Anna Quindlen bemoans the fact that Internet gossip has removed remorse from the act of gossiping. In her usual succinct fashion, she states the primary concern about Internet "trash talk."

> Don't get me wrong; there's nothing new about gawking, gossip, getting into the business of other people and being gleeful about it. Surely it was happening in caves, huts, the pyramids, the Parthenon. What's new about it is its scope and responsibility, the first vast, the second nonexistent.[3]

Quindlen's primary point is that in the old days we gossiped about someone we actually knew and someone we would personally encounter. She emphasizes that "eye contact has always had a dampening effect on trash talk. It's shame-making, quite properly so."[4] In other words, high-tech gossip takes away the human element in the activity and with it any concerns about the person(s) attacked or remorse for the action.

This acceptance of gossip makes the manager's job particularly difficult. Therefore, the following discussion explores various elements of high-tech gossip and offers a number of reasonable actions that a manager can take to minimize its destructiveness both in the organization and the work group.

## Gossip via Electronic Methods

These days, the transmission of gossip can be instantaneous. Twittering, blogging, e-mail, smartphones and texting makes the coffee shop or copy room conversations seem almost quaint. Why risk the boss watching you chat when you can shoot a tweet, an e-mail or an instant message to the intended recipient from the privacy of an office or even the restroom?

In addition, there is always the possibility that websites and blogs can be dedicated specifically to disseminating gossip in its worst possible expression. These high-tech outlets are usually industry specific like *Juicycampus.com*, a website that used to be devoted to college students and was described as "always anonymous and always juicy." It is "used to be" because its founder has repositioned himself to be a web reputation defender and has authored the book, *lol... OMG!*, a book written to help college students protect themselves on the Internet.[5]

However, managers are less concerned with the gossip industry than with the actions of individuals within their organization or work group who directly participate in Internet gossip. That includes everything from social networks like Facebook and Twitter, personal websites and blogs, and the multiple uses of smartphones. In fact, recently smartphones have gone front and center in the realm of social sharing with special apps such as Instagram, Hinge, Secret, Taptalk and Yik Yak. One description of Yik Yak, an app designed for localized intimate sharing, is particularly telling in that it is called a "breeding ground for gossip and harassment."[6]

As one might expect, there is now a new water-cooler app called Memo that allows people to gossip anonymously about their workplaces.[7] Although just recently made available to the public, it already has a substantial following with a lot of organizational griping as the primary topics.

In addition, every smartphone is equipped with a camera that can take pictures and e-mail or text message them instantly. While pictures are not inherently malicious gossip, they have that potential when they put the subject in an unfavorable light, are of a personal nature and are sent against the person's wishes.

With all of these, the stakes are incredibly high. There's hardly any location from which an employee with a smartphone can't communicate instantaneously–on the subway, in the restroom, at a table in the break room, during a conference break; from the airport or at a retreat. In other words, everywhere–and on his or her own equipment. So news, true or not, can sweep across an organization in a flash, and spread quickly to the rest of the country or even the world. Do employees think the boss screwed up on a recent deal? In 140 characters or less, any one of them can instantly send out a tweet to all of his or her followers, from one to dozens or more. Those followers can quickly send it out again until exponential numbers of people get that message. As of December 2014, there were approximately 500 million plus tweets sent every day.

That same message can be placed in a blog, making it available to others who can re-blog it countless times so that Internet search engines then pick it up. That means if someone is "googling" your company or agency, he or she can discover the blog entry easily.

In fact, the problem has become so extensive that companies have been formed for the specific purpose of protecting a person or a company's name–one's Internet reputation. Firms like DefendMyName. com will help a client know what is said about him, her or it on the Internet and provide aid in removing damaging information. This process is sometimes referred to as *googlewashing,* and the growth of the industry is clearly associated with the amount of malicious gossip found on the Web.

A critical problem, of course, is that high-tech gossip is not restricted to work hours. In other words, there is *no clear bright line* separating work from personal time, no functional difference between actions conducted on the clock as compared to those off the clock. That makes a manager's job infinitely more complicated than it was 20 years ago in terms of communication. But it also makes the job more creative and thoughtful because, used properly, tools such as texting can enhance the workplace and simplify a lot of necessary communication, binding together colleagues or teams in different work locations.

## Cyberbullying

Cyberbullying is the act of using social media to harm or harass another person, usually in a deliberate, repeated and hostile manner. Cyberbullying can be limited to posting negative rumors or tales about a person through one or more of the social media outlets. More vicious bullying may go so far as to identify victims and publish materials, including compromising pictures to defame and humiliate them severely.

Cyberbullying has been a hot topic in the media in the past few years primarily because of a number of well documented suicides linked to repeated caustic, harassing Internet messages. High school and college students are particularly vulnerable since they are heavy users of social media. The Crimes Against Children Research Center at the University of New Hampshire maintains a national database related to cyberbullying. Their most recent national survey (2011) indicated that about 2.2 million students, ages 12 to 18, experienced cyberbullying. It is clearly not a small problem.[8]

Cyberbullying can become an important issue for the manager particularly if the organization's employees are younger and/or use social media frequently. While it might be difficult if the manager does not use social media, awareness of any problem is the first step to addressing it effectively. In addition, he or she needs to inform employees clearly that attacking a fellow employee by spreading malicious gossip through social media is considered a legitimate concern that can be addressed through a personnel action, even if done on personal time and with personal technology. Combatting the problem must also include teaching employees the value of using social media to help build camaraderie and teamwork. Negative communication can be dealt with most effectively by replacing it with good, supportive interactions.

## Learning from the Pros

Blaine Sampson, the CEO of an IT consulting company in Kansas City, is well acquainted with the issues associated with high-tech communication particularly as a vehicle for gossip. Sampson says that technology has only made problems of negative communication worse. Text messaging and e-mail personify the ease with which gossips can knowingly or unknowingly lay their victims low and ruin the atmosphere of an organization with lightning speed because they encourage sloppiness and speed over thoughtfulness, and lack any real interpersonal feedback. "Everyone sends out the first draft of an e-mail," he notes dryly.[9]

Sampson and others who have studied communications have noticed a frequent phenomenon–people who pride themselves on bluntness–or what they term "honesty" in dealing with others–seldom like to get a taste of their own medicine. "They don't want anyone to communicate back to them that way. They want to send out a rocket or missile without taking any flak themselves. What I have noticed is that people who communicate face-to-face verbally have less issues of ever being misunderstood. With the advent of e-mail and instant messaging, what should be routine communication easily turns into full-blown misunderstanding. At least when people used to gossip, they were talking to someone–it was one on one. Now it's one on 1,000. With an e-mail, [a person] can pass [a juicy tidbit] on to 100 people, then [insert] it in a blog, [which then reaches] 1,000 more people. Gossip used to be somewhat restrained. Now it's viral and can't be tracked down anymore. Nowadays, where can you go to get your good name back?"[10]

We're here to warn you that most gossips in an organization will initially deny it, and may often even believe those denials. Sampson has talked many times with people who have written vicious or poisonous e-mails in an organization and listened to the person insist that he or she was just being blunt or honest. It's his job to help that person understand the harm done to the organization.

To break through that denial, he often asks people to read the nasty or gossipy message aloud: "When they hear it out loud, it's 'Oh my goodness, I can't believe it. No wonder that person got [bent] out of shape.'" In the case of one particular poison-pen e-mailer, Sampson recalled that "he could not look anyone in the face and read his own correspondence."[11]

Sampson subdivides toxic talkers into introvert gossips and extrovert gossips. He's been called into enough organizations to address communication problems that he can usually identify such office types. "Introverts gossip through e-mail," he notes, "while extroverts gossip over a latte."[12]

And he's got an opinion on which type of toxic communication is worse: "The introverted will be more viral than if I gossiped in person," he says. "E-mail has one pernicious (feature), the blind carbon copy. The passive-aggressive will use this feature viciously. Say I sent an e-mail from me to you, and I'm having an issue with how you did something. I'll pass a blind carbon copy to the vice president who is your boss, so you don't even know he's gotten it. So now someone has made an untoward remark about you, and you don't even know what I'm doing. I'll tell the VP, 'I know you like to stay on top of issues with staff,' to justify this. I don't even have the guts to let you know I've gossiped this up the line. You may send a reply back to me, 'You're wrong on all these things,' but I won't send that back to VP, and you don't even know what's going on.[13]

"E-mails simply allow passive-aggressive personalities to run amuck," he concludes. "You can be passive-aggressive out the wazoo. They'd say things in an e-mail they'd never say to your face."[14]

Sampson suggests a simple answer to this vexing problem: ban the use of blind carbon copies in your organization, period. Any minor advantage to using it–if one even exists–pales in comparison to the opportunity to halt gossip and the spread of rumor and malicious information. He (and we!) believe that any organization will be repaid many times over with better trust and higher staff morale.[15]

"It's interesting that most companies have implemented firm policies regarding the personal use of computers by employees, but utterly fail to enact any type of regulations regarding e-mail etiquette," Sampson observes. "You can send the most awful e-mail, and that's okay, but you can't watch Brittney Spears dancing on YouTube. I don't understand it. You can get away with 'murder' on these blind carbon copies, send a vicious, passive-aggressive blind carbon to some VP, but you can't buy a book on Amazon on your lunch hour."[16]

So what is an enlightened organization–be it a church or a Fortune 500 company–to do to encourage healthy, supportive and productive communication? First, if you can say something in person, don't use e-mail. If you can't simply walk down the hallway to speak with someone, pick up the phone. "E-mail is the last resort in communication, and it should be treated like a letter going out, versus something flippant," Sampson said. He himself does not list e-mails on his company's website; they prefer to make the first contact by speaking with potential clients.[17]

Second, practice waiting to send e-mails, several hours perhaps, even a day is recommended. E-mail has trained many to insist on the instant attention to their demands over thoughtfulness. But what does that really get them or their organization? Examine your own experiences. How many times have you opened a response only to see instantly that the person didn't get the point of your initial e-mail?

(And you thought to yourself, "Did they actually read that thing? How could they say that?")[18]

Third, train employees to avoid using e-mail to send sensitive information or thank you notes. "Just because you can send something via e-mail, doesn't mean you should," Sampson says. "Ask yourself, would I like to get that information in an e-mail?"[19]

Furthermore, if something vital is in an e-mail, then that e-mail can be misinterpreted. "You don't get the body language," Sampson explains. "I think we're communicating more but connecting less. I never do a meeting on the phone if I can do it person. Then my information is not open to misinterpretation."[20]

Practice waiting to send e-mails, several hours perhaps, even a day is recommended. E-mail has trained many to insist on the instant attention to their demands over thoughtfulness.

We (the authors) appreciate the balance in Sampson's comments between what not to do and what ought to be done. Interestingly, Sampson is not alone in his analysis and recommendations. In her book *Reality-Based Leadership,* Cy Wakeman provides much the same perspective on the importance of personal contact as opposed to the excessive use of the Internet and e-mail. She states:

Another way to build strong relationships and teams is to communicate face-to-face whenever possible instead of sending e-mails and memos. E-mails and memos may seem easier or faster than face-to-face conversations, but they are not the most efficient means of communication. Why? They leave your message open to interpretation in ways you cannot anticipate.... Better to take a walk down the hall and be sure of how your message is received.[21]

Similarly, one must consider the influence that emotions have on good or healthy communication. Malicious gossip is more likely when a person allows his or her emotions, such as anger or anxiety, to drive communication behavior. Fortunately, emotions fade over time, so there is a great deal of wisdom associated with allowing time to pass before communicating about a hot topic. Suzy Welch is usually recognized as the originator of the 10/10/10 rule, used to remove unwanted emotional bias from interpersonal communication. She advises people to ask three questions before speaking, writing or sending an e-mail message about an incident:

1.  How will I feel about it 10 minutes from now?
2.  How will I feel about it 10 months from now?
3.  How will I feel about it 10 years from now?[22]

While most of us will probably struggle to muster sufficient discipline to implement the 10/10/10 rule fully, using it will unquestionably help ensure more constructive, effective communication.

Given the thought and discipline required to develop good communication habits, telling employees, subordinates and colleagues not to gossip is clearly an inadequate and almost useless exercise. What managers–and coworkers–must attempt to promote is healthy communication, not just the absence of the maliciousness often associated with caustic commentary on the behavior of others.

## Organizational Control

One of the ways to reduce high-tech gossip is to implement and enforce policies that limit personal use of technology during working hours. Employees need to understand that the continual use of communication technology for personal reasons during working hours is considered theft of time and cause for discipline.

Managers who grew up without the tech devices currently available may have some difficulty understanding today's workers in their 20s or 30s. These young people have grown up posting considerable details about themselves online–even intimate details–and are completely comfortable with disclosing on blogs or recording on video blogs things that their managers consider private information about their organization. In fact, every employee will have a different idea of what constitutes acceptable behavior when using social communication tools like Twitter or cell phones.

Therefore, employees must be explicitly educated about the organization's policies regarding the use of e-mail and instant messaging. Many people are vaguely aware that the employer "owns" their e-mail in the workplace, but this often escapes their memory when it comes to transmitting gossip. The manager's task is to establish policy regarding the use of these communication channels by writing it down in the employee handbook, for instance.

Leaders/managers need to educate themselves about what current policies are in other, similar organizations. For instance, a full 54 percent of U.S. companies say they've banned workers in their companies from using social networking sites like Twitter, Facebook, LinkedIn and MySpace, while at work, according to a study commissioned by Robert Half Technology. The 2009 study[23] also notes that 19 percent of companies allow social networking use only for business purposes, while 16 percent allow limited personal use.[24]

A rather small percentage, 10 percent of the 1,400 CIOs (chief information officers) interviewed, say that employees get full access to social networks during work hours. "Using social networking sites may divert employees' attention away from more pressing priorities, so it's understandable that some companies limit access," explained Dave Willmer, executive director of Robert Half Technology.[25]

Robert Half Technology, a provider of information technology personnel, offers some common-sense guidelines to employees in using social media and modern communication while on the job. They are well worth reading, understanding and then posting in a conspicuous place.

- **Know what's allowed.** Make sure you understand and adhere to your company's social networking policy.
- **Use caution.** Be familiar with each site's privacy settings to ensure personal details or photos you post can be viewed only by people you choose.
- **Keep it professional.** Use social networking sites while at work to make connections with others in your field or follow industry news–**not** to catch up with family or friends.
- **Stay positive.** Avoid complaining about your manager and coworkers. Once you've hit submit or send, you can't always take back your words–and there's a chance they could be read by the very people you're criticizing.
- **Polish your image.** Tweet or blog about a topic related to your profession. You'll build a reputation as a subject matter expert, which could help you advance in your career.
- **Monitor yourself.** Even if your employer has a liberal policy about social networking, chose *not to use* work time checking your Facebook page or reading other people's tweets to avoid a productivity drain.[26]

Another way to keep employees aware of the organization's policies related to social networking sites is to include them in the employee handbook. Using the information they glean from their research, leaders/managers can develop clear expectations about the appropriate use of laptops, e-mail, instant messaging, blogs and video blogs. Here's a sample passage designed to help control gossip via technology by reducing the overall personal use of company computers and other electronic devices.

> High Technology Communication: There are a number of ways that technology allows us to communicate–smartphone, text messaging, e-mail, blogs and telephone. Employees should conform to the following guidelines when communicating by way of any of these devices.
>
> - When involved in professional interactions, you are expected to respond in a prompt, respectful and courteous fashion. Gossiping, derogatory comments, inappropriate innuendos and any exchange that can be considered harassment, sexual or otherwise, should all be avoided. Keep all communication as positive as possible.
> - Do not provide personal information, either about yourself or a fellow employee, to individuals outside of the company unless it has been approved by your supervisor.
> - Personal communication, whether with fellow employees or outsiders, during working hours should be minimized, unless related to emergencies or unusual situations.
> - Avoid using social media to spread gossip and negative comments about colleagues and other employees of the company.
> - Use of personal smartphones should be minimized unless they are being used for business reasons. Do not drive on company business while using a cell phone, a company phone or your own, unless you are set up to be hands free.
> - Business computers are the property of the company

> and employees have no privacy rights with regard to messages that are sent and received on them. All of your messages can be read by your supervisor or others in management. Remember that deleted messages can easily be restored. Your supervisor should be notified as to any passwords and any change in a password.

While straightforward and easily understandable, the above is pretty dry verbiage. And it's undeniable that people will rebel when simply force-fed rules with no attempt at any deeper understanding of why those rules are in place. As has been said, organizational culture trumps rules if the two diverge. What an organization needs is buy-in from its workers, a grasp of why the rules are important. If they are led to an understanding of the rules, however briefly, it can go a long way to ensuring compliance.

Compliance with the communication guidelines also ensures a more positive, high-functioning, competitive organization. On a personal level, people work at their best and feel good about where they work when they are in a place where harmful communication is kept to a minimum.

However, after coming up with a satisfactory policy and employee compliance, it is essential to stay on top of current technology even if it doesn't appear to relate to one's job. That can change in a flash. It wasn't all that long ago that cell phones didn't take pictures, e-mail was inaccessible away from the office desktop, and "twitter" was just something birds did.

While the authors are strong advocates for a clearly communicated policy on the use of high-tech channels of communication and for organizational guidelines on the appropriate use of social networks, a word of caution is needed. Under federal statute, the National Labor Relations Board (NLRB) is charged with the responsibility of protecting the right of employees to form and join a labor union. From a certain perspective, employee complaints via social networks can be viewed as a precursor to organizing a union. Discussing their employer and working conditions both good and bad on social media might legitimately be seen as a first step towards a group of employees getting together to request union representation.

It wasn't all that long ago that cell phones didn't take pictures, e-mail was inaccessible away from the office desktop, and "twitter" was just something birds did.

The NLRB has issued formal complaints against companies that have acted on what were determined to be "overbroad" social media policies. The following is a good example of NLRB action with regard to social media issues.

On May 9, [2011] the NLRB lodged a complaint against a non-profit organization in New York, saying it improperly fired five employees for Facebook posts that amounted to protected concerted activity. According to the press release, an employee posted on her own Facebook wall an allegation by a coworker that employees weren't doing enough for clients. A group of employees responded to the Facebook post, defending their job performance and complaining about their working conditions (including workload and staffing issues). The employer fired the five employees who participated in the online discussion, saying the remarks amounted to harass-

ment of the employee mentioned in the original post. The
NLRB's complaint claims the Facebook discussion was protected under the National Labor Relations Act because it
involved a conversation among coworkers about the terms
and conditions of employment, including their job performance and staffing levels.[27]

Clearly, discharging an employee for saying negative things
about the company or management on Facebook or in a tweet may
give rise to an action by the NLRB. This is not to say that employees
have free license to say whatever they want on the Internet. Since
malicious, disrespectful communication within an organization
can be subject to discipline including discharge, the same type of
interaction on the Internet can be the basis of formal action against
the employee based upon a well thought out and tightly worded policy. Obviously, managers may want to seek competent legal counsel
specializing in labor relations issues to help draft and implement
the policy.

That said, the authors still recommend crafting, communicating
and enforcing clear, specific policies for employee use of social media.

## Confidentiality Issues

Confidential and/or privileged information is a special concern
for any organization in this era of high-tech interaction. Unfortunately,
social media can provide an all too effective mode for inappropriately
transmitting confidential information. While this type of communication is usually not gossip as defined in Chapter 1, it is clearly a close
cousin and one that deserves at least a few comments.

Businesses, financial institutions, medical facilities, nonprofit
groups, government agencies and religious organizations frequently develop and store confidential information, created either
as a matter of law, business necessity or respect for personal privacy. Employees often have access to that information, and if they

contribute frequently on social media sites, the risks of improper disclosure increase significantly.

What makes leakage by social media outlets so frustratingly easy is the perceived and actual extent of anonymity. The communicator is often anonymous and can easily feel that whatever he or she discusses will not be known in its particulars by the message recipient. As a result, an employee who might not divulge confidential information in a personal interaction can easily develop an indifference to Internet disclosure.

Moreover, specific Internet outlets such as glassdoor.com encourage employees to provide anonymous reviews of their employer ("company reviews shared by real employees"). Prospective employees can check these reviews to determine whether a company and/or job is a good fit. Of course, the concern may be that the review is very one-sided and can deliberately or inadvertently reveal confidential information.

While no perfect cure exists, an employer can take a number of actions to help contain the problem. The first and most obvious is to ensure that the organization's confidentiality policy addresses prohibited communication on social media. Including the words "social media" in a list of prohibited communication actions is insufficient. Confidentiality and social media need to be addressed in sections that clearly identify the prohibited actions.

In addition, a visit to the Internet may provide insights useful in assessing and addressing any confidentiality problems. Since applications for employment usually require references, managers should also check to see what social media outlets the applicant uses. While it does not make sense to overreact to some of the more jovial and lighthearted postings, disclosures of a more intimate and personal nature might give cause for concern. At minimum, these concerns can be a subject in an interview. Similarly, a current employee's actions can raise questions about his or her respect for confidentiality.

Furthermore, where there are areas of high concern over confidentiality, a supervisor or someone in employee services might choose to review employee use of social media periodically. While clearly more draconian, random social media checking may be necessary for highly sensitive positions. For instance, Federal DOT rules require random drug testing for certain truck drivers for obvious reasons.

Another word of caution is in order. It is clearly one thing to peruse the Internet for messages available to the public; it is a distinctly different matter to require job applicants and existing employees to provide their social media logins and passwords. Recently, certain employers and colleges had made headline news by requiring that applicants and students provide access to their social media accounts. While the information about a person's character might be gleaned from a behind-the-scenes look at how he or she uses social media, these actions have been met with a strong political backlash. Maryland became the first state to prohibit the action (signed by the Governor on May 2, 2012) with a number of other states following suit. In addition, it appears that Congress[28] may move ahead with federal legislation to prohibit such requirements.

However, the state and federal legislative efforts do not in any way restrict an employer from reviewing publicly available information. Wisdom encourages an employer to have a basic understanding of how employees are using social media and be knowledgeable about matters of confidentiality and the potential problems it creates.

## Law vs. Love

The *Sydney* (Australia) *Morning Herald* recently reported on the sentencing of a young man who had published nude pictures of his ex-girlfriend on Facebook. It seems that she had ended their relationship, and he was out for some payback. He sent her an e-mail indicating that her photos were on Facebook. She demanded that they be taken down, but he refused. Her next stop was the police station.[29]

Australia, it so happens, has much stricter Internet regulation and laws than those found in the United States and most other countries. However, the words of the deputy-chief magistrate are worth noting.

> What could be more serious than publishing nude photographs of a woman on the Internet, what could be more serious? It's one thing to publish an article in print form with limited circulation. That may affect the objective seriousness of the offense, but once it goes on the World Wide Web via Facebook, it effectively means it's open to anyone who has some link in any way, however remotely.[30]

At the time of this writing, the authors are not aware of any similar criminal conviction in the United States or any other country for a personally damaging posting on the Internet. Our research indicates that the law is still struggling to find an appropriate response for deliberate harm imposed by way of social media. To paraphrase one Internet expert, the law is fully capable of responding to a case of revenge by slashing tires but, in general, has no response at all for the Internet slashing of a person's reputation.

Ultimately, we are reminded of Archbishop Desmond Tutu's often repeated statement that "love is more demanding than the law."[31] Or, to put it another way, when it comes to how we communicate about and with others, the law can at best tell us what not to do. The law is not designed to encourage supportive communication that builds community.

## Chapter 3 Summary

Technology has provided a powerful new medium by which to engage in malicious gossip. E-mails, social networking, blogs and tweets all offer a venue for rapid and extended interaction. This chapter has focused on the following primary points:

- High-tech has dramatically increased the amount of gossip in our lives and, because it now reaches a broader audience, increased its destructive impact.
- The anonymous nature of high-tech gossip makes it easier for individuals to increase the amount of gossip and its caustic tone.
- High-tech gossip has brought new players into action as previously silent introverts gossip through the Internet where they can hide while the extroverts continue to gossip at water fountains.
- A good rule for any organization is to ban the practice of sending blind carbon copies in or outside the organizational walls.
- A well-worded, not overly broad policy on the proper use of social media needs to be clearly communicated to employees as a first step towards halting its inappropriate use.
- High-tech modes of communicating have created a special area of concern related to privileged or confidential information. Employees need to be aware that they are strictly prohibited from sharing such information through social media even if it is in a disguised form.
- The law currently provides little if any help in protecting the person or the organization from reputation destroying messages sent out through social media. When paired with the appropriate corrective action, personal vigilance in monitoring and knowing what is on the Internet provides the most constructive approach to shielding the person and/or the organization from the ravages of high-tech gossip.

# Chapter 4

# GOSSIP AND GENDER

### The label "gossip" casts a critical light on women's interest in talking about the details of people's lives.
#### DEBORAH TANNEN

n April 2007, four women from Hooksett, New Hampshire, had their employment terminated for gossiping. The four ladies became known in popular media as the Hooksett 4.[1] As is so often true with gossip, the facts are somewhat fuzzy and involve allegations about a male town administrator and a female subordinate. The matter centered on the perception that the female subordinate received a questionable promotion at what some considered an inappropriately high rate of pay. As one might guess, the gossip focused on the nature of the relationship between the administrator and the employee.

After lawsuits were filed, the town settled out of court paying each woman a substantial amount of money. Two of the women received $65,000 each and had the letter of termination removed from their files. A third had her employment restored and received $65,000. Shortly thereafter she left town employment for a new position. The fourth woman received a $140,000 settlement.[2] In addition, one source indicated that the town had paid out more than $20,000 for its own legal fees though this figure was not a final tally. In other words, the town had spent considerable funds to settle an issue related to gossip.

The story of the Hooksett 4 supports two significant points. The first restates the point made in Chapter 2: *Malicious gossip costs real dollars*. Beyond the financial cost is the damage inflicted on the operation of the organization, the destructive impact on people's personal lives and the damage to reputations. In fact, it seems reasonable to conclude that recovering from the financial loss will be easier than surmounting the detrimental effects of gossip on the town and the lives of those involved.

Second, it is significant to note that the Hooksett 4 were all women. The decision to terminate the women's employment came after an independent investigator filed a fact-finding report that identified the four women as the main culprits in the dissemination of what was considered a particularly malicious piece of gossip. One published report Indicated that the town considered the women's conduct to be "insubordinate, dishonest and unsuitable, interfered with effective job performance and had an adverse effect on the efficiency of town services."[3]

Malicious gossip costs real dollars. Beyond the financial cost is the damage inflicted on the operation of the organization.

In an interview with CBS News, one of the four is quoted as stating that, "When it all filtered down, four people were fired for what literally had most of the town employees buzzing."[4] If most of the town was involved in the gossip, one has to wonder why it was that only the women were fired. Of course, we do not have a copy of the investigative report and do not know what is meant by the finding that the four were the main purveyors of the gossip. The fact remains, however, that all four were women.

Let's face it, our culture isn't filled with stories about how much men gossip. All the phrases or sayings in our language reflect the image of women as gossips. The words are so easy to call up–*cat, tattler, prattler.* Obviously, none of the images attached to the notion of women as gossips are particularly flattering. Quite the opposite, in fact. These stereotypes, which are deeply rooted in our culture, are always pejorative or negative. "She's a gossip" is an epithet that's been hurled at women for time immemorial. Can it be that the perception of "women as gossips" helped shape the eventual decision of the town council to terminate the employment of the Hooksett 4?

There is no way to have a complete answer to that question, but what follows is an exploration of the issue. Do women really gossip more than men? What is the evidence? What does it actually show? What are the implications for the workplace?

We decided to write a chapter on gossip, gender and the workplace after much deliberation. One of our concerns is that a discussion of gender differences can be volatile and might detract from the focus on the problem of malicious gossip in the workplace. We were also very concerned when our research indicated a lack of consensus with regard to the factual information. Linguist Deborah Tannen discusses the problem of accuracy in the introduction to one of her books. She resolves the problem as follows:

> Despite these dangers, I am joining the growing dialogue on
> gender and language because the risk of ignoring differences

is greater than the danger of naming them. Sweeping something big under the rug doesn't make it go away; it trips you up
and sends you sprawling when you venture across the room.
Denying real differences can only compound the confusion
that is already widespread in this era of shifting and re-forming
relationships between women and men.

Pretending that women and men are the same hurts women,
because the ways they are treated are based on the norms
for men. It also hurts men who, with good intentions, speak to
women as they would to men, and are nonplused when their
words don't work as they expected, or even spark resentment
and anger.[5]

Like Tannen, we decided to include this chapter on the grounds
that its inclusion had sufficient value to risk the dangers. We recognize that some of what we have to say is controversial and have done
our best to acknowledge the controversy while providing what we
found to be the best supported information.

It's no secret that men and women communicate differently, and
their interactions often focus on very different concerns. Numerous
books have been written about these differences including the bestseller *Men Are from Mars, Women Are from Venus* by John Gray.[6] It's
worthwhile to explore those differences and better understand the
impact of communication differences on work performance, relationships and people's lives.

## Gender Differences and Gossip

One of the authors clearly remembers a high-level male manager at a business where she worked mentioning that it bothered
him to see two females walking down a hallway talking together,
because he believed them to be invariably engaged in some form

of gossip. (Of course, he hadn't the slightest clue what they might be discussing.) And it's no secret that in more rigidly patriarchal organizations, the men in authority have an even greater tendency to label much of the communication that occurs between women as mere "gossip"; in other words, men discuss important things and women gossip. This downplays and even denigrates the significance of what women say to one another, reinforcing the superiority of male communication.

However, is it just women whose communication is suspect? Of course not! Men are far from immune to the pleasures of a juicy tidbit. It's just that men frequently label it differently, giving it the aura of greater legitimacy. Studies show that men are very interested in gossip that involves status (i.e., who is "in," who is "out" and who has authority, whether formal or informal). In fact, while celebrity-driven magazines aimed at women have exploded in recent years, so have specialized sporting magazines aimed at men who revel in insider information and "scoops."

Two related areas of great interest to men, one traditional and one cutting-edge, also traffic heavily in gossip–politics and blogging, with its frequently accompanying mediums, podcasting and tweeting. Indeed, it is fair to conclude that political operatives–whether male or female–have frequently found that harmful gossip can help bring down the opposition. A quick reading of *Scorpion Tongues,* which contains a lengthy history of the role of gossip in American politics, clearly indicates that damaging political gossip is not the exclusive purview of women. For instance, President Andrew Jackson angrily tracked a particularly malicious piece of gossip, harmful to his administration, to the male minister of his own church.[7]

Both Republicans and Democrats have accused one another of using gossip to weaken or bring down members of the opposing party. Republican Congressman Mark Foley and Democratic Congressman Anthony Weiner are just two examples. One can only imagine the amount of gossip the behavior of these two individuals has generated, and it is highly doubtful that only women shared the stories.

In the world of blogging, men revel in expressing ideas on just about any topic imaginable, and this includes discussing other people. But in many cases, because it is men talking, this falls under the label "opinion," not gossip.

It almost goes without saying that the financial industry on Wall Street thrives on gossip and rumor, from hints of lower-than-expected-earnings at a given company to what hedge-fund manager was seen secretly lunching with which high-tech CEO. Should any doubt linger about the truth of this assertion, one need only read the "Heard on the Street" column in that most august of publications, the *Wall Street Journal.* In the business world, men like to call gossip by the oh-so-respectable sobriquet, "networking."

A review of research literature reveals very little difference between genders when comparing communication habits. One study found that "71% of the women's conversations, compared with 64% of the men's conversations, were spent gossiping about others." Of course, this is just one study and the difference between 71% and 64% hardly seems worth noting since both percentages are very high.[8]

The study did point out some significant differences between men and women with regard to gossip.

> Although male and female gossip did not differ with respect to tone, significant sex differences were uncovered for characteristics of their targets of gossip. Women were much more likely than men to gossip about close friends and family members. Specifically, 56% of the women's targets but only 25% of the men's targets were friends and relatives. In contrast, men (46%) were more likely than women (16%) to talk about celebrities including sports figures as well as about other acquaintances on campus.[9] [statistical calculations omitted]

The following soliloquy by Ogden Nash paraphrases the research findings in a more poetic fashion:

> All good men believe that women would rather get rid of a
>      piece of gossip than a bulge,
> And all good women believe that gossip is a feminine
>      weakness in which men never indulge.
> Rather than give ear to scandalous rumors,
> Why, men would rather play golf in bloomers,
> And rather than talk behind each other's backs,
> They would go shopping in a mink coat and slacks
> It is one of each sex's uniquenesses
> That men's talk is all of humanity's aspirations, and
>      women's  all of their friends' weaknesses.
> Yes, this is a universal credo that no amount of evidence
>      can alter,
> Including that of Petronius, Suetonius, Pepys, Boswell,
>      the locker room of the country club, and Mrs.
>      Winchell's little boy, Walter.
> Allow me to ask and answer one question before
>      departing for Mount Everest or Lake Ossipee:
> Who says men aren't gossipy? – Men say men aren't gossipy.[10]

In short, by our definition of gossip, both men and women are fully engaged, but likely focus on different topics and call it by a different name. However, there is much more to a discussion of gender and gossip than a simple assessment of conversation topics and types of interaction. Biology also plays a part in gender differences in communication.

## Sex Differences in Communication

There are those who contend that men and women have physiological differences that have some influence on gossiping behavior. They believe that the female brain differs from the male brain in significant ways that affect communication, including issues around gossip.

Neurological studies, for example, have shown that women and men process communication acts, language and vocabulary differently. Researchers state that "the white matter in women's brains is concentrated in the corpus callosum, which links the brain's hemispheres, and enables the right side of the brain to pitch in on language tasks."[11] The more difficult the verbal task, the more global the neural participation required–a response that's stronger in females. In other words, a woman's brain structure makes it more likely that she will find communication fluid or easy.

Psychiatrist Louann Brizendine makes a strong case for the differences in the male and female brain. In her best-selling book *The Female Brain,[1]* she notes that much of the early neurological research was conducted on men with the assumption that the results applied equally to women. She takes strong exception to this conclusion and emphasizes that what little research was reported comparing the brains of men with women "suggested that the brain differences, though subtle, were profound."[12]

She draws most of her conclusions about the difference between male and female brain development based on the fact that each is bathed in different hormones. Brizendine found "that the female brain is so deeply affected by hormones that their influence can be said to create a woman's reality."[13] She summarizes the significance of the hormones at the beginning of the book.

---

1The book had its strong proponents and strong detractors. A point made by a negative review found in the October 2006 issue of *Nature* is that information is presented so that the female brain is clearly distinguished from the male brain instead of the more accurate finding of smaller differences in generally overlapping behaviors. The authors of this book have concluded that the controversies surrounding certain parts of *The Female Brain* do not diminish the value of its contribution to a discussion of gender and gossip.

Hormones can determine what the brain is interested in doing. They help guide nurturing, social, sexual, and aggressive behaviors. They can affect being talkative, being flirtatious, giving or attending parties, writing thank-you notes, planning children's play dates, cuddling, grooming, worrying about hurting the feelings of others, being competitive, masturbating and initiating sex.[14]

Drawing support from a variety of neurological research projects, Brizendine concludes that a woman's brain is more adept from birth for participating in human communication and therefore more advanced and tuned-in from the outset. She writes:

So why is a girl born with such a highly tuned machine for reading faces, hearing emotional tones in voices, and responding to unspoken cues in others? Think about it. A machine like that is built for connection. That's the main job of the girl brain, and that's what it drives a female to do from birth. This is the result of millennia of genetic and evolutionary hardwiring that once had–and probably still has–real consequences for survival. If you can read faces and voices, you can tell what an infant needs. You can predict what a bigger, more aggressive male is going to do.[15]

Note particularly the phrase "built for connection" since those who view gossip especially the positive side–as a necessary form of communication frequently describe it as a way of connecting.

While her discussion clearly ranges far beyond the topic of gossip, she raises one point that appears to parallel a prior section on gender and gossip. She summarizes data related to the impact of hormonal changes at puberty and describes some significant differences between teenage girls and teenage boys.

> Males and females become reactive to different kinds of
> stress. Girls begin to react more to relationship stresses and
> boys to challenges to their authority. Relationship conflict is
> what drives a teen girl's stress system wild. She needs to
> be liked and socially connected; a teen boy' needs to be
> respected and higher in the male pecking order.[16]

From Brizendine's perspective, these gender typical behaviors are hardwired, a reflection of how the female brain differs from the male brain both in structure and development. Interestingly, the differences outlined above have relevance to a discussion of gossip.

## Women as Gossips

In an article first published in *Women's Studies International Quarterly*, Deborah Jones initiates a discussion of women and gossip from the following perspective:

> I will initially define gossip as a way of talking between women
> in their roles as women, intimate in style, personal and domes-
> tic in topic and setting, a female cultural event which springs
> from and perpetuates the restrictions of the female role, but
> also gives the comfort of validation.[17]

Jones' definition is intriguing because instead of accusing women of being gossips, it does an about face and recognizes that in terms of style and substance there is something that can be called gossip. Moreover, this identifiable form of communication is unique to the female role. One can easily extrapolate that if there is a uniquely feminine form of communication called gossip, that there must be a male counterpart that is not gossip. Jones also spells out some of the differences between the two in the quote above–"intimate in style, personal and domestic in topic."[18] Male communication, therefore, is not intimate in style since it focuses on public topics. This conclusion is obviously consistent with the previously mentioned types of topics men tend to discuss.

Much has been written about those gender communication differences. The prominent linguist Deborah Tannen of Georgetown University provides an excellent guide to understanding them. Among other books, she is author of *You Just Don't Understand: Women and Men in Conversation*, which explores how girls and boys learn to communicate in very different ways for very different reasons from their earliest childhood.[19]

Tannen says that much of men's communication revolves around issues of status and how to improve one's position in a hierarchy, whether it be informal networks of friends or in a work setting. Men, she believes, are more prone to verbal sparring, arguing points, and taking control of the floor during meetings and debates. Studies show that even when young boys talk, they're working on being the "one up," so as not to be the low man in any pairing or group.[20] Men also value the exchange of factual information and are much less likely to engage in conversations about personal matters. In fact, long-standing friends may know little about one another's home life, including details of relationships with romantic partners or children.[21]

In contrast, communication between women has very different purposes, according to Tannen. Women's communication favors reinforcing bonds, forging intimacy, and making sure everyone is brought into the fold. They invest much less effort in discovering a person's position in a hierarchy, even in work situations. "Girls and women feel it is crucial they be liked by their peers, a form of involvement that focuses on symmetrical connections,"[22] Tannen writes. "Boys and men feel it is crucial they be respected by their peers, a form of involvement that focuses on asymmetrical status."[23] Women naturally tell each other the details of their lives, something that many men find mystifying, since they often don't discuss their personal relationships with others. Women are also more prone to mix everyday occurrences in on-the-job conversations with business, another habit that men consider a waste of time.[24]

These communication differences are so engrained that big problems can develop between the genders in both personal and professional settings when they are ignored, downplayed or simply misunderstood. But if men and women understand and account for the differences, they can adjust to and learn from each other's style.

Tannen also devotes a chapter in her book to gossip. She opens it with a short paragraph that states:

> The impression that women talk too freely and too much in private situations is summed up in a word: *gossip*. Although gossip can be destructive, it isn't always; it can serve a crucial function in establishing intimacy—especially if it is not "talking against" but simply "talking about."[25]

"Germany Sindelfingen Gossips"
Altstadt in Sindelfingen, Germany
Source: Work by Rebecca Kennison, dual-licensed under GFDL and Creative Commons Attribution 2.5

She goes on to take issue with the "negativity" associated with the concept of gossip drawing the conclusion that it "reflects men's interpretation of women's way of talking." She further notes that the "label 'gossip' casts a critical light on women's interest in talking about the details of people's lives."[26] In fact, when "people talk about the details of daily lives, it is gossip; when they write about them, it is literature: short stories and novels."[27]

Tannen's understanding of the two sides of gossip aligns with those who see a need for two different words—one that recognizes positive social interaction and a second that encompasses the dark, malicious side of human communication. Unquestionably, the climate of the workplace improves when there is a positive interest in each other's lives. Tannen reinforces this theme and highlights the fact that when women are chatting about themselves and their friends, their interaction is often viewed disparagingly as gossip even though the nature of the interaction helps to produce a sense of community and rapport.

Ultimately, she draws a clear distinction between what she labels "talking about" as opposed to "talking against." Talking about is the sharing of information, a process that she concludes builds camaraderie, community and rapport. Talking against is a way of attacking someone, putting them in their place.[28] And this raises the next question: Are women, who spend more time than men discussing the details of people's lives, more likely to stray into the area of *talking against*?

## Gender and Malicious Gossip

The literature on male and female communication indicates that very little has been done to determine if gender differences in spreading malicious gossip actually exist. One article provided this insight.

> Before accepting the validity of the stereotype according to which women are depicted as "gossips," it should be noted that gossip also has a more pejorative meaning in its popular usage. Many people associate gossip with derogatory, even scandalous, information about the lives of others. It is frequently in this context that the woman is portrayed as a gossip.[29]

> If this popular view is correct, then female conversations should be more derogatory than the conversations of their male counterparts. Our results indicate instead that both male and female gossip contained the same percentage of clearly

positive (27%) and clearly negative (25%) references to others. The difference between men and women was nonsignificant.[30] [statistical calculations omitted]

It appears, therefore, that men and women engage in equal amounts of malicious gossip and that the percentage of negativity is uncomfortably high. Beyond the above cited study, we found no other research article or credible source that suggested a gender disparity in the amount of malicious gossip.

Some additional observations about gender and malicious gossip might further inform the discussion. Gender may play a role in the spread of malicious gossip in an organization to the extent that more women occupy low power positions. As previously stated, gossip in any organization is one of the few tools available to the disenfranchised, those at the bottom of the hierarchy who feel exploited, overworked or unappreciated. It's no secret that those at the bottom are frequently women, who despite gains in recent decades, still make up a minority of managers and lag behind men in pay.

Malicious gossiping is a way for such workers to strike back against abuses, while at the same time forging a bond with one another. This is often less an indication of toxic personalities than it is of problems created by management, whether it be poorly communicated expectations, defective or nonexistent channels of communication, or outright repression. It can also reflect the inability of managers to infuse their staff with a sense of mission and purpose, no matter how humble the job. Therefore, while gender (being a woman) may be correlated to malicious gossip in an organization, the contributing factor might very likely be their low power position. In that case, men in similar positions would be equally likely to engage in malicious gossip

So what can a manager learn about controlling malicious gossip in the workplace given this information? First, it means that enlightened managers of either gender must have a good understanding of the very real difference between how men and women communicate–within certain parameters–and how each general style of communication is equally valid. It's a bit like learning a foreign language. It doesn't have to be the only language you speak for the rest of your life, but it can mean that you become much more effective on the job. Nor does it mean your own language is better than any other language; it's just different.

It also requires that managers question their unconscious assumptions about how–and why–the opposite sex communicates. Those who avoid allowing previously held preconceptions to twist what they hear or color their reactions can more effectively facilitate positive interactions among employees in any organization.

Finally, a discussion of gender and malicious gossip is not complete without some reflection on the disparate impact of malicious gossip on women as compared to men. It's worth noting that particular subcategories of gossip affect each gender differently. Coworkers use sexual innuendo as a weapon against women far more often, and it is much more damaging, whether the target be a manager or an employee. Using loaded words such as *easy, tramp, sleep around, slept with*, and so on in connection with a woman can cause quick, lasting damage. In their book, *Sex Differences in Human Communication*, Barbara Westbrook Eakins and R. Gene Eakins point out that similar terms for men are fewer in number and have more positive associations–*Don Juan, gigolo, stud, player, Casanova*.[31] Because of that, sexually tinged gossip can effectively lower the standing of any woman within a very short period, while gossip of a similar nature aimed at a man can actually raise his social standing in certain regards.

## Concluding Thoughts

There is a great banjo-picking song titled *Dirt Dishin' Daisy*. It seems that Daisy, a waitress in the local diner, serves up some spicy chili or perhaps a good beef stew accompanied by dirt. And, boy-o-boy, does Daisy know the dirt! Daisy has even been known to serve the dirt a-la-carte.[32]

Culturally, of course, it would make no sense at all to write a song about *Dirt Dishin' Dave* or *Dirt Dishin' Donald* since most people believe that women are the chief purveyors of gossip–particularly malicious gossip. Changing this perception is substantially more complicated than simply proving or disproving it. Though solid research evidence indicates that women spend a great deal more time discussing the details of people's lives, a practice historically labeled gossip, it is clear that men also gossip. They talk about "male" subjects, such as politics, religion, sports and other non-personal topics and call it *discussions* or *news* rather than gossip.

Furthermore, we found no reason whatsoever to conclude that it was important to determine the gender of the purveyor of malicious gossip since both genders engage in destructive tale-bearing. In fact, no current evidence exists indicating that the removal of malicious gossip from the workplace requires gender specific tactics. But there is overwhelming evidence confirming that both genders benefit from a supportive, connected work environment; an environment free of the spiteful, nastiness that is often the makeup of gossip.

## Chapter 4 Summary

There is a widely held view that women are the main purveyors of gossip. This view often impacts the way that women's communication is perceived and judged. Substantial objective evidence indicates that no discernible difference exists between men and women with regard to spreading malicious gossip in the workplace. Additionally, the chapter draws the following overall conclusions:

- Both genders spend a substantial amount of time in conversation that can loosely be called gossip.
- Women often communicate about different topics than men and the topics they choose (family, friends, and relationships) are the basis for viewing their communication behavior as gossip.
- Men frequently communicate to enhance status or standing, and often do not exchange much personal information, even with friends. Therefore, they don't view it as "gossip."
- Recent empirical evidence indicates that men talk as much as women in a professional setting.
- Studies of gossiping behavior in organizations indicate that men are as likely as women to engage in acts of gossip though topics differ.
- Both sexes engage equally in malicious gossip that harms a third party.
- While the negative effects of malicious gossip on the organization are not gender driven, at a personal level women are more likely to be victimized by the gossip.

# Chapter 5

## GOSSIP AND RELIGION

### "For lack of wood, the fire goes out; and where there is no whisperer, quarreling ceaseth."
**PROVERBS 26:20**

R abbi Joseph Telushkin opens the first chapter of *Words That Hurt, Words That Heal* with this short but powerful story.

In a small Eastern European town, a man went through the community slandering the rabbi. One day, feeling suddenly remorseful, he begged the rabbi for forgiveness and offered to undergo any penance to make amends. The rabbi told him to take a feather pillow from his house, cut it open, scatter the feathers to the wind, then return to see him. The man did as he was told, then came to the rabbi and asked, "Am I now forgiven?"

"Almost," came the response. "You just have to do one more thing. Go and gather all the feathers."

"But that's impossible," the man protested. "The wind has already scattered them."

"Precisely," the rabbi answered. "And although you truly wish to correct the evil you have done, it is as impossible to repair the damage done by your words as it is to recover the feathers."[1]

"It is as impossible to repair the damage done by your words as it is to recover the feathers."

The short narrative encapsulates concisely the character of malicious gossip and the irreparable damage it causes. It also illustrates the view that the world's major religions have of gossip; they universally deplore it. Therefore, adherents of these faiths who value integrity, compassion, humor, friendship, perspective, hard work and understanding in their private lives will most likely see the importance of bringing those same values to the places they work, worship and play. Furthermore, we believe that the overall conduct of any organization, no matter the size, will benefit from an understanding of the great faiths of the world, as well as from the conduct of employees who practice the tenets of their faith–especially as it relates to refraining from gossip.

While we don't advocate proselytizing on the job, we believe that wise, faith-based individuals have thought about and recorded healthy ways to communicate with other people for thousands of years. Incorporating their sage advice into our lives can help us navigate the communication maze and shape our actions, even if those sages come from a faith other than our own. In other words, an employee doesn't have to be the Pope or even Christian to appreciate the Bible's teaching on gossip. And a person doesn't need to be a Muslim to consider what the Quran has to say on the topic and use those insights to analyze his or her own behavior.

Even the briefest of surveys reveals that the great faiths have amazingly similar teachings about gossip. The commonality focuses not only on what is deplored (backbiting and slander) but also on precepts that direct followers to what they ought to be doing (loving one another).

## Religion and Gossip

The major world faiths address malicious gossip both directly and indirectly. They speak directly in that their precepts often refer specifically to the problems of gossip and indirectly in that general admonitions and encouragements towards a constructive lifestyle rule out malicious gossip. You cannot, for example, love your neighbor while engaged in slanderous communication about him or her since malicious gossip can hardly be considered a loving act.

While not all inclusive, the following are three of the dominant religious themes addressing gossip's destructive aspect, themes we found to be relatively universal.

First, Christianity, Judaism and Islam often define gossip as slander and backbiting, and view it as breaking the Golden Rule, "Do unto others as you would have them do unto you." The Christian Bible gives two versions of the rule: in the Gospel of Matthew, "In everything do to others as you would have them do to you," and in Luke, "Do to others as you would have them do to you." [2] It's hard to believe a person spreading malicious statements about a third party would want someone else to spread similar statements about him or her.

In Judaism, the Chofetz Chaim states this principle beautifully,

"Before you speak against someone else, think how you would like it if someone said the same thing about you."[3] Rumi, a 13th century poet, makes the same point from an Islamic perspective when he writes, "Veil the faults of others so that yours might be veiled."[4] Clearly, the person considering gossip should take a self-assessment test before acting. The question is: How would I feel if someone did to me what I propose to do to another person? If the action is negative, then out of respect for the well-being of others, he or she should avoid the behavior.

The second universal theme is a prohibition against dishonesty, particularly false statements about friends, neighbors and colleagues. It's put very simply in the Old Testament, so both Christianity and Judaism unite against gossip in this famous verse from Exodus 20.16: "You shall not bear false witness against your neighbor." Islam also condemns falsehood, "O you who believe, keep your duty to Allah and fear him and speak (always) the truth" (Al-Ahzaab 33:70).

Other, perhaps less well-known faiths are guided by the same, simple but eloquent principle. In *The Four Agreements*, Don Miguel Ruiz summarizes this bit of wisdom from the Toltec faith: "The word is a force; it is the power you have to express and communicate, to think, and thereby create events in your life…like a sword with two edges, your word can create the most beautiful dream, or your word can destroy everything around you."[5] The Bible makes almost exactly the same point in an affirmative fashion in Ephesians, "Let no evil talk come out of your mouths, but only what is useful for building up, as there is need, so that your words may give grace to those who hear."[6]

While the admonitions against dishonesty do not always speak directly to the problem of malicious gossip, they illustrate the belief that truthfulness and gossip are incompatible. It certainly applies in that particularly abhorrent form of untruthfulness in which people make false, derogatory statements about their neighbors (i.e., colleagues, friends and family). Numerous religious citations address the problem of unbridled chatter by warning adherents to guard their tongues. These religious injunctions recognize the danger of a loose tongue and its ability to damage relationships with friends and neighbors to the extent that the sense of community is compromised. The Christian Bible states it well in James 3:5, "So also the tongue is a small member, yet it boasts of great exploits. How great a forest is set ablaze by a small fire!"

A similar concern over the potential evils of the mouth has a unique expression among the Tuareg, a nomadic group in the Sahara desert often called the "lords of the Sahara."[7] They practice a culturally specific form of Islam that requires the men to cover their mouths at all times with a long blue scarf. The covering reflects their interest in addressing problems that originate with the mouth. Their practice of singling out the men is somewhat unusual since for most of the world a woman is usually seen as the beguiler and purveyor of malicious gossip. The following summarizes their beliefs:

> The mouth is considered the most sensual part of a man's body and the most revealing. The mouth speaks truth or falsehoods. The mouth expresses fear and love. The mouth can curse bitterly and yell ferocious hateful insults. The mouth can start wars. The mouth can be slippery and sly and woo a woman with deceitful lies. The mouth exposes the soul. It is better to keep such a powerful thing covered up.[8]

The third theme that recurs in major religions is that all call the individual to a specific lifestyle, a lifestyle inconsistent with the behaviors of non-adherents. Therefore, there is always a clear distinction between believers and non-believers, people who practice the tenets of the faith and those who do not. So when a religious creed asks its adherents to avoid spreading malicious gossip, they are expected to refrain from negative tale-bearing and speak kindly about others in spite of the behavior of non-believers in the broader community.

Rabbi Stephen Baars states Judaism's case clearly when he writes.

"In contrast with secular society, which often goes out of its way to glorify gossip, Judaism perceives it as extremely harmful. In fact, there is much Jewish literature on its divisive and insidious effects."[9]

Islam provides much the same perspective in that it calls the believer to a life consistent with Islamic teaching. An article titled "Gheebah (Gossip, Backbiting)" states the following:

> We have to set our standards much higher. They have to correspond with the teachings and understandings of Islam.
>
> All this goes to preface the idea that we have to care about each other in a way that is in line with Islam, not the lesser standards of the non-believers. Let them follow us. When we think of gheebah (gossip, backbiting), most of us think that this is the speech as defined by the non-believers–saying something negative about someone–whether truthful or not. But Islam has given it a stronger definition.[10]

Christianity provides its followers with the same basic requirements. There are tenets of the faith, including injunctions against malicious gossip, that a professing believer is expected to follow, separating him or her from the non-believer, as we see in Proverbs.

> No Christian should have the characteristics of the wicked tongue. But sadly, some do. Christians need to realize just how much God hates the sins of the tongue: "These six things doth the Lord hate: . . . a lying tongue . . . ."[11]

Christianity, of course, has many different expressions, Catholics, Eastern Orthodox, Protestants and Mormons, for instance. While universal to all expressions, the call to a higher or different lifestyle is stronger with some than with others. Joining a religious group often involves a type of separation from non-believers that comes at substantial cost to the adherent, which may include persecution and jail time in some cases.

The Quakers are clearly such a distinctive group. While numerically a small sect, they have made a lasting impression on the world with their efforts to promote social justice and the peaceful resolution of conflict. In fact, their teachings promoted human connection even in speech. George Fox, founder of the movement, encouraged followers to address another person as "friend" and called the group the "Society of Friends." Their unusual style of speaking set them apart from others, a distinction that was deliberate. The founder's intention was to correct the "many censurable defects" that characterized the way that people spoke to each other. Therefore, Quaker thinking and beliefs designate malicious gossip as anathema. The result was a gentler, more inclusive way of talking to and about others.

Fox's mission was so successful in affecting society that the Friends Service Council and the American Friends Service Committee were awarded the Nobel Peace Prize in 1947, the only religious group[1] ever to be so honored. When the prize was awarded, the presentation speech summarized the accomplishments of the group and provided the following:

> [1]The Quakers have shown us that it is possible to translate into action what lies deep in the hearts of many: compassion for others and the desire to help them–that rich expression of the sympathy between all men, regardless of nationality or race, which, transformed into deeds, must form the basis for lasting peace. For this reason alone the Quakers deserve to receive the Nobel Peace Prize today.

---

1 There are individuals such as Desmond Tutu and Mother Teresa who represented religious institutions that have received the Nobel Peace Prize, but the only religious institution so honored is the Quakers.

The Amish and the Mennonites, similar to the Quakers, have a basic belief in nonviolence. It is interesting to note the relationship between a belief in nonviolent behavior and the tenets of faith that actively promote gentler, kinder ways of communicating with each other. It hardly needs to be said that spreading malicious gossip is viewed as an act of verbal violence against another person, an act clearly contrary to the teachings of all three groups.

The examples above indicate that the theme of follower vs. non-follower highlights the distinction drawn between what we ought to be doing versus what we should not be doing. Each faith calls its members to a particular lifestyle that separates them from those who are not a part of the faith. It is an important theme that applies well in business settings since what the general population does in its private life is not necessarily a standard of behavior appropriate to the workplace.

The world's major religions have much to say about malicious gossip beyond these three themes. While substantial similarities exist, each also adds its own unique perspective on the issue.

## Christianity

Christianity's prohibitions against gossip go back for millennia, and are interwoven into the teachings of the apostles and many other great Christian thinkers. In the Apostle Paul's writing, gossiping is sin, akin to other misdeeds as grave as greed, murder and slander. In his famous letter to the Romans, he writes "They are gossips…they know God's decree, that those who practice such things deserve to die." While death is not a punishment we would endorse, it does clearly illustrate the passion Paul felt toward the transgression.

Elsewhere, the Bible has several references to gossip, the most specific include the following:

- "You shall not go about as a slanderer." (Lev. 19-16)
- "A gossip goes around telling secrets, but those who are trust-worthy can keep a confidence" (Proverbs 11:13)

- "He who goes about as a slanderer reveals secrets; therefore, do not associate with a gossip." (Proverbs 20:19)
- "Without wood a fire goes out; without a gossip a quarrel dies down. As charcoal to embers and as wood to a fire, so is a quarrelsome person for kindling strife." (Proverbs 26:20-21)
- "A perverse person stirs up conflict, and a gossip separates close friends." (Proverbs 16:28).

Most modern Christians continue to consider gossip a problem, at best unbecoming and at worst harmful, hurtful. Much of the discussion tends to center around the importance of truthfulness and the pain that hasty or caustic words cause the victim.

While gossip may not start with a lie, a thoughtful person knows how quickly facts can be distorted. Even comments about another person's performance or character can start more or less innocently but turn into slander, something antithetical to the spirit of Christianity. One Christian writer noted the inherent paradox in gossiping about the faults of others when he wrote, "Gossiping about someone's sin is really hypocritical, because you're sinning against yourself by gossiping."[12]

Christ's teachings unequivocally preclude hurting a fellow human being: "You shall love your neighbor as yourself." In other words, Christian thinking directs the believer–and we know this is a tough one–to refrain from passing on anything even mildly derogatory about another person anonymously; it is not a loving act. While the information may seem harmless, or even a little humorous at someone else's expense, remember that, like the child's game of telegraph, it's impossible to know how certain pieces of information can be twisted once hearers repeat them.

## Judaism

In his book, *Gossip: The Untrivial Pursuit*, Joseph Epstein notes that while all religions condemn gossip, he believes Judaism to be the only one that has "codified its abhorrence." He explains his position as follows:

> Coming away from reading about gossip in the Talmud, one recognizes how much a part of human nature gossip seems. But then the role of religion has never been to accept raw human nature as a completed enterprise, but to attend to tame, alter, hone, and refine the coarseness of human nature into something grander than it is.[13]

Jewish scriptures and teachings consistently present gossip as a hopelessly destructive behavior. Exodus 23:1, for example, discourages gossip entirely: "You shall not spread a false report. You shall not join hands with the wicked to act as a malicious witness." In fact, the Psalms state that anyone who desires life will not speak ill of another person, so transgressing is a serious matter. It's useful to remember that the Psalms are not simple teachings per se, but expressions of the heart that connect the individual to God. Including the injunction against slander in this context shows that the ancient Hebrews viewed gossip as seriously harmful to individuals and their communities. A Jewish proverb expands on the idea: "What you don't see with your eyes, don't witness with your mouth."[14] Once again, even spreading good gossip is discouraged–you never know how it might be relayed or twisted along the way.

Jewish teachings go even a step further: to listen passively to gossip is as reprehensible as being the one who spreads the gossip. Rabbi Stephen Baars likens malicious gossip to bad food when he writes:

There is good food and bad food. There is good talk and bad talk. Just as some things are not healthy yet taste great, so too there are some very juicy conversations we should not be listening to![15]

Later in the same article, Rabbi Baars states that, "So pernicious is gossip that it destroys the very fabric of society."[16]

Rabbi Dr. Asher Meir, of the JCT Center for Business Ethics, says in an article for the *Jewish Ethicist* that Jewish sages hold that gossip kills three: the teller, the listener and the subject. It doesn't have to be a false or slanderous story. As long as the subject of the report would prefer not to have information known, it is gossip and not fit for further dissemination or to be listened to.[17]

There is good food and bad food. There is good talk and bad talk. Just as some things are not healthy yet taste great, so too there are some very juicy conversations we should not be listening to!

Meir concedes that it can be difficult to avoid gossip in a workplace. Doing so can damage a person's position professionally and socially–even to the extent that he or she might actually be ostracized. But that is the price that must be paid, he says, quoting Rabbi Yisrael Meir HaCohen, the Chofetz Chaim, in the "classic work" on the topic: "Even if refraining from slander will cause a person to lose his job, he has no choice but to fulfill the Torah's mandate." It's also possible, Meir said, that setting a good example can cause other workers "to draw inspiration and courage from your example and also limit their tale bearing."[18]

The word gossip in Hebrew is *loshon hora,* which is best translated as "evil speech." Jewish teaching holds that gossip is wrong *even if it is true and spread without malice.* The Chofetz Chaim lists a whopping 31 commandments that may be violated when a person passes on or listens to evil speech, including "You shall not go about as a talebearer among your people." (Leviticus 19:15-16). To live the faith takes the courage to say when confronted with gossip: "I can't and I won't listen to this."[19]

Rabbi Zelig Pliskin wrote the book *Guard Your Tongue,* a title derived from the verse "Guard your tongue from evil and your lips from speaking deceit" (Psalms 34:14). In it, he explains the impact gossip has on daily life.

> Loshon hora is the source of many social ills. It has caused the dissolution of numerous friendships, the termination of countless marriages, and has generated immeasurable sufferings. The evils of hatred, jealousy, and contention spread through the medium of loshon hora, as diseases do through filth and germs. The speaking of loshon hora has resulted in people losing their incomes, and it is not an exaggeration to say that it has led to many an untimely death.
>
> The evils of loshon hora are universally recognized. Nevertheless, all too often, through various rationalizations, people condone the making of derogatory statements: "But I was only joking," "This won't hurt him," "This isn't really a loshon hora," "Everybody knows it."[20]

Jewish ethical writing also encourages adherents to judge others favorably, a perspective that comes from the Torah verse "Judge your neighbor righteously."[21] One of the usual problems with gossip is that it focuses on the shortcomings of others and, in doing so, destroys relationships. On the other hand, focusing our conversation, particularly in the workplace, on our colleagues' good qualities can have a positive impact on relationships and the group culture, offering a powerful antidote to the destructive effects of malicious gossip.

## Islam

A Muslim takes his or her authority from four different sources. The Quran is the first and primary source. The second is the words of the Prophet Mohammed; the third, the recognized sages and devout students of Islam; and the fourth, one's heart since the Prophet instructed "that in all affairs, first consult your heart." Whether a Muslim consults the Quran, the Prophet, the sages, or his or her heart, the message is clear: gossip is prohibited.[22]

The words of the Quran most often cited about the prohibitions against gossip come from chapter 49:11-12. The Sahih International translation of these two verses is as follows:

> O you who have believed, let not a people ridicule [another] people; perhaps they may be better than them; nor let women ridicule [other] women; perhaps they may be better than them. And do not insult one another and do not call each other by [offensive] nicknames. Wretched is the name of disobedience after [one's] faith. And whoever does not repent–then it is those who are the wrongdoers.

> O you who have believed, avoid much [negative] assumption. Indeed, some assumption is sin. And do not spy or backbite each other. Would one of you like to eat the flesh of his brother when dead? You would detest it. And fear Allah; indeed, Allah is Accepting of repentance and Merciful.

Central to the Islamic faith is the concept of universal brother-hood–treating every man like one's own brother. So when a Muslim gossips about another, he or she is, in effect, defying those bonds of brotherhood. Islamic sages have instructed their followers to ask three questions before anyone says something about another: 1) Is it true? 2) Is it necessary? 3) Is it kind and compassionate?[23]

One booklet, *Gossip and Its Adverse Effects on the Muslim Community*, provides extensive treatment of the topic. The writer examines what the author calls "ghibah." "Ghibah isn't an easy term to translate since no single equivalent word in English exists, although "gossip" comes closest initially. Ghibah is an interesting, all-encompassing word that includes back-biting, slandering and scandal-mongering and gives a clue as to Islam's attitude toward the behavior.

As the booklet states:

> Whichever word we chose, we cannot escape from the fact that Ghibah affects us all. We have all been victims and–we must be honest–we have all been guilty of this sin. But it is not a matter to be taken lightly–gossip can wreck lives and shatter communities. If we seek to unite as Muslims, we must combat Ghibah. Islam is a practical faith which recognizes the human condition and offers achievable remedies to the problems that beset us. Every human society faces the problem of gossip, and Islam shows us how to tackle it in a sensible and humane manner. (Interestingly enough, it is not assumed to be solely a female preserve, as popular notions would have us believe!)[24]

The Quran (49:6) also states: "You who believe, if some perverse man should come up to you with some piece of news, clear up the facts lest you afflict some folk out of ignorance and some morning feel regretful for what you may have done..."

An Islamic poet put it artfully.

"If a man is wise and fears Allah,

This will keep him too busy to concern himself

with the faults of others,

Just as the weak and sick person is so concerned

with his own pain

To think of the pain of others."[25]

And don't fool yourself into thinking that it's permissible to repeat the story to the target of the gossip. The faith has a word known as "nameemah," which in part roughly means telling somebody what others have said about him or her in order to cause trouble. So, unless opening your mouth will protect someone from harm, it's better to stay silent. The stakes are high since the Prophet said, "No person who spreads nameemah will enter Paradise."[26]

Clearly, Islam attacks malicious gossip from the standpoint of specific prohibitions against the practice, directives to speak honestly and guard one's tongue, and expressed concerns over gossip's destructive impact on Muslim communities.

## Other Religions

As noted earlier, Christianity, Judaism and Islam are not the only religions that recognize the destructive power of gossip. Buddhism and Hinduism are two of those that address issues resulting from the practice.

Buddhism, for instance, describes the person and the damage caused quite picturesquely: "Surely a person is born with an axe in her mouth, and she cuts herself with it when she speaks foolish words."[27] The Buddhist antidote to malicious gossip is the use of "right words," compassionate speech about others, as well as right intention and right actions. To that end, Buddhism's tenets encourage abandoning gossip and speaking with reasonable, moderate and beneficial words. Like the other major religions, it encourages followers to abide by a strong moral code that includes the idea of reciprocity–the Golden Rule.

In *The Noble Eightfold Path*, one of the principal teachings of Buddha, the code outlined includes *right speech, right action* and *right livelihood*. As part of that, a Buddhist shouldn't lie or engage in harsh or malicious speech, gossip and tale-bearing.[28] Comparing right speech with wrong speech provides substantial insight into the problems of malicious gossip, including the hurtful words often found on the Internet.

> Right speech is not just a personal virtue. Modern communication technology has given us a culture that seems saturated with wrong speech communication that is hateful and deceptive. This engenders disharmony, acrimony, and physical violence.
>
> We tend to think of violent, hateful words as being less wrong than violent action. We may even think of violent words as being justified sometimes. But violent words, thoughts and actions arise together and support each other. So too do peaceful words, thoughts and actions.[29]

Like most of the other major religions, Buddhism asks its followers to practice what it is teaching and, in that light, there are some basics to Right Speech which include:

1. Abstain from false speech; do not tell lies or deceive.
2. Do not slander others or speak in a way that causes disharmony or enmity.
3. Abstain from rude, impolite or abusive language.
4. Do not indulge in idle talk or gossip.[30]

Hinduism similarly condemns malicious gossip. An often repeated verse from the *Panchatantra,* an ancient Sanskrit collection of animal fables in poetry and prose, states:

In salty oceans, rivers meet their end,

In women's quarrels, bonds of kinship meet their end,

In the gossip, backbiter's secrets meet their end;

In wicked sons, families meet their end.[31]

Hinduism also offers ways to combat the human tendency to choose destructive habits. Bhakti yoga is a practice viewed as a spiritual path, intended to foster love, utter faith and surrender to God. Radhanath Swami, a respected sage, gives followers the following advice:

The practice of Bhakti-yoga requires watering the seeds of devotion within our heart. It also means to be very careful to pull out the weeds that are growing alongside. Topics of the mundane subject matters of this world are very nourishing waters to the weeds that are always eager to choke the plant of Bhakti. People tend to be fond of listening to rumors or hearing gossip. They also like to spread gossip. It is said that among all of the senses, the tongue is the most difficult to control....[32]

Notice that the swami describes how the "weeds" of mundane matters force out what is desired (Bhakti) and specifically includes gossip in the crop of weeds. His inference is that those who listen to and engage in malicious gossip force out the constructive behaviors that heal wounds and build community. He clearly agrees with the point made by other religious systems: the practice of gossip causes far-reaching damage. While the message of each religion is primarily directed at followers, the fact that they all mirror a common concern over controlling or eliminating the harmful effects of malicious gossip substantially supports the need to address the issue in the workplace.

## Concluding Thoughts

Obviously, eradicating malicious gossip is a serious matter for the world's religions, an element that gives weight to the previous discussion. We did find, however, that at times concerns about the gossip's negative impact can be expressed in a lighter, humorous fashion. Consider the following:

> Mildred, the church gossip and self-appointed arbiter of the church's morals, kept sticking her nose into other people's business. Several residents were unappreciative of her activities, but feared her enough to maintain their silence.
>
> She made a mistake, however, when she accused George, a new member, of being an alcoholic after she saw his pickup truck parked in front of the town's only bar one afternoon. She commented to George and others that everyone seeing it there would know what he was doing.
>
> George, a man of few words, stared at her for a moment and just walked away. He didn't explain, defend, or deny, he said nothing. Later that evening, George quietly parked his pickup in front of Mildred's house…and left it there all night.[33]

The story also highlights a pervasive problem: those who profess a faith that condemns destructive gossip do not always choose to act in a manner consistent with its basic tenets. As a result, the literature of each faith is usually written in a manner that recognizes the effort involved in trying to live up to the established standards. Similarly, a declaration that the workplace must henceforth be gossip free is naïve if there is no recognition that changing a toxic culture requires work.

Given the complexity of communication issues, managers need to be problem-solvers when they encounter gossip. They should aid employees who are hurt by these verbal attacks. The teachings of many faiths offer some good advice on how to proceed. First, it involves being honest with oneself by asking questions such as:

- Am I living and modeling my beliefs about speaking the truth?
- Am I using compassionate speech?
- Am I treating others with the dignity I would want shown to me?

These same questions need to be rephrased and asked in the context of the entire organization (i.e., Are we living and modeling...?). It is hard to pass on gossip or condone it with silence when managers look at it through this lens.

Rabbi Meir makes an important observation when he writes:

> Often office gossip begins because people allow their imaginations to run wild about other people's shortcomings. If we would exercise our imaginations just as much to envision their good qualities, our social environment would be completely transformed."[34]

We began this chapter with a quote from Proverbs 26:20, "For lack of wood, the fire goes out; and where there is no whisperer, quarreling ceaseth." Clearly, malicious gossip is often the source of discord and disunity in the workplace. Choosing not to engage in malicious gossip will, in fact, remove much of the strife in relationships among colleagues. However, we are indebted to Rabbi Meir for his thoughtful observation that we can go beyond simply removing strife and transform the workplace when we substitute affirmative behavior for the negative.

## Chapter 5 Summary

All of the world's great religions have something important to say about malicious gossip. Not only do they universally deplore it, they share strong prohibitions against it and admonish followers to live a lifestyle that avoids it.

- All the great religions condemn malicious gossip, putting it into the same category as other "sinful" acts.

- A universal theme found in religions is that the believer is called to a higher standard of behavior, particularly behavior that involves how we communicate with and about other people.

- A second theme related to malicious gossip is that religions instruct us not to bear false witness against our neighbor and guard against the evils of the unguarded tongue.

- In assessing whether one should engage in a specific act of gossip, religions share a common theme: they instruct the people to act towards others as they would like others to act towards them–the Golden Rule.

- Christianity views gossip as sin and enjoins believers to be loving rather than caustic and hurtful.

- In Judaism gossip is defined as loshon hora–evil speech. It is viewed as the cause of much harm in society and is heavily condemned in Jewish Law.

- Islam views gossip as abhorrent as eating the dead flesh of your brother. It prohibits the act categorically.

- The primary lesson for a manager, gleaned from the world's great religions, is that community, the sense of belonging, connectedness are all destroyed by malicious gossip, but they can be enhanced by promoting positive ways for people to talk about and to each other.

# Chapter 6

# ASSESSING THE PRESENCE OF GOSSIP

In religious and secular contexts, by standards
of morality and of decorum, loose talk about
people is deplorable. Few activities so nearly
universal have been the object
of such sustained and passionate attack.
**PATRICIA MEYER SPACKS**

S tories of office gossips abound. A colleague related an incident that occurred early in her professional career. She was employed as a project director in a marketing firm when another director approached her and shared some key information about the organization that he termed "confidential." She treated it as such and was amazed two weeks later when the director confronted her about not sharing the information. When she defended herself by noting that he had called it confidential, he seemed surprised. He had expected her to ignore that part of his message since he believed that the surest way to spread information was to tell someone that it was confidential. She retorted that if he wanted the information disseminated he should have given it to Nancy, the mail person, who visited every office on a daily basis and was a constant source of information, gossip included. A few days later, she got a visit from an angry Nancy who wanted to know why she had been accused of being a gossip.

Practically every office has at least one fount of all information, verifiable or not. Like Nancy, they are often in positions that give them ready access to a wide audience. A new employee can identify the person with reasonable certainty within days of starting a job. This person always has some nugget to share about others, and may or may not reveal the information source. Frequently, a gossip sees the behavior as a way to enhance his or her status in the office. But that doesn't mean he or she can be trusted. Even though these voluble employees may initially bestow some nugget of titillating office fare, they won't hesitate to talk about others behind their backs or share anything told them in confidence despite protests to the contrary.

It's tempting for managers to encourage the office gossip because it makes them feel that they have an open connection to the grapevine, an easy way to find out what employees are talking about. Obviously, critics play an important role in any organization, and their voices should be heard. Employees need the freedom to engage in constructive public and private conversations, but there are constructive, professional ways to express critical observations, in a safe and supportive way, particularly when something is not working. Managers, however, must realize that healthy, open communication and malicious gossip are mutually exclusive.

## Action Steps

So how does a leader assess and control this damaging communication issue? In discussion with CEOs, COOs, managers and supervisors, we found that while gossip was universally decried, very few managers or leaders have considered the magnitude of the problem within their organization. They may have a good sense of the communication practices around them and know the reputation of one or more "busy bodies," but they rarely drill deeper to determine, for example, whether employees are leaving a particular worksite because of the damage done by rampant gossip.

Clearly, leaders interested in addressing issues of gossip must gauge the scope of the problem. They will find the following three levels of assessment helpful. The first step requires looking at the overall communication climate of the organization with an eye toward determining the degree of social negativity. To what extent are employees regularly engaged in negative conversations and spreading malicious gossip?

The second focuses on individuals known as "gossips" in the negative sense of that word. Is there a person or persons whose patterns of social interaction are corrosive in the workplace? Finally, and perhaps most important, if real change is to occur, the leader must assess his or her own behavior and ask, "Am I aware of the extent to which I am personally engaging in malicious gossip?"

## Determining the Degree of Malicious Gossip

Before considering the range of positive interventions that can be implemented to reduce the negative impact of gossip, it is important to get the lay of the land. The first question to ask is, "Does the workplace inevitably have gossip as part of its basic culture?" Opinions clearly differ. Grosser, Lopez-Kidwell and Labianca assumed its presence based on their studies of several workplace environments and concluded that the majority of gossip found in the workplace is positive. At the same time, they recognized that the research on which conclusions were based uncovered a significant portion that was negative.[1]

On the other hand, Sam Chapman, author of *The No-Gossip Zone,* believes that it is possible to eradicate gossip from the business environment. Convinced of gossip's highly detrimental impact on overall team performance, his prescribed process includes discharging those employees who break the no-gossip rule.[2]

While it is doubtful that one can completely remove gossip from the workplace, leaders can consider a more realistic approach: how to tame the destructive side of gossip. The goal from this perspective is controlling the negative such that it does not become toxic. Thus, assessing the extent and egregiousness of gossip present in a work group becomes an essential step in the effort to implement effective control. The question, then, is not whether there is negative gossip present but whether the amount of gossip has become detrimental to performance and/or keeps employees from interacting in a constructive, teambuilding fashion.

Gossip can be compared at one level to alcohol consumption. An individual who drinks a little alcohol may not experience impaired

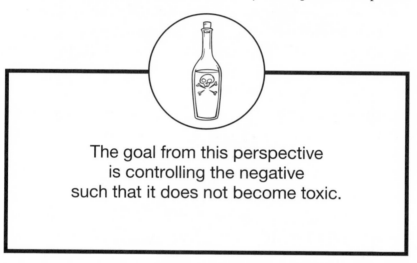

The goal from this perspective
is controlling the negative
such that it does not become toxic.

performance, but if he drinks too much, his physical abilities are substantially compromised. While we discovered no specific measure of malicious interaction, there are some approaches and reflection that managers can use to determine the extent to which gossip is a destructive element in an organization or work group.

A good way to begin an assessment is to study the current stability of the organization and how it is affecting the flow of gossip. A manager can use the set of questions found on the next page to assist in the task of evaluating a work group's vulnerability to malicious gossip.

There are also specific organizational factors that encourage gossip. For instance, an organization would be expected to have more rumors–and more gossip–in times of instability such as layoffs, reorganization, mergers/acquisitions, or changes in CEO (understood to be pastor, mayor, dean, etc.) or other top level administrator. Uncertainty and significant change can produce an outbreak of miscommunication. Gossip can also arise in response to a major negative occurrence such as an accident, building fire, or other event that elevates doubt or the likelihood of an unpredictable future.

Gossip that is the product of unusual circumstances should not be evaluated in the same negative light as the destructive interactions occurring in a culture that actively promotes malicious gossip. Usually, an organization can combat the rumor and gossip produced by significant changes through open communication and transparency. Changing a negative culture is a much more difficult and frequently long-term proposition.

Leaders interested in an actual assessment will find professors from schools of business, social psychology departments and organizational psychology divisions usually eager to conduct various forms of employee behavioral assessments. The research previously cited measuring the extent to which gossip was positive or negative in various business environments is a good example of assessment methodologies often used by college professors.[3]

Frequently, however, the manager will not be in a position to champion a formal study by an outside source. In that case, he or she can still do a great deal without external help. Administering an in-house morale or satisfaction survey, for instance, will often reveal an elevated and harmful level of malicious gossip. Whether gathered explicitly or implicitly, such instruments uncover problematic situations within the organizational unit surveyed, whether team or department.

Another factor to consider in making an organizational assessment is to look at retention rates across organizational units. Such comparisons will reveal particular units that need further scrutiny. A variety of factors may cause high turnover rates–and gossip may be one of them. Employee exit interviews also provide insight into reasons for turnover and should include something about the extent to which the individual experienced any malicious interaction.

Worksite assessment guides that compare employees across two or more dimensions can also be useful in identifying the communication practices of a team or work unit. Perhaps the best indicator that malicious gossip is creating employee unhappiness and/or turnover is an examination of the turnover ratio in the smallest unit measured (i.e., team leader, foreman, first level supervisor, sales manager, etc.).

Beyond the paper and pencil tests, the most important assessment may simply be the manager's awareness of the problem. Management

---

# ORGANIZATION RIPE FOR GOSSIP

Consider the following questions in determining whether the stage is set for gossip in your organization.

- To what extent do employees seem off task, out of their offices or away from their work site?
- To what extent is the work site characterized by cliques and/or exclusive membership groups?
- To what extent is the workplace characterized by negativity and interpersonal conflict?
- To what extent do employees identify gossip as a problem in the workplace?
- To what extent does negative communication outweigh the practice of positive communication?
- To what extent are organizational work groups characterized by "we/they" discussions?
- To what extent do employees feel in the dark about the status or direction of the organization?
- To what extent is the mood or climate of the work group or work site one of defeat, negativity and/or learned helplessness?
- To what extent do employees receive honest and timely feedback regarding their performance?
- To what extent do employees express/experience appreciation?

by walking around is an old concept that encourages a supervisor to maintain personal contact and high levels of interaction with those he or she oversees.[4] As a result, a manager who practices the art of walking around and interacting with employees should have a general sense of the extent to which employees experience the workplace as toxic (full of negative interaction) or supportive.

While management by walking around is an effective tool, a warning is in order. If your personal radar system is broken or you have developed a high level of immunity to workplace problems, walking around and talking with employees will probably have little value. Make sure to check your objectivity and ability to hear what is being said.

## Identifying a Gossip

Mark Twain once wrote: "He gossips habitually; he lacks the common wisdom to keep still that deadly enemy of man, his own tongue."[5] Does this statement remind you of a colleague or a subordinate? Focusing particularly on the two words "gossips habitually," take a moment to consider the questions in the following quiz.

One view of gossip is that it is a universal activity in which we all participate. Chapman, for instance, notes its ubiquity in the workplace.

> In a recent study performed by Randstad Corporation, employees cited office gossip as their number one annoyance in their workplace. Employers also had good reason to curb loose lips, as office gossip takes up to sixty-five hours a year of an employee's time at work according to a July 2002 survey by Equisys.[6]

So, if we're all doing it, why should a manager or supervisor be concerned with focusing on the gossiping behavior of specific employees? The answer is quite obvious; some gossips are much more destructive than others. While a manager's primary focus ought to be on substituting an affirming culture for one that has elements of maliciousness, removing a malignancy may be necessary to pave the way for and promote positive growth. Most organizations provide for

## SURVEY

Do you have an office gossip in your organization? Saying yes to any of the following questions will give you a clue.

1. Do you have a person who always wants to tell you about the problems of other members of the organization, even when they don't relate to the job at hand?
2. Is there someone you see constantly in whispered communication with others?
3. Does this person stop speaking when he or she is in a conversation with another person and you approach?
4. Does this person only want to speak in general terms when passing on some nugget of information, without identifying its source?
5. Does this person appear hypercritical of others while ignoring his or her own faults?

such eventualities by including work rules either implied or specifically stated in some form of a handbook requiring employees to avoid interacting in ways that foment division and discord. Malicious gossip obviously falls under the purview of these rules. Employees who violate the rule are rightfully subject to discipline which may warrant discharge should the problem be serious enough.

The tools for assessing the extent to which an individual employee poses a significant problem in a work group are generally the same tools used to assess the overall culture. The difference is that they are now re-calibrated to focus on one person. For example, the exit interview can include questions about the individual's relationship with the group as a whole or, when appropriate, focus on whether the departing employee has issues with a specific person. A good interviewer will know how to encourage openness without inappropriately leading the interviewee to a preset answer.

Most important, the supervisor who habitually engages and is involved with the people he or she manages will develop a sensitivity to irregularities or employee tensions. For instance, an employee whose malicious interaction is at a level that necessitates disciplinary action usually leaves a wake of unhappy, angry colleagues. The manager attuned to his or her employees will normally have little difficulty in discovering this wake. Though employees are often reticent to say negative things about a fellow employee, the undertone and overall climate of the workplace should give the supervisor a clue that the situation requires a more in-depth evaluation.

As mentioned earlier, the manager's personal radar system must be fully functioning. It is, unfortunately, easy to lose touch with the workplace climate. The everyday necessities of managing employees can create numbness to the social realities that affect the individuals in the work group.

## Self-Assessment

A basic function of management is to assess problems and implement corrections, a process of sizing up other people. However, leaders face the additional issue of assessing their own personal skills as managers, including any tendency to gossip. For all of us, it is often easier to see the faults in another than to see them in ourselves. Therefore, those in leadership must carefully cultivate self-awareness, especially since substantial evidence shows that a manager sets the emotional tone of the work group.[7] Leaders need to model expected behavior. The first and most effective step in controlling the destructive side of gossip is to begin with ourselves.

Of course, conducting a self-assessment, the process of reflecting on the nature of one's interaction with others, will be unique to each individual. Each person uses a different method. The gossip quiz found earlier in this chapter can, for example, be a helpful tool in doing a self-assessment by simply making the questions personal. The self-assessment should also include a conscious effort to be mindful about how one communicates when interacting with others.

Being mindful of these interactions includes awareness of how we listen and hear what others have to say. Genuine listening promotes healthy dialogue. Thich Nhat Hanh, a Vietnamese Buddhist monk known for promoting personal and world peace, emphasizes this point when he writes:

> Deep listening is the foundation of right speech. If we cannot listen mindfully, we cannot practice right speech. No matter what we say, it will not be mindful, because we will be speaking only our own ideas and not in response to the other person. In the *Lotus Sutra*, we are advised to look and listen with the eyes of compassion.[8]

Two self-help books were significant in shaping our thinking on this topic. The first titled *30 Days to Taming Your Tongue* by Deborah Smith Pegues, bases its 30-day process on biblical injunctions. Pegues notes that she wrote it "first and foremost for myself." She summarizes her goal as, "I desire a wholesome tongue, one that always speaks what is pleasing to God."[9]

The book presents taming sessions on topics such as the indiscreet tongue, the meddling tongue, the slandering tongue and, of course, the gossiping tongue. Pegues defines the concept of taming as the process required "to bring [something] from a state of unruliness to a state of submission."[10] Her intent is to help readers establish control (to tame) over their tongues so that they act (speak) consistently with a set of spiritual principles.

*Gossip: Ten Pathways to Eliminate It From Your Life and Transform Your Soul* by Lori Palatnik and Bob Burg is similar in theme. The primary author finds that the subject of gossip "has the greatest and most immediate impact."[11] Referencing her live presentations on gossip, she says:

> People leave being completely sensitized to the pain and destruction that gossip can bring and resolved to eliminate it from their lives. People often tell me that after the talk they suddenly become acutely aware of how much time people spend talking about other people, most often in a negative way–and how much time they spend listening to it.[12]

Both books make a couple of important points. One is that personal awareness and desire to change are essential to eliminate malicious gossip from public and private communication. So much gossip occurs as a matter of habit and without conscious awareness that those wishing to overcome it must make an honest personal assessment, an act that leads to greater insight on how "I" as an individual interact with others.

The second point is that taming gossip is not so much a process of elimination as one of positive construction. We are all social beings and will continue to interact with each other. The basic question is whether that interaction will be positive and affirming or malicious and destructive. Personal assessments raise awareness of the choices we make between engaging in negative versus constructive patterns of interaction.

While recognizing that there is undoubtedly merit in taking inventory of the negative, we want to emphasize the importance of being mindful of our positive interactions. One place to start is the expression of appreciation. In *The Five Languages of Appreciation in the Workplace*, Gary Chapman and Paul White encourage managers and supervisors to motivate their employees by appreciation (MBA).[13] The expression of appreciation, however, needs to focus on engaging others at a personal level. This requires becoming consistently aware of whether the recipient views the way in which it was expressed "as valuable."[14]

Part one of Ellen Langer's classic work *Mindfulness* begins with a chapter titled "When the Light's On and Nobody's Home."[15] Therefore, we urge supervisors and managers to turn the light on and be mindful of both instances of gossip as well as instances of positive, affirming communication in their interactions. Positive change requires mindfulness about one's personal interactions and its impact on others.

## Concluding Thoughts

Assessment is a necessary step towards gaining personal control and giving direction to our everyday communication. This is particularly true when considering some of the destructive aspects of the ways we interact. Like so many other important areas of life, assessing our communication cannot be a one-time activity; it requires periodic renewal. However, assessment is not an end in and of itself. We must remember that assessment is simply the first step towards making and sustaining desired improvements.

The two books discussed above place a heavy emphasis on making changes to destructive patterns of communication, changes that can only come with the realization that the negative patterns exist. Most important, they express a shared conviction that removing malicious, negative interaction from one's life and substituting affirming behaviors is a life changing activity. Lori Palatnik states it as follows:

> When people clean up their speech, they clean up their lives. Suddenly, a sense of control is embraced, self-respect is enhanced, and the respect of others is earned. Relationships heal, positive role modeling is in place, and peace is in the air.[16]

Recognizing that lives change for the good when the negative is removed from patterns of interaction, we, the authors, are on a mission to make the work environment a positive, constructive and affirming place through choosing to act in helpful, supportive ways.

## Chapter 6 Summary

Assessing the extent to which gossip has created a toxic environment is a useful activity for managers or supervisors concerned with extinguishing destructive communication. Assessment, however, can be both organizational and personal. This chapter provided the following insights into assessment.

- A gossip assessment can focus either on the overall culture of an organizational subdivision or determine the presence of a person who habitually engages in gossip.
- There is no single recognized evaluation tool by which to assess the degree of gossip toxicity in a culture.
- Consulting groups and university professors in related fields of study have a variety of tools for doing a general cultural evaluation of an organization. Some of these tools can and have been used to quantify problems related to malicious gossip.
- The most useful gossip assessment tool for a manager is his or her awareness of employee interaction. The manager's awareness can be enhanced by the simple process of regular interaction with subordinates sometimes called *management by walking around*. But, to be effective, the manager's personal radar system has to be fully functioning.
- The habitual gossiping behavior of individual employees may

be doing great harm to a work group. These employees need to be identified and singled out for effective disciplinary action.

- "Self-help" resources related to extinguishing gossiping behavior provide helpful insight both into ways to break the habit of gossip and an ethics/value/spiritual basis useful for encouraging personal growth in an area that can substantially improve quality of life.

# Chapter 7

---

# TAMING MALICIOUS GOSSIP

## No one gossips about other people's secret virtues.
### BERTRAND RUSSELL

J ack Levin and Arnold Arluke begin their book *Gossip: The Inside Scoop* by noting that:

> Gossip has a bad reputation around town–if not the world. Among the West African Ashanti, nasty or scandalous gossip about a tribal leader is punished by cutting off the gossiper's lips.[1]

While we do not advocate cutting off the lips of employees who gossip, we do believe that gossip is something every manager needs to be concerned about. No one is better off when management ignores the behavior.

As noted earlier, gossip has been around as long as people have been able to talk to one another. It has been used to ruin reputations, falsely accuse the innocent and spread information best left private for almost as long. Workplace gossip has caused numerous ills such as lawsuits, lost jobs and ruined relationships. More subtly, it has played a part in causing people to be passed over for promotions, often diminishing workplace cohesion. In addition, its effects on morale have undoubtedly slowed or even thwarted important initiatives, causing productivity to suffer. Worse still, it often trumps constructive forms of interaction beneficial to organizational performance.

In the face of such negative effects, one might ask why gossip is so pervasive. Unfortunately, until it hurts us personally, we are often numb to its destructive effect and view it as just part of relating to others and getting along in an organization. And, like any habitual action, it can be hard to stop–very hard. But for any manager who wants to infuse a workplace with a sense of purpose, it is critical to stem the flow in order to foster unity and good spirit within a team.

However, asserting that malicious gossip needs to be controlled is easy. The more challenging task is to conceptualize, build and implement programs and protocols for taming it. The following discussion offers leaders some tools to help develop a positive, supportive workplace.

## Concepts of Gossip Management

The pervasiveness of gossip in the workplace and the fact that it is so often an entrenched part of an organization and/or team culture make its management at minimum a worthy challenge. Fortunately, malicious gossip in the workplace can be managed effectively by constructive practices and substitution rather than elimination. Our discussion begins by providing a background in the form of six gossip management constructs.

### ➢ Our Naivety

A majority of the literature on gossip takes the position that it is naïve, unrealistic and fruitless to contemplate removing gossip from the workplace. Those who hold this view believe that critics of gossip understate its value within the organization, failing to recognize its complexity and overstating its harms. They see gossip as being an essential part of being human; we talk to each other, therefore we gossip. Thus, in the words of one gossip researcher, "It is facile to believe that gossip can be eliminated and futile for managers to attempt to do so."[2]

Whether futile or not, those who hold the opposite point of view actively look for ways to manage gossip. In fact, the demands of managers and supervisors looking for constructive ways to address the problems created by gossip fuel this perspective. In our experience, for instance, we have never heard a manager laud the presence of gossip and/or find it helpful in his or her workforce, though we frequently hear the concerns and frustration over its destructiveness.

These leadership concerns are reflected in a number of business journals with articles on how to manage it and books purporting to provide insight on how to "take control over gossip and criticism." Some of what has been written focuses on transforming the person, books such as *30 Days to Taming Your Tongue* and *Gossip: Ten Pathways to Eliminate It From Your Life and Transform Your Soul*. Secular and religious books alike espouse methods for removing gossip from one's life. In addition, we found books like *The No-Gossip Zone* that contend that a gossip-free workplace provides a healthy, high-performing work environment.

The fundamental question is whether employees can embrace an organizational culture free of malicious gossip. Martin Seligman addresses issues of change in his book *What You Can Change...and What You Can't*. He examines a variety of human foibles and behavior along with the research on whether or not lasting changes can occur. He concludes that some aspects of human behavior can be changed while others have not as yet yielded to efforts at modification.[3] Fortunately, our research and years of consulting experience indicate that a gossipy workplace can be modified into a supportive, affirming work environment. While not an easy process, it is possible.

In the same way that employees can be taught good customer service skills, employees can also learn how to help create a culture that affirms its membership. Obviously, this takes commitment on behalf of the organization, executive leadership and the individual managers, but we are convinced that it is not naïve to believe that workplaces known for positive communication can be created and sustained.

### ➤ A Higher Calling

Expecting a gossip-free workplace in a broader culture where the behavior is a mainstay does seem problematic. Can employees, who actively participate in various forms of gossip outside of the workplace, reasonably be expected to adapt their behavior to a more demanding on-the-job standard? While recognizing the challenges associated with requiring them to conform to a higher standard, the expectation is not only reasonable, it is a necessity and already commonplace.

For example, organizations already mandate that employees meet rigorous behavioral standards in the interest of improving performance and to accommodate legal requirements. Moreover, these standards often conflict substantially with an employee's personal behavior outside of the workplace. The legal requirement with regard to providing a workplace free of sexual harassment is an obvious illustration. Ribald humor about the opposite sex that brings applause from fellow patrons in a bar is likely to create substantial trouble when an employee brings that behavior to work. Similarly, there is a growing body of statutory requirements related to prohibiting behavior such as harassment, bullying and mobbing. Each of these has a verbal component that organizations must now guard against.

Of course, employment law is most often written to set a minimum requirement, not to promote an optimum experience. For instance, laws prohibiting sexual harassment are intended to prohibit unacceptable behavior but not designed as a coaching tool to bring about effective communication between the sexes. Martin Luther King, Jr. emphasized this point when he stated, "Morality cannot be legislated but behavior can be regulated. Judicial decrees may not change the heart, but they can restrain the heartless."[4]

Obviously, seeking to restrain the heartless usually accomplishes very little, particularly when the restraint is in the form of verbal admonition. And it's a mistake to say *"We're simply going to ignore it and hope it goes away."* What leadership can do is teach employees how to deal with malicious gossip with workable strategies that emphasize what they ought to be doing. This method stems the toxic tide without plunging a workplace into totalitarian negativity. Gossip taming by building and supporting constructive communication is not a passive activity; it requires conscious thought and effort.

## ➢ Condition vs. Problem

Management literature recognizes a distinct difference between a condition and a problem. In simple terms, a condition needs to be managed while a problem ought to be solved. Understanding this difference changes the way a manager thinks about an issue he or she confronts. A faulty piece of technology is a problem. Correcting that problem requires determining exactly what caused the malfunction and then fixing it. Once fixed, the problem should disappear. However, if it recurs, the problem-solver likely diagnosed it poorly or the solution was insufficient. Thus, the matter can be resolved with a better analysis and a different or more comprehensive solution.

Interestingly, basic management textbooks usually provide multiple pages if not chapters related to problem resolution approaches and skills, indicating that leaders are expected to be problem solvers. They are to address any and all problems with a rational system of fact finding, diagnosis, solution development and implementation.

A condition, on the other hand, is different from a problem in that it usually evolves out of the inherent character of a situation or the people involved, elements that can be controlled but not changed. A good example is a family-owned business where all leadership positions are reserved for family members. Therefore, primary decisions are subject to family politics with all of the pluses and minuses inherent in that environment. As a result, non-family employees of the organization can face negative consequences not present in one owned by persons with no family ties. Clearly, it is foolishness to say that family does not matter since it obviously does.

Therefore, issues developing in this context may not be problems that need solutions; they may instead result from a reality that must be confronted. Successful family-owned businesses learn how to shield non-family employees from the negative impact of family squabbles and disagreements. This requires a conscious, ongoing process that is carefully monitored and maintained, a condition to be managed, not solved.

Malicious gossip, however, has elements of both a problem and a condition. For example, a specific employee with a reputation for being the purveyor of malicious gossip can be viewed as a problem in that changing his or her behavior involves taking specific steps. Moreover, if the behavior continues and the problem is significant enough, it can often be dealt with by simply ending the employment relationship.

But malicious gossip also has the characteristics of a condition that needs to be managed. Employees are social creatures who interact with each other–sometimes negatively. We are all human, so we don't always follow our good intentions with actions consistent with our intentions and values. Or, as one of the authors stated elsewhere, we all "leak and stray";[5] we can lose our commitment and focus. Creating a culture that supports positive interaction is not a one-time fix; it is an ongoing process. A constructive workplace environment must be built and maintained over time. Slippage does occur and strategies for renewal must be developed and implemented.

## ➢ A Positive Approach

The field of positive psychology is a growing system of thought that focuses on the elements of positive human development. Not too many years ago, it would have been difficult to find articles and books that embraced this basic philosophy. Today, there are multitudes of research articles and a long list of commendable books on the topic as more and more people discover the benefits of a positive attitude and environment. Good sources include books such as *How Full Is Your Bucket?* by Tom Rath and Donald O. Clifton, *Positivity* by Barbara Fredrickson, *Authentic Happiness* and *Flourish* by Martin E. P. Seligman. While not psychology books, we would add *Different Seasons* and *Grateful Living,* titles by former *Seattle Times* columnist Dale Turner.

A well-known champion of positive psychology, Seligman begins the first chapter of *Authentic Happiness* by detailing a research project that began in 1932. It tracked a group of 178 nuns in what he calls "the most remarkable study of happiness and longevity ever done."[6] The researchers looked at many different variables. In one, the nuns were divided into four quadrants based on the extent to which they expressed positive emotions in their initial written essays that were part of the application process. Quadrant 1 contained the group of nuns who expressed the greatest degree of effervescent good cheer and positive emotion, quadrant 4 the least, with 2 and 3 ranked accordingly. When longevity of life was determined by way of the ranks,

> ...it was discovered that 90% of the most cheerful quarter was alive at age eighty-five versus only 34% of the least cheerful quarter. Similarly, 54% of the most cheerful quarter was alive at age ninety-four as opposed to 11% of the least cheerful quarter.[7]

Clearly, a positive attitude benefits life expectancy. It is also clear from observing social interactions in the broader society that malicious gossip makes no one happy. The phrase "effervescent good cheer" hardly applies. The purveyors of gossip may have some level of smug satisfaction, but it would be hard to call it happiness. Furthermore, the victims of the destructive side of gossip are just that: victims. Needless to say, the words *happy* and *victim* hardly go together.

Seligman is so convinced that his positive approach works that he asserts the following in *Flourish*:

> Positive psychology makes people happier. Teaching positive psychology, researching positive psychology, using positive psychology in practice as a coach or therapist, giving positive psychology exercises to tenth graders in a classroom, parenting little kids with positive psychology, teaching drill sergeants how to teach about post-traumatic growth, meeting with other positive psychologists, and just reading about positive psychology all **make people happier.** The people who work in positive psychology are the people with the highest well-being I have ever known.[8]

While the term *well-being* is usually applied to an individual, there is no reason it cannot be used in regard to a work group and an organization. It seems reasonable to conclude that what leadership should strive for in any organization is a high level of well-being and clearly that cannot occur in the presence of malicious gossip. However, the constructs of positive psychology leave no room for negative interaction.

➤ **The Substitution Process**

So how do leaders start ridding an organization of gossip and its toxic effects? What won't work is to assume that "no one gossips here," or that effective gossip management includes posting signs in the workplace that feature a red bar through a pair of lips. Another unworkable tactic is to establish sovereign rules of communication beginning with "Thou shalt not."

However, leaders will discover that the process of change begins with a kinder, gentler workplace, a place where employees feel valued and loved. This kinder workplace is certainly not a place where everyone walks on eggs shells, afraid to speak clearly and directly for fear of hurting someone's feelings. It is one that encourages open communication, values ethical interactions, and rewards supportive behavior and honest dealings. In this environment, employees understand that how they talk about and to each other significantly impacts their relationships and the tenor of the workplace.

The Great Places to Work Institute conducts surveys to determine what organizations are considered great places to work. To date they have completed more than 10 million surveys that clearly indicate what employees and managers view as desirable work environments. Results show that employees value most being able to trust the people they work for, having pride in what they do and enjoying the people with whom they work.[9] Managers focus on achieving organizational objectives, and having employees who give their personal best and work together as a team/family. Without question, malicious gossip subtracts from all of the elements identified as great workplace characteristics.

The survey results do offer leaders some insight into what gossip management requires. It is particularly significant that employees highly value working with people they enjoy. Therefore, managers can comfortably conclude that a focus on building positive relationships among employees will enhance the work environment more effectively than attempting to rid it of gossip. It's also safe to say that employees who enjoy working with each other do not spend time stabbing one another in the back through malicious gossip.

One of the authors has spent a substantial period of time providing consulting and training services to organizations on the topic of interpersonal conflict resolution. Early in his career, he developed a program focused on identifying the origins of conflict and offering strategies/tactics to be used in managing (i.e., reducing, eliminating) the conflict. As time passed, he became somewhat disillusioned because, while his services were usually well received and highly rated, the actual reduction of destructive conflict appeared to be almost negligible.

As a result, he began to focus on direct intervention. Instead of using a training platform, he worked specifically with the unit (i.e., team, division or program) experiencing heightened levels of conflict. The focus was not directly on the conflict but on identifying the characteristics of relationships they desired to have. Group members then explored the steps necessary to develop those relationships and concluded with a protocol in which each person committed him/herself to the relationship enhancement activities that they helped develop. Feedback from the sessions clearly showed that far more actual behavior change occurred than had resulted with the traditional training program. The altered intervention model succeeded in reducing or eliminating negative, unproductive conflict without ever directly addressing it. Group members focused instead on creating what everyone wanted in the first place–positive relationships and a supportive workplace environment.

> **Flavor of the Month**

Gerard Egan confronts the problem of what he calls "managerial fads" in the introduction to his very useful book, *Working the Shadow Side.* He writes:

> A questionable reason for focusing on the shadow side is that it is exciting–it has a catchy quality to it typical of a fad subject. *Working the Shadow Side* would be a failure were it to do nothing more than start another fad.[10]

Egan worries that his book could end up being an "expensive distraction" rather than constituting useful, viable "solutions for business problems." He concludes by noting that "great value" can be added to the business when a proposed skill set becomes "an important part of an overall managerial system" as opposed to being the flavor of the month, quickly abandoned for the next great flavor.[11]

We have a similar concern as we present an alternative technique to addressing gossip in the workplace. In fact, we would add to Egan's concerns that there is no magic in what we prescribe. Taming the practice of malicious gossip does not involve some wild new endeavor. Instead, it requires facilitating the development of a constructive workplace through predictable, persistent and positive managerial effort. The quality of relationships among employees, and between employees and management is fundamental to a productive work environment. Skills useful to help promote such an environment are not the components of a fad; they need to be a part of every manager's basic toolbox.

## Change Starts with You

Some years ago, Tom Peters and Nancy Austin opened *A Passion for Excellence* with a chapter titled, "A Blinding Flash of the Obvious." It begins with a short dialogue in which one nameless speaker tries to explain to another why reading the book might be a good idea.

> "What's new?"
> "Nothing in particular."
> "Then why read it?"
> "Because doing it isn't as easy as it sounds."[12]

Though a significant portion of what follows may also seem like a blinding flash of the obvious, at times the obvious needs to be carefully stated, repeated and emphasized. Just because it is obvious that a healthy work environment requires consistent gossip management does not necessarily mean that organizations successfully accomplish the goal–after all, "doing it is not as easy as it sounds."

Therefore, leadership throughout the organization must be the major player in building and implementing effective gossip management strategies. Individual managers or supervisors are in a position to have a powerful influence on the culture of the organization, an influence that can be exercised in three distinctly different ways: 1) removing the source, 2) creating change by example and 3) pursuing personal transformation.

## ➤ Removing the Source

Though it continues through habit, malicious gossip often stems from feelings of powerlessness, anger, estrangement and alienation. Anyone in management, supervision or other leadership positions needs to ponder the question, "Why is this happening here?" The query inevitably leads to further questions.

- Is there something about the organization that inhibits open and honest communication?
- Does my personal style as a supervisor/manager promote or create a barrier to good relationships?
- Are the attitudes of those atop the hierarchy offensive to those reporting to them?

If leaders don't encourage openness, or ignore or even punish those who do try to speak freely to them, it certainly communicates a negative message across the organization. Anyone who wants to speak frankly (not hurtfully), may, over time, feel he or she can only speak anonymously and only to others perceived to be similarly situated.

Obviously, leaders need to take steps to change managerial practices to diminish gossip that originates from feelings of powerlessness and alienation. Negative attitudes toward subordinates must be replaced with positive ones. Leadership at all levels needs to establish and maintain open channels of communication while making it a priority to cultivate quality relationships with colleagues and subordinates.

Though truly essential, the above statements seem pedantic and too obvious. Why then are there so often significant communication and relationship problems within organizations? Peters and Austin conclude that, "the number one managerial productivity problem in America is, quite simply, managers who are out of touch with their people and out of touch with their customers."[13] To this we would add that being out of touch also creates a rich venue for malicious gossip.

Since the antidote to the problem of gossip is managerial connection, the questions become quite personal.

- Have I, as a manager, established the kinds of relationships with subordinates that permit and encourage open interaction around problems that concern them?
- Do I set aside time for regular contact with my subordinates?
- What do I have to change about myself so others can change?

While not a new concept, *A Passion for Excellence* emphasizes the importance of finding creative and constructive ways of communicating with subordinates. Peters and Austin advise regular contact with subordinates in their place of work and contact that primarily involves listening. They write, "We know it as the technology of the obvious, the method by which leadership becomes effective in any well-run school, hospital, bank, single-store operation or industrial enterprise."[14] So, if all of the manager's communication with subordinates is happening in his or her office, the conversations are not likely very open, and subordinates probably limit what they will bring up for discussion.

As previously noted, this is not flavor-of-the-month advice; this is basic quality management. When a manager takes the time to maintain regular contact with subordinates, ensuring that their communication involves a great deal of genuine listening, good things happen. Productivity improves and malicious gossip is extinguished. A simple "hello" is not enough; the contact must be meaningful and include actual dialogue.

However, a word of caution is in order. The relationship between superior and subordinate can also become a rich venue for gossip. Therefore, managers need to avoid creating the perception and/or reality of a special, spicy relationship by establishing consistent contact with all subordinates, not just a small clique. Any special relationship, whether real or perceived, will undoubtedly diminish the quality of relationships with others in the work group.

> ## Creating Change by Example

In the preface to *Primal Leadership,* Goleman, Boyatzis and McKee offer what they see as a new concept of primal leadership. They state:

> The fundamental task of leaders, we argue, is to prime good feelings in those they lead. That occurs when a leader creates *resonance*–a reservoir of positivity that frees the best in people. At its root, then, the primal job of leadership is emotional.[15]

The authors believe that "this primal dimension of leadership... determines whether everything else a leader does will work as well as it could."[16] They explain that:

> In the modern organization, this primordial emotional task– though by now largely invisible–remains foremost among the many jobs of leadership: driving the collective emotions in a positive direction and clearing the smog created by toxic emotions. This task applies to leadership everywhere, from the board room to the shop floor.[17]

So where do those "toxic emotions" come from? Obviously, they are primarily the byproduct of relationships and the social environment within which people work. The leader's job, therefore, is to drive "the collective emotions in a positive direction" and by doing so help create an environment in which malicious gossip ceases.

This leads to the next question: How does a manager drive the collective emotions? Mahatma Gandhi's often quoted advice is apt; the leader "must be the change [he or she] wishes to see in the world."[18] However, as a number of commentators have pointed out, Gandhi never said those exact words. What he actually said is far more to the point.

> We but mirror the world. All the tendencies present in the outer world are to be found in the world of our body. If we could change ourselves, the tendencies in the world would also change. As a man changes his own nature, so does the attitude of the world change towards him. This is the divine mystery supreme. A wonderful thing it is and the source of our happiness. We need not wait to see what others do.[19]

Of course, in a business context, leadership *cannot* wait to see what others do because the others are waiting for leadership to express itself. If that expression is negative, subordinates will follow suit. If that expression is positive and affirming, subordinates will do the same. The basic question, therefore, for any manager concerns the "I" that is present in the workplace. Is that "I" a smog creator, helping to grow emotional toxins by spreading malicious gossip and engaging in other forms of negative communication? Or does that "I" reflect a set of positive attitudes that are supportive of colleagues and subordinates? As Gandhi said, the good news is that you don't have to wait for others in order to start setting a positive emotional tone.

In Chapter 6, we referenced Chapman and White's research on the five languages of appreciation in the workplace. The basic premise of the research is that the primary motivator for high performance and feeling good about one's work environment is being appreciated.[20] However, individual managers and even organizations often communicate appreciation infrequently, poorly or both.

Chapman and White encourage managers not only to recognize

the motivational benefits of appreciative statements but also be aware that research shows that communicating appreciation should occur in five different languages: 1) words of affirmation,[21] 2) quality time,[22] 3) acts of service,[23] 4) tangible gifts[24] and 5) physical touch.[25] Each person responds differently depending on his or her primary language. Employees feel appreciated when the manager acknowledges their value in a language that they understand.[26]

Obviously, every manager has opportunities to communicate his or her appreciation to both colleagues and subordinates. Doing so effectively, however, requires skills that must be learned and used. A good place to start is mastering Chapman and White's five languages of appreciation. In addition, there are invaluable generic skills that include hearing what a subordinate has to say and responding appropriately, expressing gratitude in a meaningful way, showing empathy, engaging in genuine dialogue and other communication skills of a similar nature. Fortunately, managers can choose to develop these skills on their own initiative. Most important, when used consistently, these skills transform the work environment because expressing appreciation is contagious. The practice nurtures goodwill, the exact opposite of the negativity promoted by malicious gossip.

### ➢ Pursuing Personal Transformation

Will Bowen begins *A Complaint Free World* with the sentence, "In your hands you hold the secret to transforming your life." What is the secret? He explains that people can transform their lives when they learn to live without engaging in "complaining, criticizing or gossiping. By becoming conscious of and, thereby, changing their words, they have changed their thoughts and begun to create their lives by design."[27] In other words, if a manager wants subordinates to arrive on time, he or she must model punctuality. Most managers realize that, even if they had an evening meeting and feel justified in arriving late, being the first one in the office or work site sends a powerful message. And, if a manager wants others to speak kindly and supportively about their colleagues, then they must see that behavior modeled. Once again, the concept is simple but often difficult to execute.

Bowen's book offers advice to those wishing to diminish or remove complaining from their everyday social interaction. He states specifically the goal is to remove any spoken "complaints, criticism and gossip,"[28] and promises that if "you stay with it, you will find that not only will you not complain, but others around you will cease to do so as well."[29]

Bowen, a minister, incorporates the popular notion that it takes 21 days to form a habit into his "transformation" process. He used the concept as the backbone of his efforts to change his own complaining behavior, and also challenged his congregation to see how long it would take to go 21 days without complaining. Those who chose to participate wore a purple band on their wrist. Every time they complained, they were supposed to move the band from one wrist to the other.

Bowen recounts his personal experiences as he tried to communicate without complaining.

> The first day, my hands got tired switching the bracelet from wrist to wrist. I realized that I was complaining all the time…. After the first week, my personal best was to have only switched the bracelet five times in one day…. Finally, after nearly a month, I had a string of three days going…. I found that I could do very well around some people but not so well around others…. I finally completed my 21 days…. More important, I found myself beginning to feel happier.[30]

Ultimately, the story of what he and the church were attempting to do appeared in a newspaper article that was reprinted in newspapers around the country. In 2007 when Bowen wrote the book, the church distributed six million purple wristbands[31] since members had agreed to give a free band to anyone who requested it. The church eventually received reports that it was taking people four to eight months to successfully make 21 days without complaining.[32] The fact that it takes so long to eliminate complaining from interpersonal communication is a good indicator that we human beings engage in much more negative interaction than we realize. As a result, changing the pattern can be quite challenging.

In *Gossip: Ten Pathways to Eliminate It From Your Life and Transform Your Soul*, Platnik highlights the difficult nature of change and emphasizes the value of the results. She writes:

> It takes effort to break a lifetime habit, as I am attempting to do, but the results are worth it. I look at the world in a completely different way now, and the world looks at me in a whole new light. All of my relationships, be they personal or business or in even brief day-to-day encounters, have improved 1000 percent.[33]

While Platnik's assertion of 1000 percent improvement seems to be a substantial overstatement, we can appreciate the sentiment and believe that relationships do improve when we rid our communication of gossip.

Though her focus was much broader than gossip, author Gretchen Rubin makes some important points about personal change. Her book, *The Happiness Project,* details the story of how she determined to invest one year into working actively on her own happiness. Dividing the year into 12 self-improvement projects, she studied what had been written about each one, and researched how she could make them part of her own life. Early in the book, Rubin observes that, "I had come to understand one critical fact about my happiness project: I couldn't change anyone else."[34] She also arrived at what she considers some basic truths about happiness and records them in her "Manifesto." In it, she states, "One of the best ways to make *yourself* happy is to make *other people* happy; one of the best ways to make other people happy is to be happy *yourself.*"[35]

Rubin recognized that much of her personal happiness was

derived from the quality of her relationships with her two daughters, husband, extended family and friends. However, she noticed that her own behavior often sabotaged that happiness. She also described how difficult it was at times to change her sabotaging behavior and noted the positive benefits that occurred when she accomplished this task. What Rubin discovered about learning to be happy can be summarized in the following three simple points:

1. We have actual control only over changing ourselves.
2. When we change ourselves and become happier, others will change around us.
3. Changing ourselves takes conscious thought and frequently requires substantial effort; we are often our own worst enemy when it comes to happiness.

Two pertinent themes about personal transformation emerge from the literature just reviewed. First, all the authors acknowledge the challenges. They concur that modifying our behavior is difficult because of a lack of awareness and because changing personal habits requires extremely consistent effort. Second, they emphasize that when we stop complaining, stop engaging in malicious gossip, stop criticizing and make the effort to engage others in positive forms of communication, we experience life in a new, more positive way.

Successful coaches use the concept of personal transformation when teaching their athletes to center their attention on what they can control. Rather than worrying about what they cannot control (the officials, the weather, etc.), the athletes achieve success by making sure they have done everything they possibly can to be fully prepared for the competition.

As team members in a different context, managers should focus their behaviors on improving the social climate of the work group. They learn to ask themselves questions such as,

- Have I done what I'm capable of doing to establish good relationships with subordinates and colleagues?

- Am I driving the emotional climate of the workplace in the right direction?
- Am I engaged in personal transformation?

Becoming a better manager is little different from becoming a better athlete. Focus on yourself and what you can change and improve.

## Change Continues with the Organization

One of our colleagues, George Suess, published a short article some time ago titled "What Would Emeril Do?"[36] The article recounts his dining experience at a Las Vegas restaurant owned by Emeril, a prominent New Orleans chef. The food was extraordinary, and he found by way of conversations with other diners that they were having similar positive reactions to both the food and service.

As he thought about it, Suess considered the challenge Emeril faced in creating the same high quality dishes in his restaurants with many different employees at multiple locations. It brought to his mind the challenges that organizations generally have as they endeavor to provide customers with products of consistent quality. The article concludes with a description of the type of training required to achieve the necessary consistency in action to meet the standards set by the owner. Suess notes that, in addition to the skills they must learn, employees at each restaurant are trained to understand that they must follow strictly the instructions given for cleanliness, food preparation and service. It is, after all, Emeril's business, and patrons must receive food and service consistent with Emeril's reputation.[37]

This holds true for any organization. Each has a unique identity and the right to establish reasonable expectations related to performance and behavioral standards. Emeril's has a well-deserved reputation because employees learn to do it Emeril's way. Most important, Emeril's has the advantage of superbly good recipes making it quite logical to demand that they be followed.

Similarly, each organization has an identity and must address the essential question of whether or not that identity works to its benefit. An organization needs "good recipes." Once those recipes are developed, tried and proven, then it has a right to demand adherence.

Consider the following additional example. There is a uniquely

An organization needs "good recipes." Once those recipes are developed, tried and proven, then it has a right to demand adherence.

American athletic activity called March Madness where basketball teams from the major colleges compete for the men's and women's national basketball championship. These single-elimination tournaments occur each spring with extensive national coverage and extraordinary fan support. As the 2011 tournament approached, Brigham Young University's (BYU) nationally ranked men's team was one of the favorites to win the national championship. Hopes for the ultimate victory faded, however, when the university chose to suspend a star player for violation of BYU's code of conduct. Among other things, the honor code required sexual abstinence before marriage, and the player had admitted to college officials that he had had sex with his girlfriend.[38]

Needless to say, sports talk radio lit up with hot debate over the decision by the school to remove the player from the team. One sports commentator put it this way, "Is getting lucky with your girlfriend really so heinous a crime that the school is willing to blow its team's dream season–and maybe even a student's academic career?"[39]

The response from the school was that every student signs the honor code and is expected to live up to his or her commitment. The issue is not whether requiring sexual abstinence is appropriate for college students but rather whether the college should enforce the honor code regardless of a student's rank or perceived value. Whether you agree or disagree with the standards, BYU distinguishes itself by enforcing an honor code regardless of the status of the student.

Likewise, work groups, programs and organizations have the same right to set a standard of excellence including the right to determine behavioral standards related to employee conduct. Those standards can certainly include the expectation that employees refrain from malicious gossip. Organizations choose numerous ways in which to communicate their behavioral expectations. The following are common to many organizations. While some provide for sanctions against malicious gossip, the primary focus is on effectively communicating positive expectations.

*The Pre-Employment Process*: The best place for an organization to begin communicating its unique identity and standards is in the on-boarding pre-employment process. Obviously, in order to craft messages that communicate positive expectations for prospective employees, the organization needs to be clear about who and what it is. Therefore, leaders need to consider questions such as:

- What messages does the organization's website express about behavioral expectations for employees?
- Is there a pre-employment interview that includes a discussion about the positive aspects of the organizational culture and how each employee is expected to act consistent with that culture?

Trinity Services, a large nonprofit organization headquartered in Illinois, includes a pre-employment letter that prospective employees must read before they are given the opportunity to fill out an employment application. That letter is reproduced below.

### Pre-Employment Letter

Dear Applicant:

On behalf of Trinity Services, I would like to thank you for considering employment with our organization. This letter is written to provide you with our Mission Statement and to share the expectations we have for our team members.

*It is our mission to be a leader in providing the highest quality, socially responsible and cost-effective services and supports to persons with disabilities, so that they might achieve their full potential and have the opportunity to live full and abundant lives.*

Trinity Services serves people with disabilities both in Illinois and Nevada. We operate such programs as a school, adult learning programs, family support services, residential programs, behavioral health services, a counseling center, vocational and competitive employment, and several support businesses.

Because of the unique nature of the services and supports we provide, it is paramount that we place significant emphasis on the selection of our employees. Therefore, we seek individuals who not only possess the necessary skills, but who share our common values and have a positive attitude and strong work ethic. It is our experience that employees who possess the following three (3) characteristics fit well into the Trinity Team:

1. *An enthusiastic attitude that promotes a positive atmosphere and a willingness to work as part of a team*
2. *A strong sense of integrity and the ability to accept personal responsibility for decisions and actions*
3. *A willingness to interact with program participants, their parents, visitors and fellow employees with respect and consideration, as they would want to be treated themselves.*

Trinity's leadership team will always provide support to employees who conduct themselves appropriately within our guidelines, policies and procedures. It is our practice to cultivate as much opportunity for employee growth, input and development as possible. The State of Illinois also requires that all persons working in a social service position possess a high school diploma or a GED.

After reading this letter, if you understand and accept the goals, philosophy and values stated above, please request an application from the Employee Services staff member. If you decide not to pursue employment with us at this time, please return this letter to the reception desk.

I would like to thank you for your time and wish you good luck in your career search.

Best regards,

Art Dykstra
President, CEO

*The Value Statement*: Many companies craft a statement of organizational values that expresses clearly the vision and purpose of the corporate entity, providing a North Star presence for behavior among coworkers at every level. It is most effective when stated simply and communicated throughout the organization since employees need to know what the company's guiding principles are.

Value statements often address behaviors such as withholding information or participating in the rumor mill by stating the importance of positive communication practices. It is not unusual to address the issue of gossip with an emphasis on "open and honest communications." What follows is an example of one organization's ten key values:

- Servant Leadership
- Serving and Supporting
- Honest and Open Communication
- Discretionary Effort
- Personal Growth
- Thinking Ahead & Following Through
- Collaboration
- Stewardship
- Achieving Outcomes
- Continuous Improvement

Each of the above can be augmented by a few sentences that explain the stated value in more detail.

Values describe the behaviors/goals the organization endorses as most important. In this light, it is difficult to conceive of a corporate statement of values that does not make reference to expectations about the quality of relationships. Clearly, by promoting positive relationships, it indirectly condemns malicious gossip. Of course, the company must go beyond simply publishing a statement of values. Those values must influence decisions and be allowed to permeate all aspects of organizational behavior. This should also include the way employees are trained.

In addition, an organization's values need to be reflected at some level in a performance evaluation system that establishes a positive relationship between those values and what is viewed as good employee performance. In other words, an employee should not be rated highly on the performance evaluation tool if he or she consistently acts contrary to the values.

*Employee Handbooks*: Almost every organization has an employee handbook that presents information intended to guide the relationship between the employee and the employer. This includes details about the structure of the organization, insurance and benefits programs, vacation and holiday time as well as a section on the rules of employment. Frequently, the tone and substance of the handbook–particularly the section on rules and discipline–focuses on what not to do rather than on how employees should conduct themselves. We crafted the following more positive handbook statement from the perspective of sending a powerful message to employees from the standpoint of expected behavior.

> Employees are required to conduct themselves in a professional manner at all times, acting in the best interests of [name of organization] and fellow employees. Therefore, each must use good judgment, common sense and a strong sense of ethics to determine the appropriateness of his or her behavior.

> Employees are expected to act in a manner that promotes harmony, good will and respect among [name of organization] employees. This includes the responsibility to recognize that differences in ethnicity, politics and religion need not divide coworkers who act with sensitivity. "In your face" attitudes, malicious gossip and other forms of negative statements and behaviors are not acceptable. Each employee is expected to act in a manner that supports high performance both for him/herself and for other [name of organization] employees.

Since employee handbooks tend to be long and at times somewhat tedious documents, messages like the above are often lost in the overall verbiage. In addition, there is the issue of a primary message vs. a secondary message. Is all information in the handbook of equal importance particularly as an instrument of instruction? Probably not. So leaders need to think carefully about how to give a message the appropriate emphasis and where to place it in the handbook. Moreover, the statement can be formatted in such a way that it highlights a specific section as a primary message.

The HR department can provide another opportunity to emphasize relational issues since it usually requires new employees to sign a statement acknowledging their receipt of the handbook and responsibility to read and live by its guidelines. It could place the above statement in a strategic part of the signature page to highlight further the importance of quality relationships and supportive interaction. Employees could then be required to read it again before signing the page.

Apart from what the organization has in writing (i.e., handbooks, policy manuals or values statements), every manager needs to communicate actively that gossip is unacceptable. This communication should occur naturally and be restated periodically since time diminishes the potency of a message. It is very important that this "touching base" occur as it provides leverage if an employee, once counseled, continues his or her gossiping behavior. Written documents, with regard to how anti-gossip messages impact employee behavior, have value only to the extent that leadership actively support them.

*Performance Reviews*: If gossiping behavior is of major concern to the organization's leaders, guidelines should not only be included prominently in the employee handbook, an evaluation of the presence or absence of the behavior should appear in the employee's performance review. It would be unwise to create a primary message around behavioral expectations (i.e., what the employee is required to do as opposed to prohibited from doing) and then ignore this primacy on performance evaluations. While performance evaluation forms vary with each organization, it appears to be reasonably easy to ensure that elements within the evaluation process assess communication behaviors that enhance or help build positive relationships

*Staff Learning Opportunities*: A learning organization that works to "continuously expand its capacity to create its future,"[40] as Peter Senge describes it, has its employees regularly involved in activities of growth and knowledge seeking. Such learning opportunities clearly vary with the size of the organization as well as with its purpose and structure. A justifiable goal for including the topic of gossip in staff learning activities is to draw attention to the destructive effects of negative gossip at every possible opportunity and work continuously to elevate the positive nature of honest and non-distorted communications. These discussions of gossip, communication and relationships help build a positive culture that benefits any business.

In the smallest of organizations, a discussion of these topics may take place before or after a staff meeting and be led by the person in charge. Organizations that employ hundreds or thousands of employees may choose both formal and informal learning activities. For instance, staff development functions as well as other venues where employees gather can highlight positive stories that carry the organization's values or mission. The "did you hear" opening gambit of gossipers can become key to building and sustaining positive culture.

Obviously, training agendas vary across organizations since they are created to address issues that arise in specific settings. Seligman describes a particularly effective one for the military in his book *Flourish*. Faced with concerns about post-traumatic stress disorder and the increasing number of suicides, the military partnered with Seligman to design a program to raise the level of active duty soldier well-being through training activities involving army sergeants. The sergeants, in turn, would help facilitate positive mental health growth in their troops. The conceptual outline that follows can be adapted for a variety of settings and issues.

The learning activities that compose the training have three primary components. The first involves encouraging personal growth or transformation in the trainees. The second consists of training in positive psychology that includes recognizing that how a person thinks and talks about an issue has a strong impact on how effectively he or she deals with it. The third involves specific verbal tool building to develop and refine communication skills useful in dealing with conflict.[41]

This brief description cannot begin to do justice to the thoughtfulness of the program design and to the implications for its application in a host of other venues. It does, however, provide an example of the on-going models of learning activities that have shown themselves effective in bringing positive change to organizational culture, change that forces malicious, destructive behavior out.

*Focus on the Positive*: While much of this section involves formal organizational tools, individual organizations are obviously free to be creative in finding ways to influence their cultures positively. One of the authors of this book published a short article several years ago that introduced the concept of a *happident*. The idea came to him when he realized that in his organization employees were required to report daily incidents, most of which were inherently negative. While many positive things occurred, they were not asked to communicate them. He knew that as CEO he needed to know about incidents that could cause current and future problems, but focusing only on the negative painted a skewed picture of what was actually going on within the organization.

So he and his leadership staff created a category called "happidents" on the daily report. The new category helped staff look for "positive accomplishments that promoted good spirits, joy and pleasure,"[42] giving them and the CEO a more realistic view of the organization's daily operations. Their experience illustrates the fact that all of an organization's efforts–whether formal, informal or creative–to promote a positive, affirming culture can have a significant impact on reducing malicious gossip.

Clearly, an organization builds and shapes its culture in many ways. As it creates a unique identity, it can, in part, shape that identity by a statement of values, its employee handbook, performance reviews, and employee learning activities. In addition, leaders invested in developing a more supportive environment for employees should remember that contradictory messages will sabotage their efforts. To facilitate positive growth, all of the above need to work in tandem–they must not work at cross purposes.

## Change Requires Dealing with the Problem Employee

As much as we hope and believe that working to create a positive team culture eliminates most malicious gossip, we realize that some employees may still appear to relish the negative, including gossiping and making disparaging remarks about colleagues. The manager cannot ignore such behavior. In some cases, the use of humor, stories, and examples facilitates constructive change. Making a joke out of an inappropriate action often provides sufficient notice to the employee that he or she needs to change that behavior. This approach should not be underestimated in coaching or developing employees.

But, when a team member remains persistently negative, the following two-step process offers an effective way to address the behavior. The first step is to attempt a constructive dialogue related to the problem communication. If the effort to resolve the issue through direct communication fails either as a result of a stubborn refusal to acknowledge the problem or because the employee is having difficulty managing his or her behavior, then formal discipline needs to be imposed with the ultimate possibility of discharge.

➤ **Step 1: Coaching the Problem Employee**

Among fundraising staff in nonprofit organizations, there is a cliché: "You won't get any money if you don't ask for it." The same could be said of dealing with malicious gossip. First, ask the person to stop the behavior. Of course, the way that a manager approaches the request has some bearing on the results. There is a significant distinction between reacting to a situation versus responding to it. Asking an employee to refrain from acts of malicious gossip should not be an angry reaction to a specific instance but rather a thoughtful, prepared communication event.

The following conversation offers some guidelines for speaking with a subordinate employee about an identified pattern of gossiping, defined as at least three instances of such behavior.

## Background

This conversation is *the first time* manager/supervisor Tom Barth has spoken with his subordinate employee Sarah Clayner. Tom has been with Milwaukee Health Care for over ten years and supervised Sarah for two. While not a superstar, Sarah is a valuable employee who performs her duties in a competent manner. Tom supervises the Quality Assurance Office that includes a staffing complement of nine individuals.

While Tom has been aware of Sarah's gossiping behavior during the time he has supervised her, he was hopeful it would be a problem that would go away or take care of itself, perhaps through feedback from another colleague or fellow worker. However, the negative communication behavior persisted, and Tom has made a decision to tackle the problem.

## The Meeting

Sarah seats herself in Tom's office where the following conversation takes place.

### Establish Non-Threatening Rapport

Tom: "Thanks for coming in this morning, Sarah. Did you have a good weekend?"

Sarah: "Yes, my husband and I went to Brad's football game on Saturday. It was homecoming, so we were hoping they would come away with a win."

Tom: "How did Brad play?"

Sarah: "Great, he had five or six tackles all by himself." [Brad is Sarah's son who plays football for Jefferson High School.]

### Leading to the Purpose of the Meeting

Tom: "Sarah, I asked to talk with you this morning regarding a concern I have within the office involving staff conversations and the ways in which staff talk about others at Milwaukee Health Care.

### Assert Respect and Caring

Tom: Quite frankly, this is something I should have raised with you earlier, but I guess I hesitated because I did not want to hurt your feelings or make you angry. As you know, I truly depend on you and you are a valued employee.

I would like to ask your assistance and commitment to increasing the positive communication practices in the office.

## The Problem

Tom: There have been several instances when I have noticed other staff in your office, sometimes just one, sometimes more. What seems to be going on are conversations that are not work or task related and in reality involve negative comments about other employees.

### The Request

Tom: Don't get me wrong, I know folks need to talk with one another to get the job done, but what I am asking you to do is to refrain from engaging in conversations that might be viewed or experienced as gossiping behavior. Gossiping is truly destructive and quite frankly, often causes hurt feelings and harmful, unintended consequences.

### Allow for Employee Response

Tom:   Does what I am sharing make sense?

Sarah: Yes, but I don't think you really know who I am. I am not a gossip, and besides, everyone does it. I remember at Christmas time I heard you telling Evelyn that you thought Mary should divorce Mark because he had a drinking problem.

Tom: I appreciate you giving me that feedback. You're right, I should not have made that comment, and I am sorry that I did.

### Acknowledgment of the Challenge

Tom: I do realize that we all make conversation mistakes, but I think it is important that we all work as hard as we can to have a positive workplace and do everything we can to avoid gossiping or harming anyone else.

### Reflection

Tom: Sarah, I would ask that you give thought to what we have talked about today. How we get along and treat each other is very important.

## The Commitment

Tom: I am asking you to pay attention to what you talk about—whether in the office or in the copy room—and also to what you listen to. As I said, you are a valuable employee; I count on you a great deal.

It is my intent to work as hard as I can so that our department is a trusting and enjoyable place to work, a place where we all establish and maintain good relationships with each other.

### Trust

Tom: There is something else I want you to know. I am not sharing this conversation with anyone else. This is feedback that I wanted to give you privately.

### Closure

Tom: My hope is that we will not have to have this conversation again and that you will take what we have discussed seriously and be a positive role model for everyone else.

Do you have any questions?

Okay, let's move on. I'll see you at our staff meeting tomorrow. Thanks for taking our time together seriously.

## Comments

The framework of the above model conversation has been taught to hundreds of employees and used successfully. As might be expected, there are innumerable variations on the theme as presented.

As a matter of approach, when talking with an employee for the first time regarding gossiping behavior, it is preferable not to share or list examples of the behavior. In most instances, the employee will "get" the message without having to identify what will feel like accusations.

The goal is not confession but rather a commitment to changed behavior. In some instances, it does become necessary to share an example. In the best of circumstances, the example should be a conversation the supervisor experienced firsthand—even if the supervisor did not call attention to the gossiping behavior when it occurred.

Sharing another person's example opens the door to more complicated interpersonal relationships. For example, stating that "Wanda told me that you told her that Margaret was having an affair with Harold" (another employee) will clearly change the relationship between Sarah and Wanda.

Because this is the first conversation with an employee regarding gossiping behavior, the consequence—future employee discipline—can usually be inferred. However, because some employees may need more explicit messages, it may be necessary to indicate that future discipline will occur if the behavior continues.

When giving an employee feedback about his or her communication practices, it is important to avoid labeling the person as a "gossip." Labels are not helpful and cause most people to become more defensive and resist changing their behavior.

Though interchanges such as the above are difficult, managers should *not* avoid them when there is an obvious problem.

Managers may enhance the results of the corrective interchange by helping the employee redirect talkative behavior by assigning him or her the job of corporate or team "town crier." The technique works best with someone who is very established, well connected to others, highly verbal, and generally viewed positively though he or she is also identified as a significant gossip. The responsibility involves bringing coworkers up to date on company news in public settings, and a manager may choose to meet with the employee before team meetings so that he or she is armed with new, positive stories. The extra bit of attention from supervisors and opportunity to speak in public often satisfies the person's need for attention. While the technique should be used with care, the authors have seen it used quite successfully in large organizations. Obviously, creative leaders can find many variations to this approach and apply them as needed.

➢ **Step 2: Disciplining the Problem Employee**

When the gossip problem persists regardless of efforts at constructive change, formal discipline must be considered. The goal of that discipline should always be to correct inappropriate behavior, so the supervisor may find that correctional action requires both punitive and non-punitive forms of discipline. If the behavior of the employee is sufficiently harmful and resists correction, then the manager will need to move through the traditional disciplinary measures of written warning, suspension, demotion and termination.

There are two possible non-punitive forms of intervention that can have significant positive results and have the additional advantage of being soft on relationship. The first is to consider site relocation, moving an employee to a different work group and supervisor. A change of supervisor can often result in a significant modification of behavior.

In addition, a gossiping employee's behavior can occasionally be diminished by moving him or her from a high traffic "easy to stop by" location to a less accessible site. A productive person prone to high levels of gossip in a job where he or she is in constant contact with people could be reassigned to paper- or computation-driven tasks.

In some organizations, an individual seems to be informally chosen or elected as the president of the "Malcontent Club." These chronically unhappy individuals may gather in someone's office or at lunch to share their misery and corporate misfortunes. Since little good comes from these relationships, a manager should confront the participating individuals along with the ring leader. However, where possible, moving the "president" to a different work group may be the single most effective strategy toward redirecting energies towards the positive.

The second non-punitive form of discipline, used extensively and successfully by one of the authors, is a "Thought Day." The approach should be given serious consideration under the right circumstances. A Thought Day works as follows:

1. To be selected for a Thought Day, an employee should have failed to respond constructively to prior discussions with his or her supervisor about inappropriate behavior. A Thought Day works particularly well to address issues such as sloppy, indifferent performance and confrontational relationships.

2. When an employee reports for work, he or she begins the day with a meeting with his or her supervisor. The supervisor discusses the employee's negative work record and provides an opportunity for him or her to offer insight into the problem.

3. At the close of the discussion, the supervisor informs the employee that he or she is being sent home with full pay for the day and an assignment. The requirement is to use the time to reflect on his or her employment, the problems that have just been discussed and how the future should unfold.

4. The supervisor also instructs the employee to report back to him or her, or a designated person on the following work day with any insights gathered during the time of reflection.

5. If part of the employee's problem is relationship issues with his or her immediate supervisor, the employee should report to a higher level manager or someone from the human services department.

6. When the employee returns to report to the supervisor or designated person, he or she shares the insights from the previous day's reflection. If the employee responds positively with thoughts about how to improve, the facilitator can provide encouragement and any available assistance. If, on the other hand, the employee responds defensively, the facilitator can conclude the meeting by stating his or her expectation that the unacceptable behavior will change and the warning that the employer will use discipline if necessary.

7. The employee then returns to his or her work group and duties.

There are a number of advantages to using a Thought Day. For one, unlike traditional discipline, it encourages an employee to make the voluntary decision to change attitudes and focus on improving his or her performance, replacing reluctant compliance with willing compliance. We cannot guarantee that a Thought Day will always produce a superior performer, but it usually provides a time for meaningful discussion and a way to encourage improved performance. The goal is not just to correct a problem but to engage in a strategy that provides the best opportunity to turn a negative into a strong positive. A marginal employee is the worst possible outcome for the discipline process, one who performs and/or behaves somewhat below expectations.

Dick Grote, author of *Discipline Without Punishment*, outlines a number of major organizations that have substituted systems of nonpunitive discipline for their old systems. In the introduction, he writes:

> Like traditional approaches, the new approach was progressive: As problems became more serious, our response became more serious. But instead of using punishments, the new system reflected our belief that every one of our employees, even our "troublemakers," was a mature, responsible and trustworthy adult who would respond like one if treated like one.[43]

Clearly, how the organization relates to the employee is a significant factor in encouraging particular behaviors. When punitive forms of discipline are a mainstay, it is difficult to grow a positive culture. On the other hand, positive cultures require employees to be and act as trustworthy adults.

Obviously, where a Thought Day doesn't work, the employer can choose to impose formal, punitive discipline. However, the discussion that follows does not address any legal or labor contract issues with regard to implementing discipline up to and including discharge. Employers can find excellent resources both online and in print related to legal concerns and the just-cause standard for discipline as found in most labor contracts. Of course, employers ought to seek competent legal advice for some questions.

Progressive discipline, a term frequently associated with administering formal discipline, promotes the philosophy that all corrective action should be remedial, not punitive. This point, of course, is somewhat difficult to defend since the actions either involve a strong sanction (written warning) or the loss of money (suspension or demotion), both of which appear to be inherently punitive. Nevertheless, if properly administered, progressive discipline focuses on remedying problems. Any act of progressive discipline, short of discharge, allows an employee to protect his or her employment if behavior is changed appropriately. At the same time, non-conformity to the employer's expectations ultimately leads to discharge. To these basics of progressive discipline, we offer the following additional analysis based on our research and experience.

First, discipline ought to be imposed only for a chargeable offense (i.e., an employee breaks a work rule, fails to perform adequately or some other action serious enough to require change). The right to impose discipline requires stating the charge in a way that identifies both the inappropriateness and seriousness of those actions. From this perspective, suspending an employee for engaging in acts of malicious gossip is probably not good form. The employer needs to link the malicious communication to specific harms regarding relationships and employee productivity. For instance, disciplinary notices should include phrases like, "Your actions have created a hostile work environment" and "Your malicious, untruthful statements about a fellow employee has undermined her well-being and made it difficult for her to perform her work." In addition, the employer needs to have evidence that these accusations are true.

Second, when a supervisor finds it necessary to address a specific employee about problems with his or her behavior or performance, the action almost inevitably creates a sense of tension and discord; relationships are strained. Therefore, since maximum performance is achieved when employees work in the context of relationships dominated by high levels of positive social regard, it is extremely important that non-punitive forms of corrective action constitute the dominant tactics used by the supervisor. When it becomes clear that non-punitive forms are not succeeding and formal steps of discipline are required, the path to discharge should be a relatively short–one formal step of discipline which, if unsuccessful, leads to discharge.

An old joke asks this question: How do you get a mule to work? The answer: You first have to hit him over the head with a two-by-four to get his attention. Once you get his attention, he will then respond to your orders. Metaphorically speaking, this is what formal discipline is all about. Where talking, coaching, training and other forms of positive intervention have failed, formal discipline gets the attention of the employee. If the employee still fails to respond constructively to the employer's expectations, then it is time to end the employment relationship.

Finally, the *hot stove rule* bears repeating in this context. The rule states that if you reach your hand towards a hot stove, you will be warned by the heat of possible negative consequences. The warning will intensify as your hand gets closer and closer to the surface. Then, if you touch the stove, consequences will be immediate. The rule illustrates the characteristics of effective discipline. There is a clear warning about the problem as the employee's behavior or performance deteriorates, followed by consequences closely associated with falling below the acceptable level. While not a perfect metaphor, the rule demonstrates the value of warnings and taking decisive action where needed.

### The Hot Stove Rule
The rule states that if you reach your hand towards a hot stove, you will be warned by the heat of possible negative consequences. The warning will intensify as your hand gets closer and closer to the surface.

It behooves managers to remember that positive methods of challenging a disruptive employee have a high probability of correcting behavior and performance problems while strengthening the relationship between the supervisor and the subordinate. However, where the positive fails to produce a desired result, the supervisor should not hesitate to impose formal discipline including, where necessary, discharge. Failing to take action has a devastating effect on the organizational culture.

## Concluding Thoughts

Some time ago, one of the authors and another colleague published an article titled "Watering the Periwinkle." Periwinkle, sometimes called vinca minor, is a plant that when fully grown forms a dense, dark green ground cover with pretty little purple flowers. The article emphasizes the fact that a healthy bank of periwinkle will crowd out all of the weeds. Similarly, a vibrant positive workplace culture will usually crowd out the negative. Or, in the context of managing communication, focusing on building a constructive, affirming culture can decimate the practice of malicious gossip in the workplace. However, as stated in "Watering the Periwinkle":

> Culture creation and change do not occur as the result of a well-worded memo or other form of directive. More than anything else, culture is the product of the shared values and beliefs of the group. The development and modification of culture, therefore, occurs primarily in the informal social interactions between group members.[44]

Since culture is primarily influenced by informal social interactions, it is imperative that these interactions be positive, not negative. Furthermore, it is only possible to gain the higher ground of a positive culture when workers understand that integrity, honesty and a desire to be authentic are crucial components of their professional lives. Their actions must flow from a genuine sense of sincerity toward coworkers and clients. They must buy into the concept of spirit in an organization. By this, we don't mean a religious flavor or a rah-rah attitude, but a sense of kindness, helpfulness, professionalism and ethical behavior, whatever a person's position within a hierarchy. On one hand, people in an organization should aspire to such behavior simply because it's the right thing to do.

But an organization and the people who make it up should do so simply because it's *good business.* When people feel supported, treated fairly, and have the ability to discuss matters freely and openly, rather than be talked about behind their backs, they tend to stay longer in a job. The dividends are obviously reduced staff turnover and training costs. It further enhances management's ability to recruit high-quality people who thrive in such an environment, and leads to better productivity.

## Chapter 7 Summary

Talking about gossip is easy; implementing a workplace program to extinguish the malicious side of gossip is difficult. This chapter provides basic approaches around which change strategies can be implemented. Included is a section on gossip management constructs, a section that challenges the leader to model the expected behavior and a section on actions needed to support the growth of a workplace environment free of malicious gossip. Key points from the chapter include:

- By law and by design the workplace has to set a standard of behavior higher than that acceptable for the general public. Organizations must actively work to protect themselves against a hostile work environment, malicious gossip included.
- It is naïve to believe that malicious gossip can be removed by formulating a workplace rule. However, it is not naïve to

conclude that gossip can be reduced through facilitating a constructive, affirming workplace culture.

- The individual manager, supervisor or program director plays a key role in shaping and building a positive culture since he or she has the power to drive the emotional climate of the work group. Thus, the leader must model the constructive behavior and emotional tone consistent with a positive culture.

- Personal transformation may be necessary in order for the leader to drive the emotional climate properly.

- The organization has numerous formal tools that it can use to help build a positive workplace culture free of malicious gossip. These tools would include a statement of organizational values, the performance evaluation process, the employee handbook and the various training activities in which employees participate.

- Ultimately, formal discipline should be used, including the possibility of discharge, when an employee fails to restrain him/herself from engaging in malicious gossip.

# Chapter 8

## CHANGING WORKPLACE TALK

# We need not bind ourselves to the old dogma that human nature cannot be changed, for we find that it can be changed.
## ALFRED KORZYBSKI

A State Department of Transportation had a mid-level management position to fill. While it offered reasonable pay, the position was certainly nothing extraordinary. The candidate selected turned out to be the son of a powerful state politician, who was fully qualified since the requirements for the position were basic and did not require any special licensure. But how had he arrived at the top of the hiring list? Almost immediately the rumor mill began to circulate tidbits of gossip; "He did not deserve this job," "He could not get a job any place else," "His father intervened in the process to ensure that he received the position," "He was not really qualified for the job," and so the gossip went. Of course, like so much hearsay, no one knew the actual truth and, once the gossip started, there was little concern about truth since bashing the new guy had become the accepted social activity of the moment.

The effect of the gossip was subtle but not insignificant. As usual, no one directly confronted him about the perception that his employment was the product of inappropriate political pressure. Instead, the office chatter primarily affected relationships. Coworkers treated the new manager with a polite coolness he found difficult to breach, a social distance he could not overcome. As a result, he never felt the genuine help and support so useful to a new supervisor even though he received responses to his inquires. The warmth and camaraderie necessary for building trust and improving the efficiency of decision-making failed to emerge. So he often felt as if he were paddling the proverbial canoe upstream.

Of course, the topic of malicious gossip usually conjures up images of a hot sexual adventure with a disastrous end–a ruined reputation, heartache and even suicide. But, from an organizational standpoint, the destructiveness of malicious gossip is usually far less dramatic and more similar to the story of the questionable political hire.

In any organizational scenario, how we think and talk about each other within an organization has a direct impact on the quality of our relationships. The residue from gossip has the same impact as putting weights on your ankles when you are playing basketball. While you can still play, the weights severely reduce the ability to run and jump so essential to effective performance. Similarly, people within organizations usually get on with their professional activities in the presence of negative gossip, but it can place a significant burden on good performance.

Words have remarkable power. In fact, the words we use in everyday conversation have a significant impact on each employee and the organization as a whole. For example, when we use words to categorize a fellow employee's hire as inappropriate, we think and act toward the person from that perspective, consistently undermining connections between coworkers and team productivity. On the other hand, when we use words to be helpful, supportive, congratulatory and affirming, we strengthen relationships and handle problems more effectively.

# Words as Destroyers

Children have long used an old schoolyard ditty to deflect the consequences of verbal assaults: "Sticks and stones may break my bones but words can never hurt me." While this statement may help keep verbal aggression from escalating into physical violence, it is an untruthful assertion at its very core. Words can be either extremely helpful or powerfully destructive. Destructive words affect both speakers and hearers in three significant ways:

- They cause personal pain.
- They limit vision, aspiration and performance.
- They create unnecessary barriers to effective relationships.

➢ **Words That Cause Pain**

Rabbi Joseph Telushkin acknowledges in the introduction to *Words That Hurt, Words That Heal* that his audiences can be quite skeptical about the claim that words are often the most painful experiences of our lives. In response to this skepticism, he writes:

> Think about your own life: unless you, or someone dear to you, have been the victim of terrible physical violence, chances are the worst pains you have suffered in life have come from words used cruelly–from ego-destroying criticism, excessive anger, sarcasm, public and private humiliation, hurtful nicknames, betrayal of secrets, rumors and malicious gossip.[1]

The simple fact is that negative statements do cause psychological pain even when the comments are true. In fact, psychological wounds from verbal assaults often linger longer than physical injuries; our bodies often heal faster than our minds.

➢ **Words That Limit**

Telushkin further illustrates the damage that words cause by citing a list of angry comments made by parents to their children. The following quotes were collected by the National Committee for Prevention of Child Abuse:

> "You're pathetic. You can't do anything right."
> "You disgust me. Just shut up!"
> "Hey, stupid. Don't you know how to listen?"
> "You're more trouble than you're worth."
> "Get outta here. I'm sick of looking at your face."
> "I wish you were never born."[2]

## Words as Destroyers

Words can be either extremely helpful
or powerfully destructive. Destructive words
affect both speakers and hearers
in three significant ways:

1. They cause personal pain.
2. They limit vision, aspiration and performance.
3. They create unnecessary barriers to effective relationships.

These words hurt deeply. More than hurting, however, they can change how we think about ourselves. Positive words can give a sense of hope and a willingness to push the boundaries. Negative words can shrink and imprison us. What we believe about ourselves and our personal potential either opens or closes doors for us. One can only imagine the type of baggage a person carries throughout a lifetime when as a small child he or she consistently heard statements like the above.

One of the authors, the first in his family to attend and graduate from college, clearly remembers an incident when he was a senior in high school, working to gain admission to college. His uncle cautioned him in a belittling fashion to remember that he was only a [family surname] and that [family surname] don't go to college. The comment made him very angry and more determined, but one wonders about the uncle who made the statement–and never went to college. While directed outward, his words may have served as belittling self-talk. If a person believes that his family does not go to college, it limits his choices in the context of a college education. Also, as evidence of the power of words, while the statement was made more than fifty years ago, it remains crystal clear in the mind of the recipient.

Another one of the authors remembers an incident as a young college professor when a student asked to schedule an office visit. When the student seemed to gather courage after some small talk, she asked him if he could help her become "mature." She said that she had been a foster child most of her life, and everyone kept telling her that she was immature. She was certain that life would be better if she could achieve the elusive goal of being mature. The irony, of course, was that she worked harder and focused more consistently on doing well than most of the other students. One has to wonder about the overall effect that her ongoing battle with "immaturity" had on her life, the constant feeling that she was not good enough.

Clearly, words have both positive and negative power. Negative words hurt and can place psychological restrictions on a person's capabilities. When we describe ourselves or hear trusted people describe us with limiting words, we are likely to believe and therefore behave in that restricted way.

➤ **Words That Create Relationship Barriers**

Consider for the moment the concept of putting emotional distance between you and someone else or drawing closer to a person. Psychological closeness encourages physical closeness and psychological distance inevitably leads to physical distance. Words clearly play an important role in facilitating either the sense of emotional closeness or distance.

The word *estrangement* is often used to describe this psychological distance between two people particularly if they are related in some fashion (i.e., two family members or two colleagues). Malicious gossip and other forms of negative communication are powerful tools for creating estrangement.

On the other hand, the word *engagement* signifies meaningful interaction between two or more individuals. In the same sense that malicious gossip and other forms of negative communication promote estrangement, positive, respectful forms of interacting promote engagement. When engaged, we can have reasonable and useful discussions.

Art Buchwald, an American humorist best known for his long-running column in *The Washington Post,* makes the case for positive engagement with the following delightful column:

> I was in New York the other day and rode with a friend in
> a taxi. When we got out, my friend said to the driver,
> "Thank you for the ride. You did a superb job of driving."
>
> The taxi driver was stunned for a second. Then he said,
> "Are you a wise guy or something?"
>
> "No, my dear man, and I am not putting you on. I
> admire the way you keep cool in heavy traffic."
>
> "Yeh," the driver said and drove off.
>
> "What was that all about?" I asked.
>
> "I am trying to bring love back to New York," he said.

"I believe it's the only thing that can save the city."

"How can one man save New York?"

"It's not one man. I believe I have made the taxi driver's day. Suppose he has twenty fares. He's going to be nice to those twenty fares because someone was nice to him. Those fares in turn will be kinder to their employees or shop-keepers or waiters or even their own families. Eventually, the goodwill could spread to at least 1,000 people. Now that isn't bad, is it?"

"But you're depending on that taxi driver to pass your goodwill to others."

"I'm not depending on it," my friend said. "I'm aware that the system isn't foolproof, so I might deal with ten different people today. If, out of ten, I can make three happy, then eventually I can indirectly influence the attitudes of 3,000 more."

"It sounds good on paper," I admitted, "but I'm not sure it works in practice."

"Nothing is lost if it doesn't. It didn't take any of my time to tell that man that he was doing a good job. He neither received a larger tip nor a smaller tip. If it fell on deaf ears, so what? Tomorrow there will be another taxi driver whom I can try to make happy."

"You're some kind of nut," I said.

"That shows how cynical you have become …."

We were walking past a structure in the process of being built and passed five workmen eating their lunch. My friend stopped. "That's a magnificent job you men have done. It must be difficult and dangerous work." The five men eyed my friend suspiciously. "When will it be finished?"

"June." a man grunted.

"Ah. That really is impressive. You must all be very proud."

We walked away. I said to him, "I haven't seen anyone like you since "The Man of La Mancha.'"

"When those men digest my words, they will feel better for it. Somehow the city will benefit from their happiness."

"But you can't do this alone." I protested. "You're just one man."

"The most important thing is not to get discouraged. Making people in the city become kind again is not an easy job, but if I can enlist other people in my campaign ...."

"You just winked at a very plain looking woman," I said.

"Yes. I know, he replied. "And if she is a school-teacher, her class will be in for a fantastic day."[3]

A kind word or a negative word–we make that choice all day long, and it is, undoubtedly, easy to underestimate the significance of that choice. Notice that in the story above the recipients of the kind and complimentary statements were skeptical ("Are you a wise guy?"). Mr. Buchwald's column establishes, in his oh-so-humorous way, the fact that positive, encouraging words can close the psychological distance and facilitate an environment of respect and accomplishment, allowing us to be engaged with others.

## Verbal Skills Toolbox

Just as a craftsman has tools useful for his craft, numerous verbal skills function as tools to help build quality relationships. Understanding the proper use of a verbal tool always requires two things: knowing how it works and knowing when to use it. Of course, experts in the communication field explain the two elements various ways.

In the book *Flourish*, Martin Seligman introduces his readers to four ways of responding to colleagues who share "a victory, a triumph, and less momentous good things that happened to them,"[4] only one of which helps build relationships. He lists the four as follows:

- Active and Constructive – strong verbal showing of interest and nonverbal display of positive emotion, (i.e., "That is a great promotion," "You completely deserve it," "I am excited for you.")
- Passive and Constructive – short, positive verbal response with little to no nonverbal emotional display, (i.e., "That's wonderful.")
- Active and Destructive – verbal response that undermines the achievement and flat or negative nonverbal emotional response such as worry or concern, (i.e., "Are you sure you can handle the responsibilities of that promotion?")
- Passive and Destructive – a non-response with disconnected nonverbal emotional demeanor, (i.e., "Where should we go to dinner tonight?")[5]

Clearly, *active, constructive responding* is the most beneficial verbal tool because it teaches employees a powerful way to help celebrate each other's achievements and in doing so strengthens relationships.

Roger Fisher and Scott Brown provide a different type of verbal and behavioral approach in their book *Getting Together.* They discuss the importance of the way in which a person responds to a colleague's verbal attack or negative behavior. Their strategy, *unconditionally constructive behavior*, helps the coworker avoid letting the negative individual set the agenda. One does not have to respond in kind. "Do only those things that are both good for the relationship and good for us, whether or not they reciprocate."[6] Examples of responses include:

- Even if they are not listening, consult them before deciding on matters that affect them.
- Even if they misunderstand us, try to understand them.[7]

At first glance, *unconditionally constructive behavior* appears to have an altruistic overtone. However, thoughtful consideration strongly argues that, rather than altruism, it is a rational approach by which a person can avoid getting caught up in the negative. Most important, this approach has the greatest possibility for long-term positive gains.

## Words and Change

In their book *How the Way We Talk Can Change the Way We Work,* professors Robert Kegan and Lisa Lahey present a change strategy they call transformational learning, learning that fundamentally changes how we think and act. The basic premise is that changing the way we talk about something significantly alters the reality of the situation. One critical area they discuss is the language of complaint, sometimes called NBC talk (nagging, bitching and complaining) or BMW (bitching, moaning and whining).[8]

They relate an incident that occurred during a session in one of their training programs. During a break, several participants were discussing how to change the language of complaint into a language of commitment. One person approached with a joke: "How do you know the difference between your dog and a direct report?" Answer, "When you let your dog into your office, he stops whining."[9]

The authors point out that the joke, itself, is a subtle form of whining and illustrates how negative patterns of interacting are deeply ingrained in each person. Thus, transformational learning is necessary if we wish to replace the negative with a positive. They further contend that making a successful shift to the positive can be built around what they call "novel language forms," defined as unique, positive ways of interacting. They describe it as follows:

> The building blocks for this new technology are novel language forms. Each language is a tool, transforming a customary mental or social arrangement into a form that increases the possibility of transformational learning. The places where

we work and live are, among other things, places where certain forms of speech are promoted or encouraged, and places
where other ways of talking are discouraged or made impossible. We are referring to how we speak to each other in public
and private conversation, in groups and informal one-on-one
communication, and perhaps more especially (at least in the
beginning) with those few others with whom we may feel the
most trust and comfort.

We are also referring to how we speak to *ourselves*, which,
though too rarely considered, is one of our most influential
and continuous conversational venues.[10]

Thus, to the extent that an organization seeks to change negative behavior, novel language forms (different ways of talking about
something) need to be promoted. The change from the negative
to the positive occurs when the organization, all the way down to
the individual teams, accept and endorse the new ways of talking.
Kegan and Lahey strongly endorse the role of leadership in promoting novel language forms.

In our view, leaders have no choice in this matter of being language leaders; it just goes with the territory. We have a choice
whether to be thoughtful and intentional about this aspect of
our leadership, or whether to unmindfully ratify the existing
drift of our community's favored forms. We have the choice
to make much of the opportunity, or little. We have the choice
to be responsible or not for the meaning of our leadership as
it affects our language community. But we have no choice
about whether we are or are not language leaders. The only
question is what kind of language leaders we will be.[11]

The phrase, "ratify the existing drift of our community's favored forms" is particularly meaningful in the context of replacing malicious gossip, negative criticism and hostile comments with the language of appreciation, respect and thankfulness.

The practice of appreciative inquiry closely parallels Kegan and Lahey's transformational learning. Appreciative inquiry is a facilitated process that helps an organization build on successes with the goal of achieving a positive result. For example, the airline industry could focus a facilitated session on how to ensure that customers have a great arrival experience instead of studying ways to correct the problem of lost baggage. And any organization, from our schools to construction companies, can change the topic from "fixing our problems" to "delivering the premium product in the industry." Rather than critiquing, assessing and fixing the negative, problems are overcome by simply using one's strength to move in the right direction.

In the book, *Appreciative Inquiry*, David Cooperrider indicates that one of the primary discoveries he has made from listening to practitioners of appreciative inquiry is that people become infected with the positive as they study and think about it. He writes:

> First, not only do the organizations we work with move in the direction of what we study and ask questions about, but also so do we as human beings. Simply put, I am not the same person when I am in a discovery mode asking in-depth questions of what leads to "joy, inspiration and hope" as I am when I do analysis of "low morale" and its causes. Inquiry and change are a simultaneous moment and we ourselves are inescapably "in it," even if the study is "out there."[12]

The simple fact is that the talk characteristic of an organization significantly influences the workplace environment and the individuals within it. Furthermore, if the communication habits are negative, they can unquestionably be redirected to the positive.

Of course, developing a positive culture does not exclude criticism. Employees need to have constructive public and private conversations. Therefore, leaders should work to develop an environment where the workforce learns helpful, professional ways to express critical observations, and managers at all levels should listen respectfully to the feedback.

## Changing Workplace Talk

However, knowing that changing the way people talk is possible has little value unless actions are taken to implement the change. The activities that follow are only a few of those available to bring about the desired communication shift. They can be used either in the form presented here or modified to fit the user's specific situation. (Additional activities can be found in such books as *Flourish* by Martin Seligman, *Positivity* by Barbara Fredrickson, and *Appreciative Inquiry* by Jane Watkins and Bernard Mohr.)

Those using the activities in this and the next chapter must understand that all of them require that participants be able to discuss various topics in a non-defensive and open fashion. Carl Rogers, the psychological guru of the '70s, has said that we all learn best in an environment of unconditional positive regard.[13] This is particularly appropriate where the purpose of the learning is directed towards implementing positive language and constructive interaction in the workplace.

# ACTIVITY 1 (1.5-2 hours)

> **Priority Circle**

This small group requires everyone to participate and gives group members the opportunity to explore non-defensively any critical issues around relationships and communication with and about each other. Some readers may feel that it is somewhat trite and superficial; however, the authors have used the activity in a number of different versions and can certify that it almost always leads to some very productive discussion.

**Step 1:** The activity facilitator writes a pertinent question about positive relationships or positive interaction on a white board, smart board or flip chart. The question should be affirmative, thoughtful and open-ended so that it elicits action steps that can be taken to accomplish a positive goal. For example:

- What can we do as a group to improve relationships and make us a better team?
- What can we do to create a happier, more personally rewarding workplace?

When the facilitator presents the question, he or she allows time to explain it and lets the participants ask questions about its meaning.

**Step 2:** After the period of discussion, each participant writes three responses to the question.

**Step 3:** The facilitator asks each participant sequentially for his or her responses and instructs them to give only one answer each time. He or she continues to go from person to person until all responses have been listed. This approach does a better job of keeping everyone involved. Then the facilitator lists all the responses on a flip chart or white board, numbering them for purposes of identification. During this phase, participants may ask questions for clarification, but discussion is not permitted.

**Step 4:** After listing all responses, the facilitator provides a short time for open discussion on the merits of the responses.

**Step 5:** After the discussion, the facilitator guides the participants through the process of identifying and then prioritizing the suggestions the group considers the most important. He or she gives each participant a piece of paper to use as a ballot and asks everyone to list his or her top three choices in order of significance.

When the participants complete their lists, the facilitator returns to the flip chart or white board and asks the group to help tabulate the choices by first identifying the suggestions they listed as most important. As each participant identifies his or her first choice in turn, the facilitator gives that item three (3) points. Then they proceed to the second most important choice, and as the participants take turns identifying that suggestion, the facilitator gives the item two (2) points. Following the same process, the participants' third choice receives one (1) point.

After adding the points that each suggestion received, the facilitator creates a second list with the item receiving the most points as number 1 (most important), the item with the second highest total as number 2, the item with the third highest total as number 3 and the item with the fourth highest total as number 4. All the rest of the suggestions are identified as number 5, the category of "all others." Limiting the new list to four top responses plus "all others" keeps the ensuing discussion focused.

**Step 6:** The facilitator gives each participant a sheet of flip chart paper and a set of color crayons. Everyone draws a large circle and turns it into a pie chart that reflects his or her assessment of the importance of each of the five. The pie chart segments should be colored to highlight distinctions. (See the sample pie chart on the next page.) The group's overall determination will usually not reflect each individual's assessment. A participant could even view the category of "all others" as more significant than any one of the top four options.

**Step 7:** The facilitator gives each participant a short time to present his or her pie chart along with the rationale for the perspective. Other participants may ask questions for clarification but cannot argue with a presenter.

**Step 8:** When all presentations have been made, the facilitator asks the group, "How can we effectively use the ideas we have created this afternoon?" After discussing implementation options, the facilitator concludes the session by reiterating the implementation steps that participants have suggested and listing the appropriate action steps.

➢ **Sample**

**Question: What can we do to create a happier, more personally rewarding workplace?**

**Top choices:**
1. Celebrate our successes as a team
2. Compliment each other's work when it deserves it
3. Give more respect and reduce teasing
4. Offer help, don't wait to be asked
5. All others

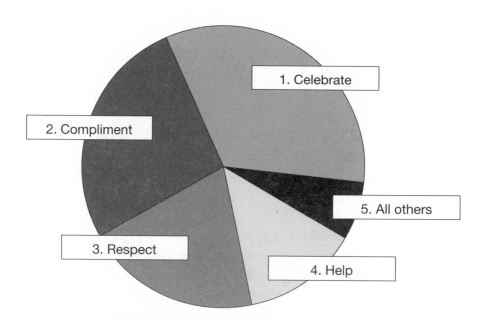

# ACTIVITY 2 (2-3 hours)

> ## ➤ Relationship Agreement

This activity is a good follow-up to the one described above. It takes some of the process from the first activity and moves it forward by asking team members to make a specific commitment to constructive behavior. The team creates a one-page, written affirmation regarding relationships and teamwork that all members can agree to and on which they will affix their signatures.

The document, a formal statement of agreement, records the team's decision to accept the challenge of doing something special and commits itself to a set of goals that will help achieve the desired end. It is therefore essential for all of the team to be part of this process.

This *agreement* has two sections: a commitment statement and a set of goals related to it. A team might, for example, construct a statement like the following:

> We, the fellow team members, working in the home of the individuals we support, are committed to making great performance a reality and the home a great place to work. We will accomplish this by realizing the following goals.

The team would then list the goals necessary for accomplishing the commitment. One of them might be:

- Should treat my colleagues and customers with the respect and dignity that I wish for myself.

A sample team *relationship agreement* is found on page 190. The document reflects the commitment of a fictitious group of employees who work in a group home on Maple Street, associated with an organization that provides services for people with intellectual disabilities.

Guiding a team through the following steps will help the members create an agreement that states their commitment and goals.

**Step 1:** To streamline the *agreement* creation process, the facilitator drafts a couple of commitment statements and a complete title to present to the group. (See the sample *relationship agreement*.) In addition, he or she should make sure that a laptop computer and printer are available for the session.

**Step 2:** The facilitator introduces the activity to the participants by drawing a distinction between process and outcome goals, and explaining that a process goal consists of an activity that is repeated, such as, "Have a monthly safety meeting with 100 percent attendance." Outcome goals, on the other hand, identify a desired result such as, "Complete the work year with zero injury accidents."

**Step 3:** The facilitator explains the concept of creating a *relationship agreement* to the participants and shows them the title and commitment statement(s) on a flip chart, smart board or laptop computer. As a group, they edit the preferred form of the commitment statement to everyone's satisfaction.

**Step 4:** The facilitator divides the participants into groups of no less than three or four, and asks each group to prepare three process or outcome goals that relate to the commitment statement. Groups should be allowed approximately 20 minutes to complete this task.

**Step 5:** As the participants present their goals, the facilitator lists them on a fresh flip chart. Then, using input from the group, he or she combines the suggestions into six or seven concise goals, allowing for plenty of discussion as participants process the list of suggestions. This may also include discussion and modifications of the original title and commitment statement so that all parts of the *agreement* are clearly integrated.

**Step 6:** The facilitator or a designated secretary enters the final, team-approved copy into an electronic document.

**Step 7:** Using the computer, the facilitator or a designated secretary prints the completed *relationship agreement* off and asks at least two participants to proofread it thoroughly to ensure that there are no typographical errors. The facilitator encourages–*never* requires–all of the participants to make their individual commitments to the *agreement* goals by signing the document. Each person who signed the document receives a copy. One copy should be framed and placed in a highly visible place within the work area.

**Step 8:** The facilitator debriefs the activity by having each participant comment on the usefulness of the session and what he or she considers meaningful. This is a powerful part of the process and helps solidify each person's commitment to the goals recorded in the *relationship agreement*.

## Team Agreement: Maple Street House

### June 1, 20___ (year)

We, the fellow team members, working in the home of the individuals we support, are committed to making great performance a reality, and the home a great place to work.

We will accomplish this by realizing the following goals:

- Assisting the residents to flourish
- Attending and participating in staff meetings with a positive, constructive attitude
- Completing all assigned tasks on a regular basis and communicating with the following shift about unusual problems and work that has not been completed
- Working with safety in mind for my colleagues, the individuals to whom we provide services and myself
- Talking to the person with whom I have an issue or concern, not to others
- Trusting others and acting trustworthy
- Treating my colleagues and the individuals to whom we provide supports with the respect and dignity that I wish for myself
- Keeping communication positive at all times.

_____         _____

_____         _____

_____         _____

_____         _____

# ACTIVITY 3

> ➢ **Coaching**

Coaching, done either one-on-one or in groups, provides a method by which to reinforce expectations about behavior and performance that have been highlighted during exercises such as the ones described above. In the context of gossip, its goal is to produce the desired positive, affirming culture. The following definition clarifies the process:

> Coaching is an ongoing process designed to help the employee gain greater competence and overcome barriers to improving performance. Coaching is appropriate when an employee has the ability and knowledge to succeed but performance is not at the level needed. The goal of coaching is to create a change in behavior, to move employees from where they are to where you want them to be. Coaching encourages people to do more than they ever imagined they could.[14]

The process helps people achieve a deeper understanding of the consequences of hurtful communication and what they can do to break the cycle. Good coaching moves a person from the hurtful to the helpful, from the damaging to the power of positive interaction. The discussion points listed below can help people break the gossip habit by making them confront language behavior they may not be consciously acknowledging.

- Why do I or others gossip? If I don't often gossip, why do I listen to those who do? Am I frightened that I will be the target of their gossip if I don't listen?
- Does gossip ever help people? Does it ever make a workplace run more efficiently?
- Can I talk about other people without being potentially hurt-

ful or harmful? What's the best way to relay personal information about another person if he or she is not present?

- What is the best way to show respect to others?
- Would I want my family or friends talked about in this fashion?
- Could I pass this information on to the person talked about face to face?
- Does it ultimately make me feel like an honorable person to pass on certain information about someone else? Is it meant to help them? What would help me have a feeling of integrity?
- Would I be embarrassed to have information I passed along revealed publicly at a meeting with me tagged as the source? Could any e-mail or text I wrote on the job be posted on a public company bulletin board? If I hit blind CC on an e-mail, would it matter who saw that message later? Does that include the subject of the e-mail?
- Does it matter whether the information is true or not when I pass it along?
- Is my private blog a place to pass on information about my organization or the people in it? Even if I'm anonymous on it? When I say negative things on my blog, how does it make me feel?
- Is the way that I am talking about my teammates creating or destroying friendship? Is it making it easier for me to work with them?

Coaching can occur at any time, so an effective supervisor is always on the lookout for the teachable moment. The process is most effective when the coach balances identifying behaviors that need to end with encouraging expected performance. The balance, however, always needs to be weighted toward the desired behavior. Pointing out what someone did wrong has little value without helpful communication about what is expected.

## Concluding Thoughts

The authors of the book *How Full Is Your Bucket?* draw on Gallup research to conclude that positivity pays. Using metaphor, they contend that each of us has an invisible bucket and, when that bucket is full, we are energized and motivated. When that bucket is empty, we are demoralized and unproductive. The various forms of positive interactions and actions fill our buckets and the buckets of those with whom we associate. Negative interactions and actions empty our buckets.[15] The authors remind us of the daily opportunity.

> So we face a choice every moment of every day: We can fill one another's buckets, or we can dip from them. It's an important choice—one that profoundly influences our relationships, productivity, health and happiness.[16]

They note that more than 15 million employees worldwide took part in the survey, and the results clearly indicate that those who receive regular recognition and praise:

- Increase their individual productivity
- Increase engagement among their colleagues
- Are more likely to stay with their organization
- Receive higher loyalty and satisfaction scores from customers
- Have better safety records and fewer accidents on the job.[17]

The authors further note that the patterns of positive interaction that fill the buckets of friends and colleagues also fill one's own bucket, and that filling buckets is a contagious activity. They strongly emphasize that:

> ...just one person can infuse positive emotions into an entire group by filling buckets more frequently. Studies show that organizational leaders who share positive emotions have workgroups

with a more positive mood, enhanced job satisfaction, greater engagement, and improved group performance.[18]

When considering the negative interactions described in previous chapters, it is clear that gossip can empty buckets very quickly. On the other hand, when one is busy filling buckets, there is no time or stomach for malicious gossip. Being caught up in the positive leaves no room for the negative.

## Chapter 8 Summary

Talk is often called cheap, meaning that what we say is of little significance or importance. This chapter promotes two major points. First, words are powerful, and they can have a negative face or a positive face. Second, the supervisor or manager can play a key role in facilitating the use of positive, supportive words in the workplace. Key points from the chapter include:

- It is not naïve to believe that it is possible to shape a workplace such that positive interaction becomes the norm, rather than an afterthought.

- Negative words including malicious gossip hurt, and they can have a long-lasting, undesirable impact on relationships and employee morale. Positive words have exactly the opposite effect.

- Negative words and malicious gossip estrange us from one another. Positive words and interactions allow us to be engaged with one another.

- Destructive words are significant in three different ways: they cause personal pain; they limit vision, aspiration and performance; and they create unnecessary barriers to effective relationships.

- Managers, program directors and supervisors are language leaders whether they want to be or not. The only question is whether they will be positive or negative language leaders.

- Positive talk does not prohibit discussion of problems and concerns within an organization. Issues can be discussed in a constructive manner and in a way that reaffirms the value of positive talk.

- Constructive change can occur in an organization by focusing on building positive behaviors; the negative is overcome by the positive without ever "fixing" the negative.

- Malicious gossip will cease when individuals are caught up in the process of building a workplace environment of respect and positive social regard.
- Filling the buckets of others simultaneously fills our own bucket. We help ourselves when we help others.

# Chapter 9

---

# REPLACING THE HABIT OF GOSSIP

## You can tell more about a person by what he says about others than you can by what others say about him.
### LEO AIKMAN

I n their book *Gossip: The Inside Scoop,* Professors Levin and Arluke share the results of a small research project they conducted on college campus gossip. They posted notices all over campus about a fictitious wedding between two nonexistent students that had supposedly occurred the day before. After one week, they interviewed students about the event and found that 52 percent of them were aware of the wedding, most having received the information from fellow students. What was particularly intriguing is that 12 percent of those responding actually claimed to have attended the nonexistent wedding and could describe the wedding dress, the limo, etc. They write:

> The implication of our experiment is clear: gossip is often used to place people at the center of attention. If you have the inside scoop about the BIG EVENT, you will be regarded as an insider. Even better, you actually attended the BIG EVENT. That makes you special.[1]

Since one of the strongest human needs is for community, people seek to be an accepted part of a group so they can feel like a valued member. In fact, a person may choose to define herself as a gatekeeper of hot information, a dispenser of secrets, to earn that position. So, when someone reveals something negative about a third party, it says to the second party: "I trust you. You are in my inner circle." And that's a heady feeling for both sides. The gossiper gets a power rush, and oddly, often feels protected in a sense because it pulls another person into her circle. The unspoken intent is to make another person look worse than the gossiper.

Meanwhile, the person that received the gossip also feels a rush of superiority based on being a part of the gossiper's inner circle: "This person trusts me with this information." A rush of adrenaline occurs as well because the human brain craves stimulation and novelty, and some hot gossip temporarily fills that niche nicely.

However, whatever the reasons for gossip, the simple fact is that it is usually not as benign as in the above fictitious wedding. It has caused highly destructive events and created toxic environments in many different arenas including the workplace.

Therefore, any effort to tame malicious gossip must deal with the psychological incentives to engage in it and address the challenging fact that it becomes a habit in many, a regular way of relating to others and getting along in an organization. And, like any habitual action, it can be hard to stop–very hard. In fact, the psychological rush that comes from gossiping may be less of a problem to correct than the habitual nature of the problem. Most of us have experienced a situation in which we made a conscious decision to change one of our behaviors only to find that habitual behavior is more powerful than the mental decision to modify it. Gossiping can be experienced in exactly that fashion. While there may be a desire to stop participating, our habits may dictate otherwise.

## Gossip as Habit

As mentioned previously, the authors of *How Full Is Your Bucket?* noted that when our metaphorical bucket is full, we are energized and motivated, but, when it is empty, we feel discouraged and lethargic. Therefore, positivity–particularly positive communication–fills our bucket and the buckets of those with whom we associate. Negativity, on the other hand, empties everyone's buckets.[2]

At this point, the question to consider is whether our positive and negative interactions are a matter of habit. Do we unthinkingly dip from the buckets of those around us and also unconsciously act in ways that fill buckets? Do we have habitual negative patterns of interaction that result in estrangement in addition to good habits that build trust and improve relationships? Barbara Fredrickson states the case as follows:

> However much we resist acknowledging it, we humans are not static. We're either on a positive trajectory or a negative one. Either we're growing in goodness, becoming more creative and resilient, or we're solidifying our bad habits, becoming more stagnant and rigid.[3]

A good understanding of the character of habits is essential for anyone who wishes to remove malicious gossip from the workplace. As Fredrickson states, both positive and negative actions can be habitual; however, we are generally choosing to "grow in goodness" or sliding inexorably into negativity. Since our concern is the process of solidifying good habits in place of the bad, it is important to understand the extensive nature of habits, explore what can be called the gossip-habit cycle and look at how keystone habits may help tame workplace gossip.

## The Pervasiveness of Habits

A habit is a "constant often unconscious inclination to perform some act, acquired through its frequent repetition; an established trend of the mind or character."[4] Substantial research indicates that old habits are hard to break and new ones hard to form because the behavioral patterns are imprinted in our neural pathways and new pathways need to be created in order to change the habit. Fortunately, research also shows that it is possible to form new habits through repetition.[5]

In his best-selling book, *The 7 Habits of Highly Effective People*, Stephen R Covey emphasizes the importance of habits in our lives when he writes:

> Habits are powerful factors in our lives. Because they are consistent, often unconscious patterns, they constantly, daily, express our character and produce our effectiveness . . . or ineffectiveness.
>
> Habits can be learned and unlearned. But I also know it isn't a quick fix. It involves a process and a tremendous commitment.[6]

When the subject of habits (neurologically imprinted behaviors) comes up, the focus is usually on the negative–bad habits. But our habits can work both for us and against us. While we may be aware of some of them, we generally ignore the fact that many essential habits help our lives run more smoothly. Charles Duhigg makes two important observations in his book, *The Power of Habit*:

1. Habits run much of our lives
2. Habits can be changed.[7]

He emphasizes the pervasiveness of habits as follows:

"All our life, so far as it has definite form, is but a mass of habits," William James wrote in 1892. Most of the choices we make each day may feel like the products of well considered decision-making, but they're not. They're habits. And though each habit means relatively little on its own, over time, the meals we order, what we say to our kids each night, whether we save or spend, how often we exercise, and the way we organize our thoughts and work routines have enormous impacts on our health, productivity, financial security, and happiness.[8]

Gossip, including malicious gossip, appears to fall very much within the above definition of a habit. While our research uncovered no information about efforts to study gossip as a habit and/or to explore its extinction, a great deal of the material we found describes it as an automatic behavior that often occurs outside conscious behavior—in other words, a habit. Therefore, if managerial staff expect to tame malicious gossip, they must understand and address its habitual nature.

Duhigg illustrates the habit changing process by telling the story of a young woman whose life was on a disastrous voyage until she began to change destructive behaviors. In an amazingly short period of time, she righted the ship by replacing bad habits with good ones. As a natural result, the good habits led to significant positive improvement in her overall well-being. We know about her journey because she was part of a study linking habits to brain function. Duhigg writes:

Eventually she was recruited into the scientists' study, and when researchers began examining images of Lisa's brain, they saw something remarkable: one set of neurological patterns—her old habits—had been overwritten by new patterns. They could still see the neural activity of her old behaviors, but those impulses were crowded out by new urges. As Lisa's habits changed, so had her brain.[9]

Clearly, management cannot expect malicious gossip to stop simply because rules are implemented and employees told not to gossip. Any effort to stop doing something may actually cause people to focus more on the behavior that they are attempting to eradicate, which, in the end, may result in more of the unwanted behavior. Duhigg's example indicates that the best way to change a habit such as gossip is to develop a new one with neural pathways strong enough to crowd out the inappropriate communication behavior.

## Gossip-Habit Cycle

Behavioral and physiological scientists have concluded that habits form in response to the brain's desire to save effort. If, for example, there had to be conscious thought for every decision needed to drive a car, the mental effort would be enormous and exhausting. However, the experienced driver's ability to start the car, shift the gears, apply the brakes and steer are all heavily dependent on well ingrained, automatic behaviors (habits).

Creating automatic behaviors, otherwise known as habit formation, is easy to understand as a habit cycle that includes a cue, a routine and a reward. A cue can be anything the brain perceives as necessitating a patterned response. A routine is the learned response that can be physical, mental or emotional. The reward results when the brain determines that the response was appropriate and necessary, and therefore remembers it for future occasions. The habit cycle can be illustrated as follows:

1. While driving a car, a person approaches a desired right turn (the cue).
2. The person performs the following physical routine: the car is slowed, and at the appropriate location in the inter-

section, the steering wheel turned to the right sufficient for a 90° turn. Then the steering wheel is returned to the straight ahead position and speed increased to the desired level.

3. The reward is the knowledge of success. The car is now traveling in the desired direction at the desired speed. This knowledge tells the brain to store the pattern enacted.

For the experienced driver, almost all of the above occurs without much, if any, conscious thought. Duhigg emphasizes the importance of understanding the habit cycle as follows:

> Over time, this loop—cue, routine, reward; cue, routine, reward—becomes more and more automatic. The cue and reward become intertwined until a powerful sense of anticipation and craving emerges. Eventually . . . a habit is born.[10]

The important point is that the habit emerges as a result of the repetition whether it is physical, mental or emotional. When the habit takes over for conscious thought, it creates efficiency–which can be either good or bad. Habits are good to the extent that they make life easier but bad to the extent that they diminish well-being. Furthermore, correcting bad habits is a difficult process. Duhigg explains:

> When a habit emerges, the brain stops fully participating in decision making. It stops working so hard, or diverts focus to other tasks. So unless you deliberately *fight* a habit–unless you find new routines–the pattern will unfold automatically.[11]

The habit of gossiping emerges in a manner fully explained by the gossip cycle. The cue comes either in the form of a juicy tidbit or fellow employee who approaches with social information to share. The routine is the sharing of the information, often done for malicious gossip in a somewhat clandestine or covert way. The reward is the psychological rush associated with being the center of attention and the sense of connection with the person listening. As the pattern is repeated over and over, it becomes automatic. Just as we drive a car without thinking much about what we're doing, we often gossip without any conscious awareness that we are harming a fellow employee and/or the organization for which we work.

## Keystone Habits

Substantial scientific evidence shows that habits are interdependent, so when a person changes or modifies one, it can impact others. The previously mentioned story of Lisa, the young woman whose life was in shambles because of bad habits, provides a perfect example. She made a radical change by replacing many bad habits with good ones when she focused on modifying a single habit.

In addition, changing some habits, called keystone habits, can trigger widespread change. Studies, for example, of physical exercise clearly show that creating a habit of regular exercise produces numerous other positive changes. These changes included eating better, becoming more productive at work, having greater patience with colleagues and using credit cards less. Go figure![12]

Obviously, it makes sense to focus on keystone habits when pursuing the goal of replacing bad habits with good ones. The problem, of course, is to identify the keystone habit. Duhigg observes that:

> If you focus on changing or cultivating keystone habits, you can cause widespread shifts. However, identifying keystone habits is tricky. To find them, you have to know where to look. Detecting keystone habits means searching out certain characteristics. Keystone habits offer what is known within academic literature as "small wins." They help other habits

to flourish by creating new structures, and they establish cultures where change becomes contagious.[13]

When considering substituting forms of positive interaction for the habit of gossiping, "contagious" is precisely the point. In other words, a habit of positive interaction can and in most cases is a keystone habit that will have many constructive spinoffs. Furthermore, positivity (relationship affirming patterns of interaction) is contagious.

## Gossip-Free Culture

Corporate culture is the invisible energizing force that reflects the collective values, attitudes and behaviors of the individuals that make up the organization. It primarily determines what is important, what gets communicated, how employees dress, how and to what extent employees socialize and acceptable performance standards.

One way of describing culture is "the way we do things around here." This phrase, among other things, implies that culture has a boundary defined by the point at which the cultural mores say "no." From this perspective, culturally acceptable values and behaviors are inside the boundary, while unacceptable values and behaviors are outside of it. Cultures tend to police their own boundaries by letting individual employees know when they have strayed too far (i.e., "That is not the way we do things here.").

As a general principle, culture development within an organization is more a reflection of the actions of team members rather than what they verbalize. Eric Allenbaugh provides a lengthy analysis of Southwest Airlines "Warrior Spirit" culture in his book *Deliberate Success*. Management did not issue a set of didactic statements about what constitutes a warrior spirit and the importance of being a warrior on behalf of Southwest Airlines. The culture evolved out of the early experiences at the airline when it had to fight for its survival. The actions related to the fight imbued the organization with its "warrior spirit." [14]

Communication patterns are also a central part of organizational culture. Is there a lot of sarcasm? Rudeness? Mockery? Teasing? Heavy judgment? Or is the communication marked with warmth, support and affirmation? Verbal instructions such as "Be polite," "Be friendly," and "Don't be negative," are less significant in establishing the organizational communication culture than the enactment of communication behavior (the action). Talking about communicating positively is not the primary force behind building culture; it is the act of communication–employees' actual communication–that shapes behavior in the environment.

Tim Sanders, the former Chief Solutions Officer at Yahoo, believes that love belongs in the workplace, and he promotes it in what he calls the "lovecat way." Described in his book *Love Is the Killer App,* a lovecat embodies the spirit of the jazz musician who makes smooth music, the polar opposite of a mad dog that attacks and/or defends ferociously. Sanders borrows a definition of love from writer Milton Mayeroff: "Love is the selfless promotion of the growth of the other."[15] Applying this definition, he writes that "when you are able to help others grow to become the best people they can be, you are being loving–and you, too, grow."[16] To be a workplace lovecat one must freely share knowledge and professional resources, and behave in a compassionate manner.

We draw three conclusions from the concept of the "lovecat way." The first is quite obvious. Malicious gossip is antithetical to compassionate behavior. The second is perhaps equally obvious: A culture marked by the free sharing of knowledge, professional resources and compassionate behavior is clearly a positive, affirming culture, the type of culture in which most of us prefer to work.

The third point simply applies the concept of the lovecat to the work group as a whole. While Sanders focuses his writing on individual behavior, the concept can also be applied to the culture of the work group where the expected behavior for all members mirrors the "lovecat way."

Eric Allenbaugh, in *Deliberate Success*, argues that the cultures of organizations can be categorized in four different ways. Using the two different variables–the human element and the bottom line–corporate cultures can be classified as follows:

4. Being
5. Surviving
6. Doing
7. Thriving[17]

The *being culture,* nicknamed the country club,[18] emphasizes the value of its people and focuses less on performance issues. While employees at first like the priority placed on good relationships, they often feel frustrated over the lack of accomplishment. Moreover, the frustration over low productivity can ultimately have a negative impact on relationships. Thus, team members may experience the irony that over-focus on relationships can ultimately be a detriment to relationships.

The *surviving culture* ("walking wounded")[19] does not value either its people or performance. The risk-averse nature of this culture makes it hard on relationships and performance. The result is that individuals hunker down and focus on getting by.

The *doing culture* ("sweatshop")[20] focuses on performance and the bottom line at the expense of the employees' well-being. This pressure cooker culture uses up people in its ever increasing effort to boost productivity. Adverse actions are more prevalent than recognition with the result that employees feel constantly scrutinized and underappreciated.

The *thriving culture* ("mastery")[21] focuses on people *and* the bottom line, mastering the process of maintaining dual targets. The energy generated by creating and sustaining good relationships is directed to performance issues. The result is a culture valued by employees both because of the high level of achievement and the relationships marked by high levels of camaraderie and good will.

Two elements of this classification system are worth noting. First, the system helps to clarify why malicious gossip is a basic issue. These spiteful interchanges inevitably sabotage efforts to build the kind of relationships that create energy that can be directed toward organizational performance. A thriving culture and malicious gossip are completely incompatible.

The second and perhaps more important element is that building a thriving culture is a matter of choice and effort. Allenbaugh emphasizes that these organizations differ only in the type of decisions they make and the focus they place on applying the principles of mastery.[22] In other words, an organization can build a positive culture that displaces malicious gossip if it chooses to do so and expends the energy.

Furthermore, the previous discussion indicates that much of our communication behavior is a matter of habits that occur automatically. It provides further evidence that building strong habits of affirming communication can force out the negative. This can occur because a strong culture establishes boundaries related to acceptable behavior and polices them, helping to shape and reinforce individual behavior.

## The Spiritual Side of Change

As noted previously, Martin Seligman became involved in a project to help the military decrease the high levels of suicide and post-traumatic stress disorder by creating a psychologically fit army. The program consists of various training and activity modules, some offered in person and others over the Internet.

One particularly insightful module concerns spiritual fitness. Seligman gives two basic reasons for the activity.

> First, the army has decided that it indeed wants its soldiers to answer to a higher moral order, so that by strengthening soldiers' morale and ethical values, the army's operations—which

present knotty moral dilemmas frequently–will be carried out ethically. Second, there is considerable evidence that a higher level of spirituality goes hand in hand with greater well-being, less mental illness, less substance abuse, and more stable marriages, not to mention better military performance–an advantage that is particularly salient when people face major adversity such as combat.[23]

Seligman explains that since the first amendment prohibits mixing religion and government, the module encourages soldiers to "search for truth, self-knowledge, right action and purpose in life: living by a code that is rooted in belonging to and serving something the

Character is a key ingredient
to spiritual energy because it fuels our ability
to live by our values even when doing so comes
at considerable cost and sacrifice.

soldier believes is larger than the self."[24] The focus is on expanding and deepening the soldiers' "spiritual core," comprised of their central values and beliefs. The activity further develops an understanding that influences decision-making both at home and in combat.

Performance psychologists Jim Loehr and Tony Schwartz argue that we all have various levels of physical, emotional, mental and spiritual energy. In *The Power of Full Engagement*, they emphasize the fact that "energy not time is the fundamental currency of high performance."[25] Understanding how to build and use these energies is essential for great performance both in our personal and professional lives.

Loehr and Schwartz find that spiritual energy "is the most powerful source of our motivation, perseverance and direction."[26] They explain:

> We define "spiritual" not in the religious sense, but rather in more simple and elemental terms: the connection to a deeply held set of values and to a purpose beyond our self-interest. At the practical level, anything that ignites the human spirit serves to drive full engagement and to maximize performance in whatever mission we are on.[27]

They further contend that character is a key ingredient to spiritual energy because it fuels our ability to live by our values even when doing so comes at considerable cost and sacrifice. Passion, commitment and integrity are all supportive elements of spiritual energy.

Duhigg made an interesting discovery when he looked into the process of replacing bad habits with good ones. He found that a person could be successfully going through the steps of building strong, positive habits only to have the success disrupted by a stressful event that caused the old negative habits to resurface. Researchers found that the word "spiritual" cropped up repeatedly when interviewing individuals who had successfully steered past the crisis and continued to build the positive habits.

Ultimately, the researchers concluded that the key ingredient was the power of belief. One of the problems with bad habits is that they lead people to believe that change is impossible. Many of those who successfully established better habits linked their ability to change with their belief in a higher power, a fact that supports the necessity of "belief." People who believe that things will get better can get through the crises. Duhigg writes:

Once people learned how to believe in something, that skill started spilling over to other parts of their lives, until they started believing they could change. Belief was the ingredient that made a reworked habit loop into a permanent behavior.[28]

This brief summary of three different perspectives on how the spiritual impacts the personal habits of individuals and ultimately the organizations within which they work demonstrates its importance in producing lasting change. The spiritual module Seligman crafted to develop psychologically fit soldiers helps emphasize the importance of deeply held values in building a thriving culture and provides a blueprint for working toward that end. In fact, malicious gossip occurs when there is a basic disconnect between our values and engaging in negative communication–particularly malicious gossip.

Likewise, Loehr and Schwartz's construct of spiritual energy seems to describe accurately what it takes to develop a highly successful organization. They conclude that spiritual energy "is the most powerful source of our motivation, perseverance and direction." Clearly, every organization benefits from having motivated employees who persevere and have purpose.

Finally, when an organization finds that the habits of communication among its employees are primarily negative, it needs a workforce that believes that building an affirming culture is possible. Fortunately, it is absolutely clear that habits can change, cultures can mature and organizations can become more successful.

## Changing Habits and Culture

Stephen Covey is credited with the thought that we all carry our own weather with us.[29] Roughly translated it means that how we experience life depends on what we habitually bring to the table. Psychologist Barbara Fredrickson also details how normal daily events can be experienced negatively or positively based only on how an individual chooses to respond to the circumstances.[30] Ultimately, in almost every case, whether or not the weather is sunny or rainy is a personal choice.

"Changing the weather" in the workplace clearly requires helping employees shift habitual negative actions and reactions to more positive behaviors. It is, of course, a process that takes a thoughtful game plan and persistent effort over time. The exercises presented below provide managers with some options for building the type of habits that promote the desired positive culture. A little additional background will help facilitators understand what enhances/creates their impact on activity participants.

First, we have already established in previous discussions that positive communication involves both the words spoken and the way they are delivered. Positive workplace interactions recognize individual worth, celebrate successes and support individual and group achievement. A predominance of this type of communication supports good relationships, builds camaraderie and fosters an environment where employees can enjoy their work.

We can also explore the question of positive communication in a different way–the ratio of positive to negative interactions. The Losada ratio, named after the academic who did the math, says that a human needs three or more positive statements for every negative statement in order to flourish. Barbara Fredrickson contends that the three to one ratio is "the tipping point, predicting whether people languish or flourish."[31] Similarly, John Gottman, well known for his work researching marital communication, has independently determined that a ratio of five or more positive statements for every negative statement is necessary "to predict a strong and loving marriage."[32]

Inherent in the Losada ratio is the recognition that life is never without some negative elements. There will always be concerns that have to be addressed and those challenges can stimulate growth. The question isn't whether the workplace will have some negative issues to confront–it will; the central question is the ratio of positives to negatives. Do administrators, managers and employees fill their lives primarily with the positive, giving them strength to deal with the negative or are they simply overwhelmed by the negative? The bottom line for the CEO, manager, supervisor or team leader is not to stifle the constructive discussion of the negative but rather to work towards ensuring that positive expression substantially outweighs the negative.

Second, among the basic assumptions underlying the activities is the fact that public statements create a type of commitment that influences future behavior. For example, a person who tells coworkers that he or she intends to contribute to the company's United Way campaign is more likely to do so than the person who simply thinks, "I should contribute." The public statement becomes a type of psychological contract. The activities are designed to allow individuals to commit themselves publicly to constructive behaviors in a non-defensive way.

Moreover, a review of the literature on persuasive messages indicates that one of the most powerful forms of persuasion is called *counter-attitudinal advocacy.*[33] It is a type of self-persuasion in that the research establishes a constructive shift in attitude when an individual presents positive aspects of something that he or she views as primarily negative. An example could be an overall negative attitude towards a political candidate. If a person grudgingly provides in writing or states verbally some of the candidate's positive characteristics or accomplishments, there is a measurable positive shift in attitude. A skilled facilitator regularly uses this fact as a way to get a group to reconsider an overall negative position on the subject under discussion.

The effectiveness of the six activities provided in this book (three in this chapter and three in the last chapter) comes in part as a result of creating psychological contracts and using counter-attitudinal advocacy. In either case, individuals are not forced to change, instead they grow into change.

Finally, all the activities are designed to facilitate a process of exploring core values, since linking daily behaviors to those values is a powerful way to realize a shift towards positive, affirming behaviors. Moreover, the warm feeling associated with positive behaviors becomes the reward in the habit loop that encourages the behaviors. As the loop continues to cycle, it generates positive habits. Or, returning to the bucket metaphor, helping to fill someone's bucket feels good, and the good feeling encourages more bucket filling. Ultimately, as the cycle continues, bucket filling becomes a habit.

In addition, as Seligman has noted, spiritual energy, psychological fitness and the ability to resist negativity in times of crisis are all heavily dependent on an individual's ability to align thoughts and actions consistently with his or her core values. The resulting behaviors will be positive because the person who explores his or her core values will identify positive values. Though some might consider the above a naïve expectation, Seligman's spiritual module offers concrete proof. When asked to craft a eulogy for a fallen friend and then their own eulogy, soldiers inevitably described positive values at the spiritual core. While we do not have personal access to what was written, it is highly doubtful that anyone was eulogized for his or her active role in malicious gossip. Malicious gossip does not emanate from anyone's core values.

With these concepts in mind, managers can use the following activities in any work group to initiate a shift to a more positive culture. Of course, all of these activities can be modified to meet the particular circumstances of a given situation.

# ACTIVITY 1

### ➢ What-Went-Right Journal

Adapted from exercises described in Seligman's *Flourish*, this activity has life-changing potential if set up appropriately and employees participating follow through consistently. Seligman used it with both schoolchildren and soldiers and achieved equally positive results. One of the authors of this book has used it with some of his grandchildren and personally vouches for its impact. This activity can be readily adapted for almost any group that chooses to meet on a regular basis (i.e., a work group, church group, school class or book club).

Most important, of the six activities that are provided in this book, this one can be done by the reader. We strongly assure anyone willing to take the time for a reasonable duration that it will positively affect how you experience your work life and your relationships at work.

**Step 1:** The facilitator introduces the activity to the group by discussing the findings of positive psychologists that people grow best when they focus on the good things in their lives. He or she explains that one of the ways of helping oneself see the world more positively is to take time each day to remember positive events. Group members should be encouraged to participate in the activity but not compelled to do so. They also need to understand that continued participation in the activity with the group depends on their completing the assignment.

The facilitator notes that participants are asked to do the focus exercise for a month, preferably beginning on the first day of the month. Of course, the activity may be designed for a different time span with the understanding that it must last long enough to gauge the effect on participant focus.

**Step 2:** The facilitator gives a blank journal to each person who agrees to take part in the month-long activity. The journals must be completely blank so that participants can create their own unique version of the assignment.

**Step 3:** The facilitator asks participants to take some time each evening before going to bed to list three good things that happened that day at work. These can be incredibly minor or very significant. What has worked for one of the authors is to ask employees to identify two from work and one from home. The facilitator encourages the participants to complete this daily activity in a quiet space where they can give full attention to what they write and the reasons for the choices made.

Since the impact of the activity depends on consistent daily entries, the facilitator and participants should create a plan for reminders and encouragement during the month.

**Step 4:** At the end of the designated time period, the facilitator and participants meet to debrief the activity. It is best to do this in small groups numbering at most nine or ten. The facilitator asks the members of the group to share some of what they have recorded along with their observations about how the activity is influencing the way they are experiencing their work.

**Step 5:** The facilitator concludes the session by discussing whether or not participants want to continue with the activity and how often they want to meet for purposes of debriefing. If it is not a required activity, then debriefing sessions do not necessarily have to be on company time.

# ACTIVITY 2

## ➢ Positive Communication Survey

One of the authors has used the following activity in training sessions as part of an overall training program. It has many iterations and the one presented here focuses on thoughts about positive communication with a heavy emphasis on gossip. The activity can be used in many different situations but usually works best with a large audience where smaller groups can be formed for discussion purposes.

The discussions are usually more meaningful when a supervisor is not a member of the discussion group. Discussions tend to go equally well whether group members are total strangers or regular coworkers.

**Step 1:** The facilitator hands out the survey found on the following page. He or she asks the participants to read the instructions carefully at the top of the page and then respond appropriately to the ten items. Participants need sufficient time to complete the task.

**Step 2:** When the task is complete, the facilitator divides the group into smaller discussion units–five people to a group is ideal. Participants should discuss one item at a time and share their responses along with their thoughts about why answers differ. The facilitator should encourage the groups to avoid rushing through the process, and he or she should walk around and listen in on the group discussions. The insights gathered can inform the final debriefing.

**Step 3:** Finally, the facilitator debriefs the activity with the whole group. He or she should also ask questions and seek comments that help the group see the value of speaking positively about coworkers and see the harm in destructive statements.

➢ **Activity 2 Illustration**

---

# WORKPLACE COMMUNICATION QUESTIONNAIRE

Listed below are a number of statements. Each represents a commonly held opinion and there are no right or wrong answers. You will probably agree with some items and disagree with others. Read each statement, then indicate the extent to which you agree or disagree by marking the appropriate number in the margin.

|  | 5 | 4 | 3 | 2 | 1 |
|---|---|---|---|---|---|
| **If you:** | Strongly Agree | Agree | Don't Know | Disagree | Strongly Disagree |

1. ____Some workplace gossip is good and some is bad.
2. ____I perform better at work when the communication around me is positive, and we all support each other.
3. ____What is true is not gossip.
4. ____I resent it when other employees talk about me behind my back.
5. ____I feel equally comfortable initiating communication with people above me and below me in the authority hierarchy.
6. ____Gossiping is bad for workplace relationships.

7. ＿＿I prefer not to gossip, and I am uncomfortable around people who gossip a lot.

8. ＿＿Talking negatively about your coworkers should be prohibited and those who do so should be disciplined.

9. ＿＿Some people have a habit of always talking negatively while others have habits of talking positively.

10. ＿＿Gossiping is just socializing, and we all need to gossip at some time.

When you have completed this questionnaire, you will be divided into groups and asked to discuss your responses to these statements. You should pay particular attention to the extent to which people respond differently to each one. Ask every member of the group to explain his or her reaction to the statement in question, including any personal experiences related to it. There should be a facilitated, large group debriefing after the small group discussions.

# ACTIVITY 3

> **My Values**

One of the authors taught a college public speaking class in which he asked students to give an informative speech about a closely held personal value. The goal was to help the audience understand the value of and reason for the speaker's choice.

Frequently, frustrated students approached the professor during the preparation period, indicating that they found the assignment difficult because they could not identify a strong personal value. Usually, a short discussion with a few questions brought about a personal revelation–they had values. Interestingly, in every class that included this assignment, the students identified it as their favorite.

The following exercise is adapted from the college assignment. It works best when included as part of a series of activities such as a set of activities about what it means to be psychologically fit as an employee or how to improve one's performance by being psychologically fit. This activity is also an excellent follow-up to the *What-Went-Right Journal* activity.

**Step 1:** The facilitator discusses the concept of core values with the group. The discussion should include an analysis of the difference between a core value and a value.

**Step 2:** The facilitator then asks the participants to prepare some thoughts to share with the larger group about a personal core value that has proven important/essential in the workplace. They can use a series of short questions to help guide the preparation process:
- What is my core value?
- How did I acquire it?
- Why is it important for the work that I and my coworkers do?
- How has it impacted my work performance?

The facilitator also explains that the presentations are informal, so the speaker may choose to stand or sit. He or she also assures participants that their core value remarks need not be rushed–and can instead be savored–since additional time can be scheduled for speakers.

**Step 3:** Each person presents his or her core value. When the speaker completes the presentation, the facilitator opens the floor for discussion. This "debriefing" should occur after each participant's presentation.

## Concluding Thoughts

Thich Nhat Hanh states our concluding thought with simple elegance in his wonderful book, *Being Peace,* when he writes:

> If we are not happy, if we are not peaceful, we can't share peace and happiness with others, even those we love, those who live under the same roof. If we are peaceful, if we are happy, we can smile and blossom like a flower, and everyone in our family, our entire society, will benefit from our peace.[34]

What we are learning from positive psychology is that being happy and at peace is often a reflection of good habits. They are the products of an automatic way of thinking about life and about the people we encounter. In other words, we can build habits of happiness and peace. Those habits include choosing to communicate in a manner that helps build positive relationships both at home and at work, benefitting everyone around us in powerful ways.

# Chapter 9 Summary

A substantial amount of human behavior exists outside of our conscious awareness and is often referred to as habits. The collective set of habits for the individuals within a work group and/or the larger workplace is the major contributor to the culture of the group and/or the organization. Creating an affirming culture requires that negative communication habits be replaced with positive. Key points include:

- Much of our communication–including gossip–happens as a result of habits. We can habitually engage in negative communication just as we can habitually engage in positive communication.

- Habits are repeat patterns of behaving, thinking or feeling that occur without conscious thought. Gossip is often a habitual behavior because it happens without the individual's making a conscious decision that he or she desires to engage in gossip.
- Old gossip habits are hard to break and new habits of positive interaction are hard to form because the behavioral patterns we repeat are imprinted in our neural pathways.
- While a challenge, new habits can be created and strengthened such that they crowd out the old.
- A "thriving" culture requires a dual concern over people and the bottom line. Emphasizing one over the other reduces overall performance.
- Malicious gossip is antithetical to a thriving culture as it reduces the energy that comes from high levels of camaraderie and positive relationships.
- Attitudes shift and solidify in the direction of public statements espousing a personal position on an issue. Therefore, public statements become a form of commitment.
- Spiritual energy is created when we act consistently with our most deeply held values and beliefs.
- A changed habit is more durable when it is accompanied by a strong belief that change is both possible and desirable.

# Chapter 10

## PUTTING IT ALL TOGETHER

Be Impeccable With Your Word. Speak with integrity. Say only what you mean. Avoid using the word to speak against yourself or to gossip about others. Use the power of your word in the direction of truth and love.

**MIGUEL ANGEL RUIZ**

C. S. Lewis, a well-known British novelist, literary critic and Christian apologist, is widely known for exploring the characteristics and consequences of good and evil in his novels for both adults and children. One of his lesser known works, a relatively small allegory titled *The Great Divorce*, tells the story of a few residents of Hell who take a bus ride to Heaven where they are met and counseled by people who dwell there. The proposition is that they can stay on the condition that they successfully confront and separate themselves from a personal issue that keeps them from experiencing life in its most meaningful and joyful way, a separation requiring a "great divorce." The story is told by an individual on the bus, who is given a teacher to help him understand what is happening once he arrives in heaven.

In the preface, Lewis' assures the reader that the book is fantasy, the product of his own imagination. It is not even a "guess or a speculation at what may actually await us."[1] He has no intention "to arouse factual curiosity about the details of the afterworld."[2] Rather, his purpose is to focus attention on the results of everyday choices.

He advances the basic supposition that those consequences move us either in the direction of hell or heaven–hell defined as that which diminishes us and heaven, the state of experiencing life in its most joyful, fulfilling expression.

Lewis does not describe people who committed transgressions that brought great harm. Instead, he identifies obvious faults that have a negative effect on a person's life and his or her relationships, because these everyday thoughts and actions clearly have a positive side but can become twisted and ultimately more difficult to confront successfully than the "deadly sins."[1]

For example, most people would agree that a mother's love for her children is a good, constructive quality, the ultimate expression of self-sacrifice and positive, nurturing support. Yet, Lewis cleverly details how that love can be warped to the point that it becomes manipulative, controlling and divisive. He describes how this destructive twist separates the participants from the warmth and affection of the genuine. To make matters worse, the mother finds it much more difficult to recognize the damage her daily behavior causes because its genesis is positive. She cannot see that her expressions of "love" have made it impossible for her to experience the quality of relationships with her children that would bring a deeper level of joy and meaning into her life.[3] Not being able to recognize the tyranny of the negative, her ability to change to the positive becomes almost impossible. Lewis, using the teacher as the expounder, writes:

> There is always something they insist on keeping even at the price of misery. There is always something they prefer to joy– that is to reality.[4]

---

1 Greek monastic theologian Evagrius of Pontus was a 4th century Christian monk and ascetic. Charles Panati, in his book _Sacred Origins of Profound Things_, {(New York: Arkana, The Penguin Group, 1996), 180}.comes to the conclusion that Evagrius was the first to draw up a list of deadly sins. For Evagrius there were eight "offenses and wicked human passions" that made the list. They were, in order of increasing seriousness: gluttony, lust, avarice, sadness, anger, acedia (indifference, apathy), vainglory, and pride.

The word "reality" reflects Lewis' belief that a positive, fulfilling existence is not a fairy tale; it is actually a certainty if we understand and address the choices that separate us from joy. It is a certainty, for instance, that a mother's love freely given in its most positive expression is a powerful force for real, unquestionable good in all of our lives.

Of course, the distortion of mother love described above is only one example of the many ways we humans can sabotage our life experience through everyday behaviors that separate us from a joyful reality. The list of destructive behaviors is long because we hang on to grudges, are too proud to ask for forgiveness, take perverse pleasure in our own unhappiness and insist on gratifying personal desires. Lewis leaves us, however, with a sense of hope when the question, "Is there really a way out of Hell into Heaven?" arises.[5] He insists that the positive is inherently stronger than the negative. The teacher makes the point when he states:

> Can you really have thought that love and joy would always
> be at the mercy of frowns and sighs? Did you not know they
> were stronger than their opposites?[6]

Lewis' insightful thinking is easily transferable to the matter of gossip. Every day human interactions, such as interchanges with families, colleagues and friends, can degenerate into gossip. Our normal, healthy interactions bind us together while conversations that become twisted and self-serving can turn into backbiting and slander. As Lewis emphasizes in *The Great Divorce*, the individual engaging in acts of backbiting and slander can very well have a sense of self-justifying righteousness and indignation, a sense that allows the gossiper to ignore any misery or suffering created by his or her behavior. Worse, the sense of being right blinds the person from seeing how the action diminishes him or her as a person and progressively undermines real life fulfillment. Promoting constructive change is impossible when a person feels righteous about his or her destructive actions.

Pope Francis addressed the issue of destructive interactions in his 2014 Christmas message. He drew worldwide attention with his blunt honesty and call for significant change in the conduct of his subordinates. Yet, as emphasized in a *Chicago Tribune* front-page editorial, it was a message with which we all can resonate and use to critique our own behavior.

> We all navigate through life as best we can. But we also gossip. We envy others. We chase the latest gadgets, the bigger home, the fancier car. These are normal impulses that can be channeled for good or ill, for healthy pursuit or destructive obsession. The pope's words invite us to examine how we live, how we pursue our goals and–most important–how we treat others.[7]

The sentence, "These are normal impulses that can be channeled for good or ill, for healthy pursuit or destructive obsession," mirrors what C. S. Lewis says in *The Great Divorce*. So much of our everyday behavior can be channeled toward a positive or directed toward the negative. It is normal for all of us to discuss with others what is going on in our lives and in our relationships. But, when those discussions turn to the malicious, our interactions can have a destructive impact on individuals and on an organization be it a nonprofit, a private business, a government bureau or a church. What is particularly significant about Pope Francis' Christmas message is the heavy emphasis he placed on the destructive role of gossip amongst his subordinates and his concern for the debilitating impact of gossip on administrative effectiveness; how gossip destroys important relationships and negatively impacts the mission of the church. That emphasis is summarized in the *Chicago Tribune* editorial.

> He talked about the "terrorism" of gossip, which he labeled
> a disease that could destroy a reputation "in cold blood." He
> urged them [his subordinates] to be "conscientious objectors"
> to gossip.[8]

Gossip, that ordinary, everyday activity has a toxic side that can be extremely harmful. As both C. S. Lewis and Pope Francis state, part of the harm is the fact that it can appear to be normal since everyone does it. Fortunately, there is a way out of hell into heaven; we can create workplaces without malicious gossip that resonate with the positive. Achieving that outcome starts by recognizing the problem and being able to envision the possibilities.

C. S. Lewis is one of many who have explored significant philosophical and theological questions through fantasy. On May 25, 1977, George Lucas introduced the movie *Star Wars* to what became a worldwide audience. *Star Wars* was followed by *The Empire Strikes Back* and *The Return of the Jedi*. Light sabers, Wookies, the Jedi and the Force became an overwhelming part of popular culture. Of these, the concept of the Force has had the most lasting impact, having become a part of everyday speech and the subject of full length books. Philosophy professors Kevin Decker and Jason Eberl have edited a collection of philosophical articles written about the metaphysics of *Star Wars* with a special focus on the Force. Titled *Star Wars and Philosophy: More Powerful Than You Can Possibly Imagine*, it contains an article by professor Jan-Erik Jones on the Force. In it, he writes:

> The reason why the Force in **Star Wars** has such a grip on the
> viewer's imagination is because it makes us ask the fundamen-
> tal metaphysical questions that have driven science and phi-
> losophy from the beginning; questions about cause and effect,
> the laws of nature, the possibility of foreknowledge, and the
> relationship between the mind and the physical world.[9]

The movie audience is first introduced to the concept of the Force by the ancient Jedi warrior Obi-wan Kenobi when one of the main heroes, Luke Skywalker, seeks to understand what it is. Obi-wan explains that "[t]he Force is what gives a Jedi his power. It's an energy field created by all living things. It surrounds us, it penetrates us, it binds the galaxy together."[10]

Jungian psychologist Stephen Galipeau, the author of the book *The Journey of Luke Skywalker: An Analysis of Modern Myth and Symbol*, expands on the definition of the Force by stating:

> The force, like any symbol can have numerous meanings. I would like to suggest here that it is a symbol for the whole of psychic energy, for what Jung called the collective unconscious, an aspect of psychic reality that all people share and from which a religious experience, myth, symbol, and art emerge.[11]

The *Star Wars* tale centers on an intergalactic struggle that has gone on for millennia between the Jedi warriors, who exercise the positive side of the force in defense of truth, justice, peace and freedom, and the Sith, who seek power through the use of the dark side of the Force and are indifferent to any harms associated with its use. The dark side represents an aspect of the Force not practiced by the Jedi who view it as evil.

The philosophical discussions of the Force primarily focus on the interplay between the positive and negative sides. A Jedi's power comes from the positive side and as Yoda, a Jedi Master, explains, "a Jedi uses the Force for knowledge and defense. Never for attack."[12] On the other hand, the Sith find that there is more power in the dark side. The dark side is primarily energy drawn from strong negative emotions such as fear, hate and anger. The *Book of Sith* explains that "a warrior's true strength lies not in muscle but in anger."[13] The Wookepedia provides a more comprehensive overview of the dark side when it states:

By channeling tense negative emotions, such as anger, jeal-ousy, or greed, into the Force, individuals can attain powers of the Force more easily, but as a consequence: they gain lust for power, and become increasingly self-aggrandizing. Followers of this path are always depicted as corrupt and wicked, engag-ing in a never-ending, self-centered pursuit of power.[14]

A number of significant similarities exist between the charac-ter of the Force and gossip. The most obvious is the fact that gossip is a communication act and the ability to communicate unites our human experience. Like the Force, communication has both a con-structive and negative side. In the same sense that the Force has a dark side, gossip has a dark, destructive side. It is the dark side that impacts organizational performance. It is what Pope Francis, finds so destructive amongst his administrative staff and what events involv-ing people such as the Hooksett 4 illustrate.

There are other similarities. For instance, the Sith do not see the practice of the dark side to be wrong. In fact:

The Sith view the dark side as pragmatic, demonstrating one of *Star Wars* creator George Lucas' central observations that "most bad people think they are good people."[15]

The same can be said for gossipers; at the time of gossiping, most would probably not think that what they were doing was bad. They are just sharing information that justifiably needs to be shared. And, to the extent that it passes judgment on an absent person's behavior, the judgment is appropriate and most likely deserved.

Another similarity between the character of gossip and the Force is the fact that Lucas constantly uses dialogue in the movie to show that much of the struggle between the positive and negative sides is an internal struggle within each Jedi knight.

Lucas uses "the dark side," and "paths to the dark side," as devices to suggest the distinction between good and evil is not a distinction between 'us' and 'them' … but rather a battle within ourselves, reflecting the frailty of human nature and our own competing (and equally compelling) internal impulses towards kindness on the one hand, and cruelty on the other.[16]

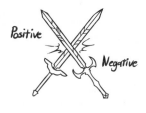

Like the Force, communication has both a constructive and negative side. In the same sense that the Force has a dark side, gossip has a dark, destructive side. It is the dark side that impacts organizational performance.

All of us experience this same struggle that often manifests itself in how we talk about and to each other. We can choose to engage in malicious gossip or be conscientious objectors and focus on the positive.

A more important similarity is the supposition that when a person gives in to the dark side it begins to change who he or she is as an individual. The Sith obtain power from the dark side–hatred, anger, resentment, fear. But in doing so, they lose touch with positive emotions such as compassion, love and forgiveness. Losing touch with the positive allows a person to engage in actions harmful to others with great indifference. As Yoda explains to Luke, "Fear is the path to the dark side. Fear leads to anger, anger leads to hate, hate leads to suffering."[17]

Positive actions and emotions have exactly the opposite effect; they affirm and build positive expressions of the individual. Judith

Barad, another contributor to *Star Wars and Philosophy*, explores what she calls the Jedi's "handbook of virtue" and writes:

> When Luke meets his father for the second time in real battle, he succeeds in overcoming his anger and hatred by seeing the good in his father. His vision of this good results in for-giveness and compassion, such that he refuses to kill Vader. At this moment, Luke experiences the ultimate triumph of the Jedi Knight. The Jedi Knight resists evil, but does so motivated by a compassion that remains open to forgive-ness and reconciliation.[18]

Obviously, a similar conclusion can be drawn about malicious gossip and the gossiper. An ultimate triumph can be experienced by the individual who resists the opportunity to engage in malicious gossip and instead interacts from a positive point of view. This type of interaction leaves the individual open to building camaraderie and good will into his or her relationships.

Lewis and Lucas clearly excel in the use of story to provide insight into human behavior. Powerful stories, however, can be much simpler than those that involve the afterlife or intergalactic struggles. Jon Gordon, who specializes in providing meaningful instruction in positive psychology, is the author of *The Positive Dog*. It is the story of two dogs, Matt and Bubba, who currently reside at a local dog shelter. Matt has had a very tough life before being rescued and is now up for adoption. He very much wants to be adopted by a loving family, but his earlier experiences left him feeling angry and sad, emotions that affect his behavior. Every time a family comes to the shelter for the purpose of adopting a dog and visits with Matt, he acts withdrawn, unhappy and mean. He doesn't get adopted nor is it likely to happen.

Fortunately for Matt, Bubba, a wise, old dog residing at the shel-ter, spends most of his exercise time with him. Bubba takes it upon himself to help Matt become an affectionate dog that a family would want to adopt. He begins to teach him the principles of positive psychology and explains that in each of us there is a positive dog and a negative dog; "One dog is positive, happy, optimistic, and hopeful. The other dog is negative, mad, sad, pessimistic, and fearful. These two dogs often fight inside us…."[19]

Matt, of course, wants to know which dog usually wins and Bubba answers:

> "The dog who wins is the one you feed the most," Bubba exclaimed. "You have to feed the positive dog inside you and starve the negative dog. The more you feed the positive dog, the more it grows. The more you starve the negative dog, the more it shrinks and weakens. You become the dog you feed, so feed the positive dog and your big problems will give way to big blessings and a bright future."[20]

So what dog does malicious gossip feed? The places where we work, play, socialize and worship take on the energy of those present. We all suffer the consequences when the negative dog is the dominant resident. On the other hand, if our communal energy primarily comes from the positive dog inside each of us, we all benefit from the effervescent, affirming outcome.

## Concluding Thoughts

While discussing the topic of malicious gossip some time ago, a column in the *Seattle Times* on gracious living caught our attention. The author challenges readers to imitate one of her grandparents who epitomized graciousness when interacting with other people. She acknowledges that "graciousness may be hard to define, but it's easily recognized in someone's manner."[21] Most important, the individual who interacts with a gracious person walks away feeling affirmed and supported. When these types of interactions replace malicious gossip in the workplace, employee morale improves and enhances overall performance.

Dale Turner, an author and retired minister, wrote a column for the Saturday religion page of the *Seattle Times* for 20 years. His columns were filled with warmth, wisdom and inspiration. When he died at the age of 88, his passing made the front page of the newspaper. He communicated his positive message so well that the *Seattle Times* saw fit to reprint a number of the flood of letters it had received in his memory. One writer echoed the common theme in all of the letters.

> His message [referencing a specific article] gave me hope. I cut it out, highlighted his words of wisdom, and kept it in my billfold at all times for many, many years until it became so tattered and illegible that only his wisdom and faith remained.... My children, my grandchildren and their offspring will benefit from his life.[22]

Turner was colleague and friend to all three of the authors of this book. He was an inspiration to us as his personal life mirrored the words of his columns. We constantly saw how words can inspire, give hope and make life better. For these reasons, we saw fit to dedicate this book to his memory.

Turner was keenly aware of the power of words and how they reflect our view of the world. He constantly urged his readers to speak with kindness and to be conscious of the harm that can happen when we fail to guard against the unkind word. He wrote: "It is not easy to bridle the tongue, but it is important that we learn to do so."[23] In his writing, he emphasized the relationship between how we experience life and what we have to say. He wrote:

> The heart of the matter is that speech is an index to the mind. The tongue reflects what the mind thinks. It shows where our minds have been feeding. When we use words, we are vocalizing our thoughts.[24]

Words do matter. They set the atmosphere in which we live whether in our personal lives or in the workplace. They either add to or subtract from our lives. We can choose whether to build communication habits that enrich our personal lives and the places in which we pursue our professional activities, or whether we allow negative habits of communication to dominate the cultures of our institutions.

Turner was well known for using poetry in his columns and in his speaking engagements. He loved the simple statement. One of his favorites, often used in his presentations and a reflection of his own life, is an Irish verse that serves to challenge each of us.

> Give me a sense of humor, Lord.
> Give me the grace to see a joke,
> To get some pleasure out of life
> And pass it on to other folk.
> Give me sympathy and sense
> And help keep my courage high.
> Give me calm and confidence,
> And, please, a twinkle in my eye. [25]

# Afterthought

## GOSSIP: THE ACADEMIC-PRACTITIONER CONFLICT

Gossip is no longer the resource
of the idle or the vicious, but has
become a trade, which is pursued
with industry as well as effrontery.
### LOUISE BRANDEIS AND SAMUEL WARREN

W hen the authors began the work of researching and writing this book, we thought that the task could be completed in a relatively short period of time. That turned
out not to be the case because gossip is a subject that can
be amorphous and hard to define, a topic with many facets and
perspectives, with tentacles reaching into questions of organizational performance, law, gender, social networking and religious
teachings. While generally condemned, it permeates almost every
aspect of our lives.

We were certain from the outset that our goal was to focus less on
describing the problem of malicious gossip and more on the importance of replacing it with positive communication. A primary concern was to avoid presenting a simplistic condemnation of gossip that
ignored the realities of everyday communication. We are all social
beings and our usually positive everyday interactions with each other
can often be considered gossip. Yet what affirms our humanity can be
a source of personal pain and unhappiness since gossip has a destruc-

tive side. Thus, a critical task for us was to be clear about the type of gossip we wished to replace.

After completing and reviewing an initial draft of the book, there emerged a growing sense that more should be said about the debate that is ongoing over its destructive or constructive value–a debate overviewed in the first chapter.

## The Perspectives of Gossip

Throughout the preceding chapters, we have stated clearly that we believe gossip within an organization to be hurtful, destructive and preventable. We have also consistently taken the stance that pro-hibition alone is insufficient and ineffective. Replacing gossip with constructive behavior is essential for the organization to obtain a sig-nificant positive benefit. In espousing this view, we are fully aware of the academic and research information that places gossip in a posi-tive light and pokes fun at practitioners who suggest otherwise. In Chapter 1, we cited a number of academics who postulated a con-structive role for gossip in the organization and claimed that negative attacks on the practice are for the most part superficial and naïve.

So how is it that with all of these apparently well established and supposedly helpful attributes of gossip, we remain adamant that a destructive side to gossip exists and needs to be tamed? Is it facile and simplistic for practitioners to view gossip in the organization as harmful, a problem that needs to be addressed? We have dedicated most of this "Afterthought" to providing a more detailed response to these two questions. Though the subtitle, "The Academic-Practitioner Conflict," denotes a focus on the difference in perspective between those who study gossip (academics) and those who have to deal with it (practitioners), we also acknowledge that their positions on some aspects of gossip are not always mutually exclusive. In addition, even differing perspectives on either side may add value to our under-standing of the practice.

Based on the information provided in the previous ten chapters, we provide a rebuttal to the claim that gossip will always be with us and the accusation that any effort by practitioners to remove gossip from the workplace or other organizational setting is naive and counterproductive. We contend that a polar opposite is true; a failure to address problems with malicious gossip can leave the organization badly compromised and ineffective.

## Two Definitions of Gossip

There is an academic-practitioner disagreement over the impact of gossip on an organization. In using the word "academic," we refer primarily to university professors who conduct research into social behavior, and study and write about gossip. Their work is most often recorded in professional journals. Practitioners (i.e., business consultants, human resource managers and others) who directly experience the impact of negative gossip in the workplace generally publish their articles in trade journals or blogs. The term "practitioner" also

Academics researching social behavior disagree with practitioners in business settings about the impact of gossip in an organization.

includes employees that make up the workforce. Surveys have constantly shown that they view gossip in the workplace as a problem. For example, 36 percent of respondents to a large survey indicated that gossip was their "biggest workplace pet peeve."[1]

As is often true of disagreements, the two groups may not be talking about the same thing. In fact, a review of the academic literature and of the extensive practitioner literature related to gossip finds that there is an obvious problem of definition. Each academic research project we reviewed had its own definition. They ranged from gossip as any and all social interaction (chatting about life is gossip) to the narrower sense of two people talking, whether positively or negatively, about a third person not present for the conversation.

We observed, however, that with only one or two exceptions the research articles we reviewed did not attempt to draw a distinction between the impact of positive gossip versus negative gossip. In Chapter 1, we noted that gossip has generally had a pejorative meaning that ignored the positive. In fact, we quoted Louise Collins who suggested that we needed two different words for gossip—gossip and guossip. She chose to use gossip for the negative element of social interaction and guossip for the positive that builds relationships and helps form community. As to the relationship between the two, she writes:

> In my view, only some gossip is malicious and malicious gossip is parasitic on ordinary gossip, as lying is parasitic on sincere discourse.[2]

This simple statement mirrors the problem that we have with much of the research that suggests a positive role for gossip in organizational dynamics. Obviously, no organization can function without sincere discourse, and it is equally obvious that dishonesty undermines the value of discourse. Thus, if research conducted for the purpose of studying the importance of discourse to organizational effectiveness lumps honest and dishonest discourse together, it would produce flawed results. Similarly, we question the results of any research that fails to draw a distinction between gossip and guossip (malicious and non-malicious social interaction).

Studies also differ on the prevalence of malicious gossip. For example, a study cited in Chapter 5 found no statistical difference between males and females with regard to the percentage of negative gossip versus positive with approximately 25 percent of all gossip statements for both genders classified as negative.[3] Another study conducted in England concluded that only five percent of all gossip was malicious.[4]

We suspect that the actual amount of malicious gossip in the workplace is a factor of the culture specific to each organization. As a result, the measurable amount of malicious gossip would change from one organization to another. Whatever the amount, we are convinced that the impact of the malicious is substantially different from that of the positive. Therefore, any research that does not accommodate or address this distinction provides results that have little or no value.

While most research does not draw a distinction between good and bad gossip, the work of Weber State University professor Susan Hafen is an exception. She found some forms of beneficial gossip and other forms that hurt the organization. More specifically, she draws a distinction between "organizational citizenship behaviors (the positive) and "workplace deviance behaviors" (the negative). Ultimately, Hafen concludes:

> The question is not whether to gossip or how to eliminate it, but how to foster an ethical workplace environment that promotes positive forms of gossip by male and female employees.[5]

Hafen's research also clearly indicates that some forms of gossip are harmful to the organization and that we do not have to accept that harm as inevitable.[6] Her conclusion supports our view that building the "ethical workplace environment" requires substituting positive, supportive communication.

While not specifically referencing a research project, Harvard Business School professor John Kotter discusses the matter of personal effectiveness and the role of communication in his book *Power and Influence*.[7] He states that he wrote it "to provide assistance to the many people who are trying to foster excellence, innovation, and responsibilities in their organizations, despite the many forces that promote bureaucracy, parochial politics, and destructive power struggles."[8]

Kotter is particularly concerned with the fact that organizations often have individuals with great ideas that never see the light of day. He links this failure to a misunderstanding of how power and influence work in an organization and to the person's failure to acquire the skill set necessary to work effectively within that organization. He writes:

> After studying this problem for over a decade now, I think I understand why it is that some people are incredibly effective in providing leadership in getting things done inside complex organizations, while most of us are not. It begins with a certain way of thinking about the social milieu in which one operates.[9]

Kotter emphasizes the fact that employees in the modern, complex organization are substantially interdependent, meaning that each person must depend on others in order to be successful at what he or she does.[10] Thus, an essential component to effectiveness within an organization is the ability to build meaningful relationships. He explains:

> Good working relationships based on some combination of respect, admiration, perceived need, obligation, and friendship are a critical source of power in helping to get things done..... Furthermore, since these relationships serve as important information channels, without them one may never be able to establish the information base one needs to operate effectively.[11]

Melding the work of Hafen and Kotter offers valuable insight into the kind of environment that promotes effective performance. Kotter links personal effectiveness to recognition of the importance of the social milieu in which people work. A milieu characterized by quality relationships and healthy interdependence provides employees with a much greater ability to influence and control outcomes. In fact, Kotter consistently reiterates the value of interpersonal communication skills as part of what he calls the soft use of power.[12] While Kotter does not speak directly to the problem of malicious gossip, it is significant that he never suggests that speaking maliciously about a colleague behind his or her back promotes personal effectiveness.

Hafen recognizes the importance of good citizenship behaviors in the organization and the destructiveness of deviant behaviors, and notes that good citizenship behaviors build relationships while deviant behaviors destroy them. Notably, both Kotter and Hafen contend that positive behaviors can be identified and discussed separate from the negative, urging leadership to encourage the constructive while concurrently controlling the negative.

## Gossip and Organizational Performance

Organizations exist to accomplish a purpose. Practitioners, whether in a church, business or nonprofit, are concerned with how well an organization is fulfilling its purpose. We have previously discussed, for example, Pope Francis' concerns about gossip and the administrative effectiveness of the Catholic Church (page xxx). He leveled the very serious charge that the work of Vatican administrators "can take a downward spiral into mediocrity, gossip and bureaucratic squabbling."[13] He further challenged:

… Vatican officials to exercise "conscientious objection to gossip.

"Let us all be conscientious objectors, and mind you I am not simply moralizing! Gossip is harmful to people, our work and our surroundings."[14]

The Pope's observation clearly illustrates the interface between dysfunctional administration and gossip. He understands how gossip can add to administrative incompetence.

Organizational success depends heavily on individual and group performance. Most organizations measure productivity by assessing three primary elements of performance: quantity, quality and timeliness of work. Is gossip an asset that promotes a more productive workplace? Does the quantity, quality and timeliness of work produced by employees increase or decrease in the presence of gossip? Research indicates that there is no simple answer to these questions.

A review of the literature indicates that some academics–particularly those that believe the presence of gossip in the workplace is an inevitable and necessary phenomenon–tend to avoid discussing the extent to which gossip, especially malicious gossip, increases or decreases the amount of output. Rather, they focus heavily on how gossip plays a role in positively socializing individuals within the organization. While it is possible to make an argument that the socialization process produces more productive employees, it is not presented by those who advocate a constructive role for gossip in the organization. In fact, they never suggest that as gossip increases so does output.

So, is gossip an asset to management decision making? Since one of the functions of management is to make decisions, this question is all about the quality of management work–good decision-making. The problem in answering it is once again definitional and, to a great extent, based on whether one separates good from bad gossip. It is hard to believe that malicious gossip, particularly the completely dishonest type, would assist in a management decision-making process. However, if one is looking just at the positive side of gossip then the above conclusion is clearly defensible. Or, to put it another way, would the elimination of malicious gossip negatively impact the ability of management to make good decisions? Our review of the literature impels us to answer the question with an emphatic "no."

The gap between the perspectives of academics who view gossip as a positive socializing influence and practitioners who see it as detrimental is very much related to the focus on organizational performance. Practitioners make the relationship between gossip and performance a major concern. In an article titled "Office Gossip: An HR Challenge," Susan Dunn writes:

> Some gossip is relatively benign; other forms are malicious and can turn right into slander and libel.
>
> Unchecked, it's not going to go away and can be disruptive to productivity and morale.
>
> Office gossip generally centers around which employees management is dating, and who's about to get fired, transferred, promoted or demoted. Particularly malicious gossip is used for personal or political gain within the organization.[15]

The assessment above is common to most practitioners. While the article adds little specific, measurable information about the relationship between work performance and malicious gossip, it does provide a clear example of a practitioner's focus on the negative side of gossip and the concern with its disruptive impact on output. With almost no exceptions, practitioners link poor morale and reduced performance to malicious gossip.

Another practitioner article titled "Gossip Poisons Business–HR Can Stop It" states that "whisper campaigns ruin a workplace" and that the HR professional should and can take steps "to squelch the rumors and clear the air." The author believes that "there is no way to measure how common or destructive office gossip is," but "it is clear that it can wreak havoc in an organization."[16]

The author emphasizes that when not effectively controlled "gossip can not only cause deep personal pain but also lead to turnover, conflict, and lawsuits."[17] He includes numerous examples of the type of hurtful statements made about fellow employees that have a destructive impact on the organization. Under the heading "Confronting the Problem," he also offers a list of suggested steps that HR can take to remove gossip from the workplace.[18]

These two articles are part of an almost endless list of short, workplace-based pieces, addressing the problem of gossip. They illustrate the type of analysis that at least one academic has called facile and superficial, noting that they promote futile attempts to remove negative interactions.[19] We, however, believe it is worth repeating that the difference between the two camps (academic and practitioner) primarily comes about because the practitioner focuses on the destructive effects of malicious gossip on organizational performance.

## Gossip as Catharsis

Other students of gossip feel that it serves the positive function of helping employees release the stresses and pressures found in the workplace. One article, for example, discusses how "gossiping about patients and colleagues helps nurses let off steam and cope with the stresses of work."[20] The research project involved interviewing 100 nurses about their habits of gossip in the workplace, all conversations that occurred behind closed doors. The author concludes that:

> .... on the positive side there is no doubt that gossiping behind closed doors helps nurses manage their emotions and cope with the demands of working in a pressurized, stressful and sometimes distressing environment.[21]

There is also a new app for smartphones called Memo that purports to offer a venue for similar "stress relief." Memo allows participants to "gossip anonymously about their workplace woes," but requires them to use their workplace e-mail addresses. The app creator believes that "allowing employees to complain without fear of reprisal"[22] will provide workers with a positive, cathartic experience.

However, the conclusion that "private" bitching and moaning about one's workplace relieves unhealthy stress is questionable to say the least. We found no study using a control group that demonstrates a positive effect for the group allowed to make anonymous negative comments about colleagues and their workplace when compared to employees who do not make such negative statements. In addition, no study actually shows that bitching and moaning makes a person feel better when compared to people who do not complain.

Furthermore, stating that venting by making negative statements actually produces a positive end result directly contradicts much of the work of positive psychologists such as Martin Seligman. Also, research indicates that while there are constructive ways to discuss a problem, negative venting (sometimes called catharsis theory) can often lead to increased unhappiness and even rage. The more people talk about the problem, the angrier they get.[23] Therefore, we side with positive psychologists and contend that learning to discuss problems from a positive perspective empowers an individual and provides a much better perspective on life.

## Gossip as Social Outlet

One of the dominant themes in much of the academic litera-ture is that gossip provides a fundamental and positive element in the socialization process. Gossip helps an individual belong to the in-group, feel liked and exert influence. It also makes the job more interesting, helps relieve the pressures of the job, and allows low power employees to feel better about themselves and their status within the organization.

Articles written by practitioners, on the other hand, generally do not discuss a positive role for gossip from a socialization perspective or any other point of view. At best, these articles present workplace gossip as a benign, though somewhat time-wasting, activity. In gen-eral, however, when practitioners address organizational problems that need a solution, gossip tends to be one of those problems. In fact, we found no practitioner article that viewed gossip as a fix for a problem.

The difference between the two perspectives, however, is not a clash of opposites. The academics primarily take a more global view of an organization and evaluate how people informally communicate, establish relationships and make decisions. Practitioners, on the other hand, focus narrowly on specific problems typically caused by negative or malicious gossip. To a certain degree, practitioners and academics are simply writing about different things.

A broader term, phatic communication, denotes a type of interaction between individuals that is social in nature and can include gossip. Phatic communication is defined as:

> Small talk: the nonreferential use of language to share feelings or establish a mood of sociability rather than to communicate information or ideas....[24]

Phatic communication is often referred to as the oil of relationships since it is essential in helping to reduce friction between people. For instance, we talk with each other at work, and share information about our families, our pets, the weather, sports and our pastimes. Phatic communication can easily be viewed as a waste of time by an organization since it has nothing to do with the work itself. Clearly, time spent talking about the weather, our pets and other non-work-related topics does not get the job done.

Much of what is considered phatic communication could also be called guossip or positive gossip. Sharing little stories with our colleagues about our children's adventures and misadventures, for example, would be gossip. After all, our children are not present and might not even want us to share the story. And, of course, discussing our children at work can hardly be considered a task-oriented activity. However, these social activities can have great significance in building trust, promoting camaraderie and cementing relationships.

Sociologist Erving Goffman has written that "[t]he gestures which we sometimes call empty are perhaps in fact the fullest things of all."[25]

That said, recognizing the significance of social interaction, including the role of positive gossip, does not alter our thinking about malicious interactions. It does not build trust, teamwork and camaraderie to circulate a story about how a coworker is using male prostitutes or bedding the boss, as in examples previously cited. It tore President Andrew Jackson's cabinet apart when an untruthful story circulated about the wife of his Secretary of War having had and then killing her illegitimate child in order to protect her reputation.[26] Lumping positive and malicious gossip into one category and then declaring it a general good simply does not work.

Clearly, wherever people are present, social interaction that includes gossip will occur. It does occur, and it is simplistic to suggest that it should be eliminated from the workplace. We concur with one author who responded to the charge that gossip was unprofessional by stating:

> When managers warn us not to be unprofessional, they're really saying that when we show up for work, they expect us to leave behind the emotional and social parts of who we are. But we're unable to leave our humanity at the door. We react to things emotionally, we form bonds with people, we gossip. To pretend otherwise makes things worse.[27]

But do we have to bring both the positive and the negative to work? From the authors' perspective, there is a significant difference between sharing affirming communication about our lives and malicious attacks on fellow employees. The first is essential and a reflection of our humanity while the second is destructive and exposes the worst part of who we are as humans.

## Big Picture Gossip

Another recurring theme in the study of gossip as a positive social activity involves a big picture view of its impact. That is, gossip has value in that it helps shape and protect the values and rules of a culture. We gossip about individuals who break the rules and in doing so reaffirm the rules and our commitment to them. In fact, Noon and Delbridge conclude that gossip is a social process that helps to protect and perpetuate organizations.[28] Or, as another academic put it:

> Gossip shepherds the herd. It says: these are the boundaries and you're crossing them. You're not abiding by the rules and you'd better get back in step… [29]

From the big picture view, the harm an individual experiences as a result of gossip is justified in that the person is being punished for breaking the rules. Moreover, the value of gossip as related to a culture maintenance function substantially outweighs the costs paid by the individual being gossiped about. One article clearly asserts this point:

> Unless you acknowledge the powerful good that gossip can give, you are not confronting the issue…. The primary reason gossip has a bad name (in secular or religious life) is that the benefits of gossip are diffused among many people (though they are better informed, they have little incentive to speak up for the value of gossip) while the price of gossip is concentrated on individual subjects who have a huge incentive to tamp it down.[30]

We take exception to this conclusion. That we can learn from the mistakes of others is obvious, but we question whether gossip is the best mode of communication by which to impart lessons in cultural norms and rules. More importantly, we question whether the costs associated with gossip have been calculated properly by those who extoll its positive benefits. For example, what is the actual cost to our society when competent individuals choose not to go into public service because they have no interest in having their private lives become fodder for the tabloids? Or, what is the actual cost to the organization when untruthful, malicious gossip stands as a barrier to an individual's receiving a promotion, encouraging him or her to seek employment elsewhere? We strongly question any conclusion that the positive benefits of gossip are broadly distributed while the harm caused to the individual gossiped about remains localized. In truth, malicious gossip actually hurts the whole organization.

Even when you look at a large societal picture, it is still very difficult to find a sum total of social good that outweighs malicious gossip. Former Secretary of State Colin Powell in his recent book, *It Worked for Me in Life and Leadership*, makes a significant statement about the relationship between the paparazzi, gossip and public service. At one point, he relates the story of contacts with Princess Diana primarily during joint participation in charitable fundraising activities. Of her untimely death, he writes:

> The celebrity of her position as the People's Princess created the conditions that led to her death. Paparazzi, tabloids, the expansion of the Internet, the explosion of social networks, the introduction of cameras into phones and ever smaller cases make everyone in public life much more vulnerable. Intrusions by the media are no longer an occasional irritation; they're constant. All of this feeds an insatiable, often vicious appetite for the celebrification of our society. The more outrageous, misanthropic, and narcissistic the behavior, the more it sells. We suck it all up. The news and gossip cycles now move so fast that a falsehood goes around the world at the speed of light and is imbedded in a million depositories. The correcting truth seldom

gets that kind of distribution. And so what? Another story has
already grabbed people's ever-roaming attention.[31]

Needless to say, it is extremely difficult to find some larger social
good in the role that the paparazzi and Internet gossip played in the
death of Princess Diana.

Or, take another example, the recent story of a 15-year-old
British Columbia schoolgirl who took her own life in response to an
instance of Internet gossip and cyberbullying. The story, as presented
in a lengthy article found in the *Seattle Times*,[32] included the fact that
"she was lured by a stranger to expose her breasts on a webcam and
the picture ended up on a Facebook page made by the stranger, to
which her friends were added." Shortly before her death, she posted a
nine-minute video in which she did not speak "but told her story in
haunting detail in a series of handwritten notes that she held up to the
camera." The video added great poignancy to her death.

As we noted previously, malicious gossip and bullying can often
be closely linked together. In the above case, we consider the posting
of the intimate picture an act of malicious Internet gossip. The message is the picture and the picture sends a message to a third party
undesired by the young woman. The Internet can be a particularly
devastating medium because the gossiper can send the gossip to a
large audience almost instantaneously. (See Chapter 3.)

Big picture gossip theory tells us that we should be mindful of
the social good that comes from gossip because it reinforces our cultural values. One could argue that thousands of people have heard
this story and/or watched the video, and it emphasized a message to
young women that modesty is a virtue. Moreover, it reminds all of
us that sending intimate pictures by way of the Internet is a foolish
action. Therefore, because of the incident, we are all better prepared
to deal with the stratagems of Internet strangers.

While these arguments have some merit, they ignore the full
social and personal costs. The gossiper's actions were despicable and

any attempt to find a greater good is deplorable. Bluntly stated, there are better ways to communicate cultural values and mores than with the malicious posting of intimate material against the wishes of the interested party, particularly when that person is a highly vulnerable teenager. Furthermore, the stance that only one person (the young women) was hurt by the gossip is irrational. Obviously, the tragic events negatively impacted her family, her friends, her community and the larger society.

The same may be said of the workplace. The harms associated with malicious gossip affect the whole work group rather than damaging just the person who is the victim.

## Final Thoughts

Masaru Emoto, a Japanese author and researcher, became well known for his work photographing water crystals. His water crystal experiments consisted of exposing water to different words, pictures or music, and then freezing it. Next, he examined the appealing properties of the resulting ice crystals using microscopic photography. His best known work is the book *The Hidden Messages in Water,* a *New York Times* bestseller. In the prologue to the book, he writes:

> In Japan, it is said that words of the soul reside in a spirit called kotodama, or the spirit of words, and the act of speaking words has the power to change the world. We all know that words have an enormous influence on the way we think and feel, and that things generally go more smoothly when positive words are used. However, up until now we have never been able to physically see the effect of positive words.[33]

Emoto asserts that positive words created beautiful, harmonious crystals, and he provided hundreds if not thousands of photographs in support of this assertion.

*Ice crystal associated with the words "love and gratitude"*
*Source: © Office Masaru Emoto, LLC*

His statement that "the act of speaking words has the power to change the world" is certainly inspiring, and we agree completely. While Emoto's claim that beautiful words such as "love" and "gratitude" will shape beautiful ice crystals has not been demonstrated under rigorous scientific conditions, the same cannot be said about the effect of positive words on people. We have extensively used the work of positive psychologists like Barbara Fredrickson and Martin Seligman to establish the powerful impact on the human experience when positive ways of thinking and talking dominate our lives. While it may be questionable to conclude that ice crystals formed in the presence of positive words will always be aesthetically beautiful, it is not a stretch for a manager to see the destructive impact of negative words on a work team and determine to engage in a planned course of action by which to substitute the power of the positive for malicious gossip.

It is a challenge that we believe managers should undertake and one that promises substantial payoffs to the organization. Words do have a "spirit," and the workplace is better off when the dominant spirit of our words shores up relationships, builds higher levels of cooperation and support, thereby working to produce a joyful workplace.

# ENDNOTES

## INTRODUCTION

1. Abigail Van Buren, "Dear Abby: Flow of Office Gossip Is Impossible to Stanch (June 26, 2006)," *Uexpress*, http://www.uexpress.com/dear-abby/2006/6/26/flow-of-office-gossip-is-impossible.

2. Barbara L. Fredrickson, *Positivity: Groundbreaking Research Reveals How to Embrace the Hidden Strength of Positive Emotions, Overcome Negativity and Thrive* (New York: Three Rivers Press, 2009), 15.

## CHAPTER 1

1. "Gossip." *Wikipedia: The Free Encyclopedia*, accessed April 20, 2015, http://en.wikipedia.org/wiki/Gossip.

2. Louise Collins, "Gossip: A Feminist Defense," in *Good Gossip*, ed. Robert F. Goodman and Aaron Ben-Ze'ev (Lawrence: University Press of Kansas, 1994), 106.

3. Gail Collins, *Scorpion Tongues: Gossip, Celebrity, and American Politics* (New York: Harper Perennial, 1998), 6.

4. Nan DeMars, *You Want Me To Do What? When, Where and How to Draw the Line at Work* (New York: Touchstone, 1998), 191.

5. Patricia Meyer Spacks, *Gossip* (New York, Alfred A. Knopf, 1985), 25.

6. Louise Collins, "Gossip: A Feminist Defense," 108.

7. Alexander Pope, "Temple of Fame," The Works of Alexander Pope (London: W. Bowyer, 1717), 183.

8. Devin Hakala, "The Poison of Workplace Gossip," in *Healthy Profits: The 5 Elements of Strategic Wellness in the Workplace*, ed. Sandra Larkin (Chicago: Yellow Duck Press, 2009), 163.

9. Nicholas DiFonzo and Prashant Bordia, *Rumor Psychology: Social and Organizational Approaches* (Washington, DC: American Psychological Association, 2007), 22.

10. Gordon Allport and Leo Postman, *The Psychology of Rumor* (New York: Henry Holt, 1947), 75-115.

11. Tomatsu Shibutani, *Improvised News: A Sociological Study of Rumor* (Indianapolis: Bobbs-Merrill, 1966), 9-17.

12. Bob Smith, "Care and Feeding of the Office Grapevine," *Management Review* 85, no. 2 (1996): 6.

13. Gretel C. Kovach, "Highway to Hell," *Newsweek*, December 10, 2007, 58.

14. Ibid.

15. Ibid.

16. David Sloan Wilson and Kevin M. Kniffin, "Utilities of Gossip Across Organizational Levels: Multilevel Selection, Free-Riders, and Teams," *Human Nature* 16, no. 3 (2005): 279-280.

17. See, for example, F. Aureli, C. van Schaik and J. van Hooff, "Functional Aspects of Reconciliation Among Captive Long-Tailed Macaques (Macaca Fascicularis)," *American Journal of Primatology* 19 (1989): 39-51.

18. Wilson and Kniffin, "Utilities of Gossip Across Organizational Levels," 280-281.

19. Ibid., 284-285.

20. Ibid., 285.

21. Patricia Meyer Spacks, *Gossip* (New York: Alfred A. Knopf, 1985), 26.

22. Ralph L. Rosnow and Gary Alan Fine, *Rumor and Gossip: The Social Psychology of Hearsay* (New York: Elsevier Scientific, 1976), 86.

23. Giuseppe (Joe) Labianca, "It's Not 'Unprofessional' to Gossip at Work," *Harvard Business Review* 88, no. 9 (2010): 28.

24. Mike Noon and Rick Delbridge, "News From Behind My Hand: Gossip in Organizations," *Organization Studies* 14, no. 1 (1993): 32, 35.

25. Nicholas DiFonzo and Prashant Bordia, "Rumor, Gossip and Urban Legends," *Diogenes* 54, no. 1 (2007): 19-35.

26. Noon and Delbridge, "News From Behind My Hand," 33.

27. Ilsa M. Glazer and Wahiba Abu Ras, "On Aggression, Human Rights, and Hegemonic Discourse: The Case of a Murder for Family Honor in Israel," *Sex Roles: A Journal of Research* 30, no. 3-4 (1994): 269-288.

28. Martin E.P. Seligman, *Authentic Happiness: Using the New Positive*

*Psychology to Realize Your Potential for Lasting Fulfillment* (New York: Free Press, 2002), xi.

29. Ibid., 13.

## CHAPTER 2

1. "Can Office Gossip Be Banned?" BBC News Talking Point, last modified July 24, 2001, http://news.bbc.co.uk/2/hi/talking_point/1446679.stm.

2. Gail Collins, *Scorpion Tongues: Gossip, Celebrity and American Politics* (New York: Harper Perennial, 1998), 203-206.

3. "Gary Hart Asked Me to Marry Him," *National Enquirer* (Boca Raton, FL), June 2, 1987.

4. Gail Collins, *Scorpion Tongues*, 220.

5. Doris Kerns Goodwin, 109th Landon Lecture, Landon Lecture Series at Kansas State University, Manhattan, KS, April 22, 1997, http://www.k-state.edu/media/newsreleases/landonlect/goodwintext497.html.

6. Mark Twain, *Following the Equator: A Journey Around the World* (Hartford: American Publishing, 1897), http://www.twainquotes.com/Slander.html.

7. Louise Collins, "Gossip: A Feminist Defense," in *Good Gossip*, ed. Robert F. Goodman and Aaron Ben-Ze'ev (Lawrence: University Press of Kansas, 1994), 108.

8. Barbara Fredrickson, *Positivity: Groundbreaking Research Reveals How to Embrace the Hidden Strength of Positive Emotions, Overcome Negativity and Thrive* (New York: Three Rivers Press, 2009), 9.

9. Eric Berne, *Games People Play* (New York: Grove Press, 1967), 110-112.

10. Robert Post, "The Legal Regulation of Gossip: Backyard Chatter and the Mass Media," in *Good Gossip*, ed. Robert F. Goodman and Aaron Ben-Ze'ev (Lawrence: University Press of Kansas, 1994), 67.

11. E.L. Godkin,"The Rights of the Citizen: To His Reputation," *Scribner's Magazine*, July 1890, 65.

12. Melvin v. Reid, 112 Cal.App. 290 (1931).

13. Florida Star v. B.J.F., 491 U.S., 524 (1989).

14. Ken Hardin, "False Workplace Gossip Can Result in Company Liability," *IT Policies, TechRepublic*, last modified March 3, 2003, http://www.techrepublic.com/article/false-workplace-gossip-can-result-in-company-liability.

15. Ibid.

16. Ibid.

17. State of Oregon, Department of Environmental Quality, Anti-Mobbing Policy No. 50.110. (2002), http://www.mobbing-usa.com/

resources/legal-resources/state-of-oregon-department-of-environmental-quality-anti-mobbing-policy-no-50-110.

18. John Holusha, "Students Killed by Gunman at Amish Schoolhouse," *New York Times* (New York, NY), Oct. 2, 2006.

19. Melody Simmons, "After Shooting, Amish School Embodies Effort to Heal," *New York Times* (New York, NY), Jan. 31, 2007.


## CHAPTER 3

1. Jason George, "Gossip's Hurtful Sting Is Sharpened on the Web: But Rumor Sites Now Face Backlash," *Chicago Tribune* (Chicago, IL), March 2, 2008.

2. Ibid.

3. Anna Quindlen, "In Today's World, Everyone Can Gossip Without Remorse," *Herald-News* (Joliet, IL), March 1, 2007.

4. Ibid.

5. Matt Ivester, *lol...OMG! What Every Student Needs to Know About Online Reputation Management, Digital Citizenship and Cyberbullying* (Seattle: Amazon/CreateSpace Independent Publishing Platform, 2011), xv-xx.

6. Kaila White, "Controversial Yik Yak 'Gossip' App Gains Popularity," USA Today Network, last modified December 24, 2014, http://www.usatoday.com/story/news/nation-now/2014/12/24/yik-yak-app-college-arizona/20856275.

7. Kaja Whitehouse, "Water-Cooler App Draws Ire from Companies," *USA Today*, last modified January 16, 2015, http://www.usatoday.com/story/tech/2015/01/16/app-google-ibm-ebay-amazon-wattercooler-anonymous/21815669.

8. "Cyberbullying Facts," *Cyberbullying Research Center*, accessed May 7, 2015, http://cyberbullying.us/facts.

9. Blaine Sampson, telephone interview by Elaine Porterfield, April 12, 2009.

10. Ibid.

11. Ibid.

12. Ibid.

13. Ibid.

14. Ibid.

15. Ibid.

16. Ibid.

17. Ibid.

18. Ibid.

19. Ibid.

20. Ibid.

21. Cy Wakeman, *Reality-Based Leadership: Ditch the Drama, Restore Sanity to the Workplace, and Turn Excuses into Results* (Hoboken, NJ: Jossey-Bass, 2010), 138.

22. Chip Heath and Dan Heath, *Decisive: How to Make Better Choices in Life or Work* (New York: Crown Business, 2013), 160.

23. We recognize that in the field of high technology the results of a 2009 study is ancient history, but it is the most comprehensive we could find at the time the book went to print. This is likely a changing field with the ever increasing use of social media and with industries using social media for marketing purposes. However, the problem of employee misuse of time as it relates to on-the-clock use of social media is still a major issue for employers, and we believe that the problem will most likely increase, not decrease.

24. "Whistle - But Don't Tweet - While You Work," *Robert Half Technology*, last modified October 6, 2009, http://rht.mediaroom.com/index.php?s=131&item=790.

25. Ibid.

26. Ibid.

27. Megan Erickson Moritz, "NLRB Continues Aggressive Response to Employers' Social Media Policies It Deems Overbroad," *Social Networking Law Blog.com*, June 21, 2011, http://www.socialnetworkinglaw-blog.com/2011_06_01_archive.html.

28. "Demanding Facebook Passwords May Be Illegal, Senators Warn Bosses," *Jim Tait, "You're That H.R. Guy,"* Blog Archives, Opi, https://hr2012.wordpress.com/tag/employers.

29. Heath Aston, "Man Jailed over Nude Facebook Photos," *Sydney Morning Herald* (Sydney, Australia), Apr. 22, 2102, http://www.smh.com.au/technology/man-jailed-over-nude-facebook-photos-20120421-1xe2c.html.

30. Ibid.

31. Desmond Tutu, "Quotes," *Goodreads*, accessed May 14, 2013, http://www.goodreads.com/author/quotes/5943.Desmond_Tutu,

## CHAPTER 4

1. Found in numerous places on the web including Sara Gandy, "New Hampshire Town Fires 4 Employees for Gossiping," CBS 42, last modified May 23, 2007, http://keyetv.com/watercooler/watercooler_story_143100705.

2. "Town Settles Federal Employment Lawsuit," *Boston Globe* (Boston, MA), Nov. 2, 2008, http://www.boston.com/news/local/articles/2008/11/02/

rollover_car_crash_on_pike_kills_man_23.

3. Greta Cuyler, "Two of Hooksett 4 File Federal Lawsuit," *Union Leader* (Manchester, NH), Sept. 22, 2007.

4. Lloyd Vries, "N.H. Town Fires 4 Employees for Gossiping," CBS News, last modified May 23, 2007, http://www.cbsnews.com/news/nh-town-fires-4-employees-for-gossiping.

5. Deborah Tannen, *You Just Don't Understand: Women and Men in Conversation* (New York: William Morrow, 1990), 16. We have drawn material from Tannen for this section from several chapters of her excellent book on how the genders communicate, particularly chapters 1 and 2.

6. John Gray, *Men Are from Mars, Women Are from Venus: The Classic Guide to Understanding the Opposite Sex* (New York: HarperCollins, 1992), 3-5.

7. Gail Collins, *Scorpion Tongues: Gossip, Celebrity, and American Politics* (New York: Harper Perennial, 1999), 40.

8. Jack Levin and Arnold Arluke, "An Exploratory Analysis of Sex Differences in Gossip," *Sex Roles: A Journal of Research* 12, nos. 3/4 (1985), 283.

9. Ibid., 284.

10. Linell Nash Smith, ed., "Don't Even Tell Your Wife, Particularly," *The Best of Ogden Nash* (Chicago: Ivan R. Dee, 2007), 56-57.

11. Hara Estroff Marano, "The New Sex Scorecard," *Psychology Today*, July/August 2003, 39.

12. Louann Brizendine, *The Female Brain* (New York: Broadway Books, 2006), 2.

13. Ibid., 3.

14. Ibid., xvii.

15. Ibid., 21.

16. Ibid., 34-35.

17. Deborah Jones, "Gossip: Notes on Women's Oral Culture," in *The Feminist Critique of Language*, ed. Deborah Cameron (New York: Routledge, 1990), 243.

18. Ibid.

19. Tannen, *You Just Don't Understand*, 13-22.

20. Ibid., 24-25.

21. Ibid., 119

22. Ibid., 108.

23. Ibid.

24. Ibid., 117.

25. Ibid., 96.

26. Ibid., 96.

27. Ibid., 97.

28. Ibid., 119-120.

29. Levin and Arluke, "An Exploratory Analysis of Sex Differences in Gossip," 283.

30. Ibid.

31. Barbara Westbrook Eakins and R. Gene Eakins, *Sex Differences in Human Communication* (New York: Houghton Mifflin, 1978), 113.

32. Erin McGrane and Jeff Freling, "Dirt Dishin' Daisy," from *Victor & Penny: Antique Pop*, V&P Productions, LLC, 2011, compact disc.

## CHAPTER 5

1. Joseph Telushkin, *Words That Hurt, Words That Heal: How to Choose Words Wisely and Well* (New York: Harper, 1996), 3.

2. Matthew 7:12 and Luke 6:3. All Bible quotations are taken from the Harper Collins Study Bible, (New York: Harper Collins, 1989), unless otherwise noted.

3. Yisrael Meir HaCohen, Chofetz Chaim (1873) as quoted by Stephen Baars, "All About Gossip," *Torah Portion: Tazria, aish.com*, accessed May 29, 2006, www.aish.com.

4. Franklin Lewis, *Rumi: Past and Present, East and West: The Life, Teachings and Poetry of Jalal al-Din Rumi* (London: Oneworld Publications, 2008), 409.

5. Miguel Ruiz, *The Four Agreements: A Practical Guide to Personal Freedom* (San Rafael, CA: Amber-Allen, 1997), 26.

6. Ephesians 4:29.

7. Richard Engel, "Timbuktu: A Journey to Africa's Lost City of Gold," NBCNews.com, accessed February 2, 2013, http://www.nbcnews.com/id/39563268/ns/world_news-africa/t/timbuktu-journey-africas-lost-city-gold/#.VRL-t-FUWYU.

8. Ibid.

9. Stephen Baars, "All About Gossip," *Torah Portion: Tazria, aish.com*, accessed May 29, 2006, www.aish.com.

10. Shariffa Al Andalusia, "Gheebah," accessed May 29, 2006, www.islamawareness.net/Backbiting/gheebah.html.

11. Proverbs 6:16.

12. "The Sin of Gossip and Tale Bearing," accessed May 29, 2006, www.wolfeborobible.com.

13. Joseph Epstein, *Gossip: The Untrivial Pursuit* (New York: Houghton Mifflin Harcourt, 2011), 214.

14. Original printed source and author unknown.

15. Stephen Baars, "All About Gossip," *Torah Portion: Tazria*, www.aish.com.

16. Ibid.

17. Asher Meir, "How to Protect Yourself from Listening to Office Gossip," *JCT Center for Jewish Ethics, aish.com*, accessed October 13, 2005, www.aish.com.

18. Ibid.

19. Tracey R. Rich, "Speech and Lashon Ha-Ra," *Judaism 101*, accessed May 29, 2006, http://www.jewfaq.org/speech.htm.

20. Ibid.

21. Leviticus 19:15.

22. Jamal Rahman. Interview by Timothy Williams, Seattle, Washington, April 7, 2009.

23. Ibid.

24. Husayn al-Awayishah, *Backbiting and Its Adverse Effects* (Riyadh: International Islamic Publishing House, 2009), 12.

25. Ibid., 55.

26. Al Andalusia, "Gheebah," www.islamawareness.net/Backbiting/gheebah.html.

27. Sutta Nipata 657.

28. Barbara O'Brien, "Right Speech: The Buddha's Words," accessed May 13, 2015, http//Buddhism.about.com/od/theeightfoldpath/a/eightfoldpath.htm.

29. Ibid.

30. Ibid.

31. The original Sanskrit Panchatantra is attributed to Vishnu Sharma and was composed around the 3rd century BC, according to scholars.

32. Radhanath Swami, "Bahagavad-gita," accessed September 5, 2012, www.radhanathswami.com/tag/bhagavad-gita.

33. Anonymous story passed around on the Internet.

34. Meir, "How to Protect Yourself from Listening to Office Gossip," www.aish.com.

## CHAPTER 6

1. T.J. Grosser, V. Lopez-Kidwell and G. Labianca, "A Social Network Analysis of Positive and Negative Gossip in Organizational Life," *Group & Organization Management* 35 (2010):177-212.

2. Sam Chapman and Bridget Sharkey, *The No-Gossip Zone: A No-Nonsense Guide to a Healthy, High-Performing Work Environment* (Naperville, IL: Sourcebooks, 2009), 9-10.

3. Giuseppe (Joe) Labianca, "It's Not 'Unprofessional' to Gossip at Work," *Harvard Business Review* 88, no. 9 (2010): 28.

4. This is an old concept practiced by many. An overview appears in Thomas J. Peters and Robert H. Waterman, Jr., *In Search of Excellence:*

*Lessons from America's Best-Run Companies* (New York: Harper Business, 2006), 122.

5. Mark Twain, *Mark Twain's Letters from Hawaii* (Honolulu: University of Hawaii Press, 1975), 144.

6. Chapman and Sharkey, *The No-Gossip Zone*, 1.

7. One good source is Daniel Goleman, Richard Boyatzis and Annie McKee, *Primal Leadership: Learning to Lead With Emotional Intelligence* (Boston: Harvard Business Review Press, 2013), 7.

8. Thich Nhat Hanh, *The Heart of Buddha's Teaching: Transforming Suffering into Peace, Joy and Liberation* (New York: Broadway Books, 1998), 86.

9. Deborah Smith Pegues, *30 Days to Taming Your Tongue* (Eugene, OR: Harvest House, 2005), 7.

10. Ibid.

11. Lori Palatnik and Bob Burg, *Gossip, Ten Pathways to Eliminate It from Your Life and Transform Your Soul* (Deerfield Beach, FL: Health Communications, 2002), xix.

12. Ibid.

13. Gary Chapman and Paul White, *The Five Languages of Appreciation in the Workplace: Empowering Organizations by Encouraging People* (Chicago: Northfield Publishing, 2011), 25.

14. Ibid., 21.

15. Ellen J. Langer, *Mindfulness* (Cambridge, MA: Perseus Books, 1989), 9.

16. Palatnik and Burg, *Gossip: Ten Pathways to Eliminate It*, xix.

## CHAPTER 7

1. Jack Levin and Arnold Arluke, *Gossip: The Inside Scoop* (New York: Plenum Press, 1987), 3.

2. Mike Noon and Rick Delbridge, "News from Behind My Hand: Gossip in Organizations," *Organization Studies* 14, no. 1 (1993): 35.

3. Martin E. P. Seligman, *What You Can Change and What You Can't: The Complete Guide to Successful Self-Improvement* (New York: Vintage Books, 2007), 4-5.

4. Martin Luther King, Jr., address at Western Michigan University "Conscience of America" Symposium, Kalamazoo, MI, December 18, 1963. Available from many sources including Marcus D. Pohlmann, *African American Political Thought* (New York: Routledge, 2003), 34.

5. A concept developed in Art Dykstra's book *Outcome Management: Achieving Outcomes for People with Disabilities* (Homewood, IL: High Tide Press, 1995), 14-15. Skills and abilities dissipate over time if not

renewed (leaking), and we can lose our concentration on goals and objectives (straying).

6. Martin E. P. Seligman, *Authentic Happiness: Using the New Positive Psychology to Realize Your Potential for Lasting Fulfillment* (New York: Simon & Schuster, 2002), 3.

7. Ibid., 4.

8. ___, *Flourish: A Visionary New Understanding of Happiness and Well-Being* (New York: Free Press, 2012), 2.

9. Michael Burchell and Jennifer Robin, *The Great Workplace: How to Build It, How to Keep It and Why It Matters* (San Francisco: Jossey-Bass, 2011), 7-11.

10. Gerard Egan, *Working the Shadow Side: A Guide to Positive Behind-the-Scenes Management* (San Francisco: Jossey-Bass, 1994), xiii-xiv.

11. Ibid., xiv.

12. Nancy Austin and Thomas J. Peters, *A Passion for Excellence: The Leadership Difference* (New York: Grand Central, 1989), 3.

13. Ibid., 8.

14. Ibid., 9.

15. Daniel Goleman, Richard Boyatzis and Annie McKee, *Primal Leadership: Realizing the Power of Emotional Intelligence* (Boston: Harvard Business School Publishing, 2002), ix.

16. Ibid.

17. Ibid., 5.

18. Attributed to Mahatma Gandhi. Original printed source unknown.

19. Mahatma Gandhi, *The Collected Works of Mahatma Gandhi*, Vol. 13 (Electronic book) (New Delhi: Publications Division Government of India, 1999), 241.

20. Gary Chapman and Paul White, *The Five Languages of Appreciation in the Workplace: Empowering Organizations by Encouraging People* (Chicago: Northfield Publishing, 2011), 11.

21. Ibid., 47.

22. Ibid., 61.

23. Ibid., 77.

24. Ibid., 89.

25. Ibid., 101.

26. Ibid., 21-22.

27. Will Bowen, *A Complaint Free World: How to Stop Complaining and Start Enjoying the Life You Always Wanted* (New York: Doubleday, 2007), 1.

28. Ibid., 3.

29. Ibid., 4.

30. Ibid., 14-15.

31. Ibid., 17.

32. Ibid.

33. Lori Palatnik and Bob Burg, *Gossip: Ten Pathways to Eliminate It From Your Life and Transform Your Soul* (Deerfield Beach, FL: Health Communications, 2002), xvii-xviii.

34. Gretchen Rubin, *The Happiness Project: Or, Why I Spent a Year Trying to Sing in the Morning, Clean My Closets, Fight Right, Read Aristotle and Generally Have More Fun* (New York: Harper, 2011), 40.

35. Ibid., 297.

36. George Suess, "What Would Emeril Do?" *Perdido: Leadership with a Conscience*, Winter 2006, 15.

37. Ibid., 17.

38. McKay Coppins, "Here's Why BYU's Honor Code Outranks March Madness," *Business Insider,* last modified March 4, 2011, http://www.businessinsider.com/heres-why-byus-honor-code-outranks-march-madness-2011-3?op=1.

39. Ibid.

40. Peter M. Senge, *The Fifth Discipline: The Art & Practice of the Learning Organization* (New York: Doubleday, 1990), 14.

41. Seligman, *Flourish*, 152-181.

42. Art Dykstra, "Why Not Happidents," *Perdido: Leadership with a Conscience*, Summer 2004, 2.

43. Dick Grote, *Discipline Without Punishment: The Proven Strategy That Turns Problem Employees into Superior Performers* (New York: AMACOM, 1995), 1-2.

44. Timothy Williams and Martie Geltz, "Watering the Periwinkle," *Perdido: Leadership with a Conscience*, Spring 2003, 16-17.

## CHAPTER 8

1. Joseph Telushkin, *Words That Hurt, Words That Heal: How to Choose Words Wisely and Well* (New York: Harper, 1996), xviii.

2. Ibid., xix.

3. Art Buchwald, "Love and the Cabbie," *Chicken Soup for the Soul 20th Anniversary Edition*, ed. Jack Canfield and Mark Victor Hansen (Cos Cob, CT: Chicken Soup for the Soul, 2013), 55-57.

4. Martin E.P. Seligman, *Flourish: A Visionary New Understanding of Happiness and Well-Being* (New York: Simon & Schuster, 2011), 48.

5. Ibid., 49.

6. Roger Fisher and Scott Brown, *Getting Together: Building Relationships As We Negotiate* (Boston: Houghton Mifflin, 1988), 38.

7. Ibid.

8. Robert Kegan and Lisa Laskow Lahey, *How the Way We Talk Can Change the Way We Work: Seven Languages for Transformation* (San Francisco: Jossey-Bass, 2001), 18.

9. Ibid., 19.

10. Ibid., 7.

11. Ibid., 8.

12. David Cooperrider, foreword to *Appreciative Inquiry: Change at the Speed of Imagination,* Jane Magruder Watkins and Bernard J. Mohr (San Francisco: Jossey-Bass/Pfeiffer, 2001), xxviii.

13. One of the authors first heard Carl Rogers express this point on an old audio tape which is no longer accessible. Wikipedia, in a lengthy article on Rogers provides an outline of his basic theory in a 19-point summation and then adds that "Rogers is known for practicing 'unconditional positive regard,' defined as accepting a person "without negative judgment of.... [a person's] basic worth." http://en.wikipedia.org/wiki/Carl_Rogers.

14. Karen Lawson and Karen M. Miller, *Improving Workplace Performance Through Coaching* (West Des Moines, IA: American Media, 1996), 12.

15. Tom Rath and Donald O. Clifton, *How Full Is Your Bucket?* (New York: Gallup Press, 2004), 5.

16. Ibid.

17. Ibid., 17.

18. Ibid.

## CHAPTER 9

1. Jack Levin and Arnold Arluke, *Gossip: The Inside Scoop* (New York: Plenum Press, 1987), 16.

2. Tom Rath and Donald O. Clifton, *How Full Is Your Bucket?* (New York: Gallup Press, 2004), 15.

3. Barbara L. Fredrickson, *Positivity: Groundbreaking Research Reveals How to Embrace the Hidden Strength of Positive Emotions, Overcome Negativity and Thrive* (New York: Three Rivers Press, 2009), 17.

4. "Habit," *The American Heritage Dictionary of the English Language* (Boston: Houghton Mifflin, 1979), 590.

5. Charles Duhigg, *The Power of Habit: Why We Do What We Do in Life and Business* (New York: Random House, 2012), xiv-xv.

6. Stephen R. Covey, *The 7 Habits of Highly Effective People: Restoring the Character Ethic* (New York: Simon & Schuster, 1989), 46.

7. Duhigg, *The Power of Habit*, xv-xvii.

8. Ibid., xv-xvi.

9. Ibid., xiv.

10. Ibid., 19.

11. Ibid., 20.

12. Ibid., 109.

13. Ibid., 109.

14. Eric Allenbaugh, *Deliberate Success: Realize Your Vision with Purpose, Passion and Performance* (Franklin Lakes, NJ: Career Press, 2002), 50.

15. Tim Sanders, *Love Is the Killer App: How to Win Business and Influence Friends* (New York: Crown Business, 2002), 12.

16. Ibid., 12.

17. Allenbaugh, *Deliberate Success*, 55.

18. Ibid., 60.

19. Ibid., 61.

20. Ibid., 57.

21. Ibid., 64.

22. Ibid., 67-90.

23. Martin E.P. Seligman, *Flourish: A Visionary New Understanding of Happiness and Well-Being* (New York: Free Press, 2011), 149.

24. Ibid., 150.

25. Jim Loehr and Tony Schwartz, *The Power of Full Engagement: Managing Energy, Not Time, Is the Key to High Performance and Personal Renewal* (New York: Free Press, 2003), 4.

26. Ibid., 110.

27. Ibid.

28. Duhigg, *The Power of Habit*, 85.

29. *Carry Your Own Weather* is a training video that is used as part of a signature program by The Franklin Covey Company.

30. Barbara L. Fredrickson, *Positivity: Groundbreaking Research Reveals How to Embrace the Hidden Strength of Positive Emotions, Overcome Negativity and Thrive* (New York: Three Rivers Press, 2009), 3-9.

31. Ibid., 32.

32. Selgiman, *Flourish*, 67.

33. Gerald R. Miller and Michael Burgoon, *New Techniques of Persuasion* (New York: Harper and Row, 1973), 14.

34. Thich Nhat Hanh, *Being Peace* (Berkeley: Parallax Press, 1987), 13.

## CHAPTER 10

1. C. S. Lewis, *The Great Divorce* (New York: HarperSanFrancisco, 1946), x.

2. Ibid.

3. Ibid., 98-104.

4. Ibid., 71.

5. Ibid., 68.

6. Ibid., 132-133.

7. "Blunt Words from Pope Francis," *Chicago Tribune* (Chicago, IL), Dec. 24, 2014.

8. "Ibid.

9. Jan-Erik Jones, "Size Matters Not: The Force as the Causal Power of the Jedi," in *Star Wars and Philosophy: More Powerful Than You Can Possibly Imagine*, ed. Kevin S. Decker and Jason T. Eberl (Peru, IL: Carus, 2005), 132.

10. Ibid.

11. Steven A. Galipeau, *The Journey of Luke Skywalker: An Analysis of Modern Myth and Symbol* (Chicago: Open Court, 2001), 29.

12. "The Force," *Wookieepedia: The Star Wars Wiki*, accessed March 2, 2015, http://starwars.wikia.com/wiki/The_Force.

13. "Book of Sith," *Wookieepedia, The Star Wars Wiki*, accessed March 2, 2015, http://starwars.wikia.com/wiki/Book_of_Sith.

14. "Dark Side (Star Wars)," *Wikipedia: The Free Encyclopedia*, accessed March 2, 2015, https://en.wikipedia.org/wiki/Dark_side_%28Star_Wars%29.

15. Ibid.

16. Ibid.

17. Ibid.

18. Judith Barad, "The Aspiring Jedi's Handbook of Virtue," in *Star Wars and Philosophy: More Powerful Than You Can Possibly Imagine*, ed. Kevin S. Decker and Jason T. Eberl (Peru, IL: Carus, 2005), 63.

19. Jon Gordon, *The Positive Dog: A Story About the Power of Positivity* (Hoboken, NJ: John Wiley & Sons, 2012), 3-4.

20. Ibid., 4.

21. Jodi Detrick, "'Gracious Living' Refers to How You Treat Others, Not to What You Own," *Seattle Times* (Seattle, WA), Sept. 1, 2007.

22. "Letters to the Editor: The Revered Dale Turner," *Seattle Times* (Seattle, WA), June 10, 2006.

23. Dale Turner, *Imperfect Alternatives: Spiritual Insights for Confronting the Controversial and the Personal* (Homewood, IL: High Tide Press, 2005), 93.

24. Ibid.

25. ___, *Different Seasons: Twelve Months of Wisdom and Inspiration* (Homewood, IL: High Tide Press, 1997), xvi.

## AFTERTHOUGHT

1.  "Biggest Workplace Pet Peeves," Ipsos Public Affairs-Randstad Survey, *USA Today*, June 9, 2010.

2.  Louise Collins, "Gossip: A Feminist Defense," in *Good Gossip*, ed. Robert F. Goodman and Aaron Ben-Ze'ev (Lawrence: University Press of Kansas, 1994), 108.

3.  Jack Levin and Arnold Arluke, "An Exploratory Analysis of Sex Differences in Gossip," *Sex Roles: A Journal of Research* 12, nos.3-4 (1985): 283.

4.  Kathleen Kelleher, "Pssst! Heard the Latest About Gossiping? Can You Believe It?" *Los Angeles Times* (Los Angeles, CA), May 19, 1998.

5.  John Kowalewski, "Psst…Have You Heard the Latest on Gossip?" *Weber State University*, last modified October 17, 2005, http://www.weber.edu/WSUToday/101705gossip.html.

6.  Ibid.

7.  John P. Kotter, *Power and Influence: Beyond Formal Authority* (New York: Free Press, 1985), 117-168. Part III of the book focuses on the life cycle of an employee in an organization and repeatedly addresses the need to achieve power and influence through effective positive communication and the development of healthy relationships.

8.  Ibid., vii.

9.  Ibid., 9.

10. Ibid., 17-18.

11. Ibid., 40.

12. Ibid., 88.

13. Nicole Winfield, "Pope Warns Against Mediocrity, Gossip in Vatican," *AP: The Big Story*, last modified December 21, 2013, http://bigstory.ap.org/article/pope-warns-against-mediocrity-gossip-vatican.

14. Ibid.

15. Susan Dunn, "Office Gossip: An HR Challenge," *WebProNews*, last modified November 12, 2002, http://www.webpronews.com/office-gossip-an-hr-challenge-2002-11.

16. Samuel Greengard, "Gossip Poisons Business: HR Can Stop It," *Workforce* 80, no. 7 (2001), http://www.workforce.com/articles/print/gossip-poisons-business-hr-can-stop-it.

17. Ibid.

18. Ibid.

19. Mike Noon and Rick Delbridge, "News From Behind My Hand: Gossip in Organizations," *Organization Studies* 14, no. 1 (1993), 35.

20. "Gossip: A 'Necessary Evil' at Work," *Nursing Standard* 17, no. 31 (2003), 6.

21. Ibid.

22.   Kaia Whitehouse, "Water-Cooler App Draws Ire from Companies," *USA Today*, last modified January 16, 2015, http://www.usatoday.com/story/tech/2015/01/16/app-google-ibm-ebay-amazon-wattercooler-anony-mous/21815669.

23.   See, for example, Robert D. Nye, *Conflict Among Humans: Some Basic Psychological and Social Psychological Considerations* (New York: Springer, 1973).

24.   Richard Nordquist, "Phatic Communication," *About.com*, accessed December 16, 2012, http://grammar.about.com/od/pq/g/phaticterm.htm.

25.   Marshall Berman, "Weird and Brilliant Light on the Way We Live Now," *New York Times* (New York NY), Feb. 27, 1972.

26.   There are two sources for this bit of history and the gossip had many different versions. Jon Meacham, *American Lion: Andrew Jackson in the White House* (New York: Random House, 2008), 89-90, 114-115, and Gail Collins, *Scorpion Tongues: Gossip, Celebrity, and American Politics* (New York: Harper Perennial, 2007), 41.

27.   Guiseppe (Joe) Labianca, "It's Not 'Unprofessional' to Gossip at Work," *Harvard Business Review* 88, no. 9 (2010): 29.

28.   Noon and Delbridge, "News from Behind My Hand." 35-36.

29.   Ralph L. Rosnow and Eric K. Foster, "Rumor and Gossip Research," *American Psychological Association, Psychological Science Agenda* 19, no. 4 (April 2005), http://www.apa.org/science/about/psa/2005/04/gossip.aspx.

30.   Luke Ford, "Gossip as a Gauge of a Religion's Commitment to Reality," *Luke Ford* (blog), accessed April 30, 2015, www.lukeford.net/Dennis/indexp271.html.

31.   Colin Powell, *It Worked for Me: In Life and Leadership* (New York: HarperCollins, 2012), 241.

32.   Jeremy Hainsworth and Toby Sterling, "Suspect Arrested in Cyber-Harassment Death," *Seattle Times* (Seattle, WA), Apr. 18, 2014, http://www.seattletimes.com/nation-world/suspect-arrested-in-cyber-harassment-death.

33.   Masaru Emoto, *The Hidden Messages in Water* (New York: Atria Books, 2001), xxvi.

# BIBLIOGRAPHY

Al Andalusia, Shariffa. "Gheebah." Accessed May 29, 2006. www.isla-mawareness.net/Backbiting/gheebah.html.

al-Awayishah, Husayn. *Backbiting and Its Adverse Effects*. Riyadh: International Islamic Publishing House, 2009.

Allenbaugh, Eric. *Deliberate Success: Realize Your Vision with Purpose, Passion and Performance*. Franklin Lakes, NJ: Career Press, 2002.

Allport, Gordon, and Leo Postman. *The Psychology of Rumor*. New York: Henry Holt, 1947.

Aston, Heath. "Man Jailed over Nude Facebook Photos." *Sydney Morning Herald* (Sydney, Australia), Apr. 22, 2012. http://www.smh.com.au/technology/man-jailed-over-nude-facebook-photos-20120421-1xe2c.html.

Aureli, F., C. van Schaik and J. van Hooff. "Functional Aspects of Reconciliation Among Captive Long-Tailed Macaques (Macaca Fascicularis)." *American Journal of Primatology* 19 (1989): 39-51.

Austin, Nancy, and Thomas J. Peters, *A Passion for Excellence: The Leadership Difference*. New York: Grand Central, 1989.

Baars, Stephen. "All About Gossip," *Torah Portion: Tazria. aish.com*. Accessed May 29, 2006. www.aish.com.

Barad, Judith. "The Aspiring Jedi's Handbook of Virtue." In *Star Wars and Philosophy: More Powerful Than You Can Possibly Imagine*, 57-68. Edited by Kevin S. Decker and Jason T. Eberl. Peru, IL: Carus, 2005.

Berman, Marshall. "Weird and Brilliant Light on the Way We Live Now." *New York Times* (New York NY), Feb. 27, 1972.

Berne, Eric. *Games People Play*. New York: Grove Press, 1967.

"Biggest Workplace Pet Peeves." Ipsos Public Affairs-Randstad Survey. *USA Today*, June 9, 2010.

"Blunt Words from Pope Francis." *Chicago Tribune* (Chicago, IL), Dec. 24, 2014.

Bowen, Will. *A Complaint Free World: How to Stop Complaining and Start Enjoying the Life You Always Wanted*. New York: Doubleday, 2007.

Brizendine, Louann. *The Female Brain*. New York: Broadway Books, 2006.

Buchwald, Art. "Love and the Cabbie." *Chicken Soup for the Soul 20th Anniversary Edition*, 55-57. Edited by Jack Canfield and Mark Victor Hansen. Cos Cob, CT: Chicken Soup for the Soul, 2013.

Burchell, Michael, and Jennifer Robin. *The Great Workplace: How to Build It, How to Keep It and Why It Matters*. San Francisco: Jossey-Bass, 2011.

"Can Office Gossip Be Banned?" BBC News Talking Point. Last modified July 24, 2001. http://news.bbc.co.uk/2/hi/talking_point/1446679.stm.

Chapman, Gary, and Paul White. *The Five Languages of Appreciation in the Workplace: Empowering Organizations by Encouraging People*. Chicago: Northfield Publishing, 2011.

Chapman, Sam, and Bridget Sharkey. *The No-Gossip Zone: A No-Nonsense Guide to a Healthy, High-Performing Work Environment*. Naperville, IL: Sourcebooks, 2009.

Collins, Gail. *Scorpion Tongues: Gossip, Celebrity, and American Politics.* New York: Harper Perennial, 1998.

Collins, Louise. "Gossip: A Feminist Defense." In *Good Gossip*, 106-114. Edited by Robert F. Goodman and Aaron Ben-Ze'ev. Lawrence: University Press of Kansas, 1994.

Cooperrider, David. Foreword to *Appreciative Inquiry: Change at the Speed of Imagination.* Jane Magruder Watkins and Bernard J. Mohr. San Francisco: Jossey-Bass/Pfeiffer, 2001.

Covey, Stephen R. *The 7 Habits of Highly Effective People: Restoring the Character Ethic.* New York: Simon & Schuster, 1989.

Cuyler, Greta. "Two of Hooksett 4 File Federal Lawsuit." *Union Leader* (Manchester, NH), Sept. 22, 2007.

"Cyberbullying Facts." *Cyberbullying Research Center.* Accessed May 7, 2015. http://cyberbullying.us/facts.

"Demanding Facebook Passwords May Be Illegal, Senators Warn Bosses." *Jim Tait, "You're That H.R. Guy."* Blog Archives. Opi. https://hr2012. wordpress.com/tag/employers.

DeMars, Nan. *You Want Me To Do What? When, Where and How to Draw the Line at Work.* New York: Touchstone, 1998.

Detrick, Jodi. "'Gracious Living' Refers to How You Treat Others, Not to What You Own." *Seattle Times* (Seattle, WA), Sept. 1, 2007.

DiFonzo, Nicholas, and Prashant Bordia. "Rumor, Gossip and Urban Legends." *Diogenes* 54, no. 1 (2007): 19-35.

___. *Rumor Psychology: Social and Organizational Approaches.* Washington, DC: American Psychological Association, 2007.

Duhigg, Charles. *The Power of Habit: Why We Do What We Do in Life and Business.* New York: Random House, 2012.

Susan Dunn. "Office Gossip: An HR Challenge." *WebProNews.*" Last modified November 12, 2002. http://www.webpronews.com/office-gossip-an-hr-challenge-2002-11.

Dykstra, Art. *Outcome Management: Achieving Outcomes for People with Disabilities.* Homewood, IL: High Tide Press, 1995.

__. "Why Not Happidents." *Perdido: Leadership with a Conscience,* Summer 2004.

Eakins, Barbara Westbrook, and R. Gene Eakins. *Sex Differences in Human Communication.* New York: Houghton Mifflin, 1978.

Egan, Gerard. *Working the Shadow Side: A Guide to Positive Behind-the-Scenes Management.* San Francisco: Jossey-Bass, 1994.

Emoto, Masaru. *The Hidden Messages in Water.* New York: Atria Books, 2001.

Engel, Richard. "Timbuktu: A Journey to Africa's Lost City of Gold." NBCNews.com. Accessed February 2, 2013. http://www.nbcnews.com/id/39563268/ns/world_news-africa/t/timbuktu-journey-africas-lost-city-gold/#.VRL-t-FUWYU.

Epstein, Joseph. *Gossip: The Untrivial Pursuit.* New York: Houghton Mifflin Harcourt, 2011.

Fisher, Roger, and Scott Brown. *Getting Together: Building Relationships As We Negotiate.* Boston: Houghton Mifflin, 1988.

Ford, Luke. "Gossip as a Gauge of a Religion's Commitment to Reality." *Luke Ford* (blog). Accessed April 30, 2015. www.lukeford.net/Dennis/indexp271.html.

Fredrickson, Barbara L. *Positivity: Groundbreaking Research Reveals How to Embrace the Hidden Strength of Positive Emotions, Overcome Negativity and Thrive.* New York: Three Rivers Press, 2009.

Galipeau, Steven A. *The Journey of Luke Skywalker: An Analysis of Modern Myth and Symbol.* Chicago: Open Court, 2001.

Gandhi, Mahatma. *The Collected Works of Mahatma Gandhi,* Vol. 13. (Electronic book.) New Delhi: Publications Division Government of India, 1999.

Gandy, Sara. "New Hampshire Town Fires 4 Employees for Gossiping." CBS

42. Last modified May 23, 2007. http://keyetv.com/watercooler/water-cooler_story_143100705.

"Gary Hart Asked Me to Marry Him." *National Enquirer* (Boca Raton, FL), June 2, 1987.

George, Jason. "Gossip's Hurtful Sting Is Sharpened on the Web: But Rumor Sites Now Face Backlash." *Chicago Tribune* (Chicago, IL), Mar. 2, 2008.

Glazer, Ilsa M., and Wahiba Abu Ras. "On Aggression, Human Rights, and Hegemonic Discourse: The Case of a Murder for Family Honor in Israel." *Sex Roles: A Journal of Research* 30, no. 3-4 (1994): 269-288.

Godkin, E.L. "The Rights of the Citizen: To His Reputation." *Scribner's Magazine*, July 1890.

Goleman, Daniel, Richard Boyatzis and Annie McKee. *Primal Leadership: Learning to Lead with Emotional Intelligence.* Boston: Harvard Business Review Press, 2013.

Goodwin, Doris Kerns. 109th Landon Lecture, Landon Lecture Series at Kansas State University, Manhattan, KS, April 22, 1997. http://www.k-state.edu/media/newsreleases/landonlect/goodwintext497.html.

Gordon, Jon. *The Positive Dog: A Story About the Power of Positivity.* Hoboken, NJ.: John Wiley & Sons, 2012.

"Gossip." *Wikipedia: The Free Encyclopedia.* Accessed April 20, 2015. http://en.wikipedia.org/wiki/Gossip.

"Gossip: A 'Necessary Evil' at Work." *Nursing Standard* 17, no. 31 (2003): 6.

Gray, John. *Men Are from Mars, Women Are from Venus: The Classic Guide to Understanding the Opposite Sex.* New York: HarperCollins, 1992.

Greengard, Samuel. "Gossip Poisons Business: HR Can Stop It." *Workforce* 80, no. 7 (2001): 24-28.

Grosser, T.J., V. Lopez-Kidwell and G. Labianca. "A Social Network Analysis of Positive and Negative Gossip in Organizational Life." *Group & Organization Management* 35 (2010): 177-212.

Grote, Dick. *Discipline Without Punishment: The Proven Strategy That Turns Problem Employees into Superior Performers*. New York: AMACOM, 1995.

HaCohen, Yisrael Meir. Chofetz Chaim (1873). In "All About Gossip," *Torah Portion: Tazria*. By Stephen Baars. *aish.com*, Accessed May 29, 2006. www.aish.com.

Hainsworth, Jeremy, and Toby Sterling. "Suspect Arrested in Cyber-Harassment Death." *Seattle Times* (Seattle, WA). Last modified April 18, 2014. http://www.seattletimes.com/nation-world/suspect-arrested-in-cyber-harassment-death.

Hakala, Devin. "The Poison of Workplace Gossip." In *Healthy Profits: The 5 Elements of Strategic Wellness in the Workplace*, 163-166. Edited by Sandra Larkin. Chicago: Yellow Duck Press, 2009.

Hanh, Thich Nhat. *Being Peace*. Berkeley: Parallax Press, 1987.

___. *The Heart of Buddha's Teaching: Transforming Suffering into Peace, Joy and Liberation*. New York: Broadway Books, 1998.

Hardin, Ken. "False Workplace Gossip Can Result in Company Liability." *IT Policies, TechRepublic*. Last modified March 3, 2003. http://www.techrepublic.com/article/false-workplace-gossip-can-result-in-company-liability.

Heath, Chip, and Dan Heath. *Decisive: How to Make Better Choices in Life or Work*. New York: Crown Business, 2013.

Holusha, John. "Students Killed by Gunman at Amish Schoolhouse." *New York Times* (New York, NY), Oct. 2, 2006.

Ivester, Matt. *lol...OMG! What Every Student Needs to Know About Online Reputation Management, Digital Citizenship and Cyberbullying*. Seattle: Amazon/CreateSpace Independent Publishing Platform, 2011.

Jones, Deborah. "Gossip: Notes on Women's Oral Culture." In *The Feminist Critique of Language*, 242-245. Edited by Deborah Cameron. New York: Routledge, 1990.

Jones, Jan-Erik. "Size Matters Not: The Force as the Causal Power of the

Jedi." In *Star Wars and Philosophy: More Powerful Than You Can Possibly Imagine*. Edited by Kevin S. Decker and Jason T. Eberl, 132-143. Peru, IL: Carus, 2005.

Kegan, Robert, and Lisa Laskow Lahey. *How the Way We Talk Can Change the Way We Work: Seven Languages for Transformation*. San Francisco: Jossey-Bass, 2001.

Kelleher, Kathleen. "Pssst! Heard the Latest About Gossiping? Can You Believe It?" *Los Angeles Times* (Los Angeles, CA), May 19, 1998.

King, Martin Luther, Jr. Address at Western Michigan University "Conscience of America" Symposium, Kalamazoo, MI, December 18, 1963.

Kotter, John P. *Power and Influence: Beyond Formal Authority*. New York: Free Press, 1985.

Kovach, Gretel C. "Highway to Hell." *Newsweek*, December 10, 2007.

Kowalewski, John. "Psst...Have You Heard the Latest on Gossip?" *Weber State University*. Last modified October 17, 2005. http://www.weber.edu/WSUToday/101705gossip.html.

Labianca, Giuseppe (Joe). "It's Not 'Unprofessional' to Gossip at Work." *Harvard Business Review* 88, no. 9 (2010): 28-29.

Langer, Ellen J. *Mindfulness*. Cambridge, MA: Perseus Books, 1989.

Lawson, Karen, and Karen M. Miller. *Improving Workplace Performance Through Coaching*. West Des Moines, IA: American Media, 1996.

Levin, Jack, and Arnold Arluke. "An Exploratory Analysis of Sex Differences in Gossip." *Sex Roles: A Journal of Research* 12, nos. 3/4 (1985), 281-286.

___. *Gossip: The Inside Scoop*. New York: Plenum Press, 1987.

Lewis, C. S. *The Great Divorce*. New York: HarperSanFrancisco, 1946.

Lewis, Franklin. *Rumi: Past and Present, East and West: The Life, Teachings and Poetry of Jalal al-Din Rumi*. London: Oneworld Publications, 2008.

Loehr, Jim, and Tony Schwartz, *The Power of Full Engagement: Managing*

*Energy, Not Time, Is the Key to High Performance and Personal Renewal.* New York: Free Press, 2003.

Marano, Hara Estroff. "The New Sex Scorecard." *Psychology Today*, July/August 2003.

McGrane, Erin, and Jeff Freling, "Dirt Dishin' Daisy." From *Victor & Penny: Antique Pop*, V&P Productions, LLC, 2011, compact disc.

Meir, Asher. "How to Protect Yourself from Listening to Office Gossip." *JCT Center for Jewish Ethics. aish.com.* Accessed October 13, 2005. www.aish.com.

Meacham, Jon. *American Lion: Andrew Jackson in the White House.* New York: Random House, 2008.

Miller, Gerald R., and Michael Burgoon. *New Techniques of Persuasion.* New York: Harper and Row, 1973.

Moritz, Megan Erickson. "NLRB Continues Aggressive Response to Employers' Social Media Policies It Deems Overbroad." *Social Networking Law Blog.com*, June 21, 2011. http://www.socialnetworkinglawblog.com/2011_06_01_archive.html.

Noon, Mike, and Rick Delbridge. "News From Behind My Hand: Gossip in Organizations." *Organization Studies* 14, no. 1 (1993): 23-36.

Nordquist, Richard. "Phatic Communication." *About.com.* Accessed December 16, 2012. http://grammar.about.com/od/pq/g/phatic-term.htm.

Nye, Robert D. *Conflict Among Humans: Some Basic Psychological and Social Psychological Considerations.* New York: Springer, 1973.

O'Brien, Barbara. "Right Speech: The Buddha's Words." Accessed May 13, 2015. http//Buddhism.about.com/od/theeightfoldpath/a/eightfold-path.htm.

Palatnik, Lori, and Bob Burg. *Gossip: Ten Pathways to Eliminate It from Your Life and Transform Your Soul.* Deerfield Beach, FL: Health Communications, 2002.

Pegues, Deborah Smith. *30 Days to Taming Your Tongue*. Eugene, OR: Harvest House, 2005.

Peters, Thomas J., and Robert H. Waterman, Jr. *In Search of Excellence: Lessons from America's Best-Run Companies*. New York: Harper Business, 2006.

Pohlmann, Marcus D. *African American Political Thought*. New York: Routledge, 2003.

Pope, Alexander. "Temple of Fame." *The Works of Alexander Pope*. London: W. Bowyer, 1717.

Post, Robert. "The Legal Regulation of Gossip: Backyard Chatter and the Mass Media." In *Good Gossip*, 65-71. Edited by Robert F. Goodman and Aaron Ben-Ze'ev. Lawrence: University Press of Kansas, 1994.

Powell, Colin. *It Worked for Me: In Life and Leadership*. New York: HarperCollins, 2012.

Quindlen, Anna. "In Today's World, Everyone Can Gossip Without Remorse." *Herald-News* (Joliet, IL), March 1, 2007.

Radhanath Swami. "Bahagavad-Gita." Accessed September 5, 2012. www.radhanathswami.com/tag/bhagavad-gita.

Rath, Tom, and Donald O. Clifton. *How Full Is Your Bucket?* New York: Gallup Press, 2004.

Rich, Tracey R. "Speech and Lashon Ha-Ra." *Judaism 101*. Accessed May 29, 2006. http://www.jewfaq.org/speech.htm.

Rosnow, Ralph L., and Eric K. Foster. "Rumor and Gossip Research." *American Psychological Association, Psychological Science Agenda* 19, no. 4 (April 2005). http://www.apa.org/science/about/psa/2005/04/gossip.aspx.

Rosnow, Ralph L., and Gary Alan Fine. *Rumor and Gossip: The Social Psychology of Hearsay*. New York: Elsevier Scientific, 1976.

Rubin, Gretchen. *The Happiness Project: Or, Why I Spent a Year Trying to Sing in the Morning, Clean My Closets, Fight Right, Read Aristotle and Generally Have More Fun*. New York: Harper, 2011.

Ruiz, Miguel. *The Four Agreements: A Practical Guide to Personal Freedom*. San Rafael, CA: Amber-Allen, 1997.

Sanders, Tim. *Love Is the Killer App: How to Win Business and Influence Friends*. New York: Crown Business, 2002.

Seligman, Martin E.P. *Authentic Happiness: Using the New Positive Psychology to Realize Your Potential for Lasting Fulfillment*. New York: Free Press, 2002.

___. *Flourish: A Visionary New Understanding of Happiness and Well-Being*. New York: Free Press, 2012.

___. *What You Can Change and What You Can't: The Complete Guide to Successful Self-Improvement*. New York: Vintage Books, 2007.

Shibutani, Tomatsu. *Improvised News: A Sociological Study of Rumor*. Indianapolis: Bobbs-Merrill, 1966.

Simmons, Melody. "After Shooting, Amish School Embodies Effort to Heal." *New York Times* (New York, NY), Jan. 31, 2007.

"The Sin of Gossip and Tale Bearing." Accessed May 29, 2006. www.wolfe-borobible.com.

Smith, Bob. "Care and Feeding of the Office Grapevine." *Management Review* 85, no. 2 (1996): 6.

Smith, Linell Nash, ed. "Don't Even Tell Your Wife, Particularly." *The Best of Ogden Nash*. Chicago: Ivan R. Dee, 2007.

Spacks, Patricia Meyer. *Gossip*. New York, Alfred A. Knopf, 1985.

Suess, George. "What Would Emeril Do?" *Perdido: Leadership with a Conscience*, Winter 2006.

Tannen, Deborah. *You Just Don't Understand: Women and Men in Conversation*. New York: William Morrow, 1990.

Telushkin, Joseph. *Words That Hurt, Words That Heal: How to Choose Words Wisely and Well*. New York: Harper, 1996.

"Town Settles Federal Employment Lawsuit." *Boston Globe* (Boston, MA), Nov. 2, 2008. http://www.boston.com/news/local/articles/2008/11/02/rollover_car_crash_on_pike_kills_man_23.

Turner, Dale. *Different Seasons: Twelve Months of Wisdom and Inspiration.* Homewood, IL: High Tide Press, 1997.

___. *Imperfect Alternatives: Spiritual Insights for Confronting the Controversial and the Personal.* Homewood, IL: High Tide Press, 2005.

Tutu, Desmond. "Quotes." *Goodreads.* Accessed May 14, 2013. http://www.goodreads.com/author/quotes/5943.Desmond_Tutu,

Twain Mark. *Following the Equator: A Journey Around the World.* Hartford: American Publishing,1897. http://www.twainquotes.com/Slander.html.

___. *Mark Twain's Letters from Hawaii.* Honolulu: University of Hawaii Press, 1975.

Van Buren, Abigail. "Dear Abby: Flow of Office Gossip Is Impossible to Stanch (June 26, 2006)." *Uexpress.* http://www.uexpress.com/dear-abby/2006/6/26/flow-of-office-gossip-is-impossible.

Vries, Lloyd. "N.H. Town Fires 4 Employees for Gossiping." CBS News. Last modified May 23, 2007. http://www.cbsnews.com/news/nh-town-fires-4-employees-for-gossiping.

Wakeman, Cy. *Reality-Based Leadership: Ditch the Drama, Restore Sanity to the Workplace, and Turn Excuses into Results.* Hoboken, NJ: Jossey-Bass, 2010.

"Whistle - But Don't Tweet - While You Work." *Robert Half Technology.* Last modified October 6, 2009. http://rht.mediaroom.com/index.php?s=131&item=790.

White, Kaila. "Controversial Yik Yak 'Gossip' App Gains Popularity." *USA Today Network.* Last modified December 24, 2014. http://www.usa-today.com/story/news/nation-now/2014/12/24/yik-yak-app-college-arizona/20856275.

Whitehouse, Kaja. "Water-Cooler App Draws Ire from Companies." *USA Today*. Last modified January 16, 2015. http://www.usatoday.com/story/tech/2015/01/16/app-google-ibm-ebay-amazon-wattercooler-anonymous/21815669.

Williams, Timothy, and Martie Geltz. "Watering the Periwinkle." *Perdido: Leadership with a Conscience*, Spring 2003.

Wilson, David Sloan, and Kevin M. Kniffin. "Utilities of Gossip Across Organizational Levels: Multilevel Selection, Free-Riders, and Teams." *Human Nature* 16, no. 3 (2005): 278-292.

Winfield, Nicole. "Pope Warns Against Mediocrity, Gossip in Vatican." AP: The Big Story. Last modified December 21, 2013. http://bigstory.ap.org/article/pope-warns-against-mediocrity-gossip-vatican.

# INDEX

# H

# W

# ABOUT THE AUTHORS

**ART DYKSTRA**, President and CEO of Trinity Services, Inc., as well as author and speaker, began his career with the Illinois Department of Mental Health and Developmental Disabilities. Over a period of 20 years, he assumed positions of greater responsibility, including serving as director for two state-operated developmental centers, Chicago Regional Administrator for Developmental Disabilities and public policy advisor to the Director of the Department of Human Services.

In 1987, he became the executive director of Trinity Services, a small school that served children and adults with developmental disabilities. Since that time, Trinity has grown into a statewide organization, developed programs in Reno, NV, expanded services to persons with mental illness, and now operates over 12 major programs and several support businesses.

Art has also taught classes at the undergraduate and graduate level in psychology, public administration and executive leadership at several state and public universities. He is a frequent speaker at local, state and national conferences, sharing ideas on such topics as leadership, organizational culture, strategic planning and systems thinking. In addition, Art has authored numerous journal articles, publications and thought pieces. He is perhaps best known for *Outcome Management*, a book providing insights and person-centered applications for those leading disability organizations.

He attended Bethel University in St. Paul, MN, and received a master's degree in clinical psychology from Bradley University. He has served as President of the Board on The Council on Quality and Leadership (CQL), and president of the Illinois Chapter of the American Association on Intellectual and Developmental Disabilities (AAIDD), the Illinois Council of Executive Directors of the ARC, and the Illinois Association of Rehabilitation Facilities (IARF). He currently serves on numerous boards and advisory councils and is a fellow of the national American Association on Intellectual and Developmental Disabilities.

These leadership positions, including his work as the CEO of Trinity Services, have given him numerous opportunities to experience the destructive effect of malicious gossip in different organizations. They have also provided a venue within which he could work with staff to help build a positive, values affirming workplace culture.

Art and his wife, Anita, reside in New Lenox, IL. In his spare time, he enjoys fishing, gardening and catching frogs.

**TIMOTHY WILLIAMS**, an arbitrator, educator and speaker, is a practicing dispute resolver with 41 years of experience as a mediator, ombudsperson, facilitator, fact-finder and arbitrator. During that time, he has worked to resolve more than 1,500 labor disputes, including discipline cases involving gossip. He has provided services in both public and private organizations, designing and implementing dispute prevention/resolution systems.

He has taught courses in conflict management, organizational communications, negotiations, and interpersonal communications at Hamline University, the University of Minnesota, Southern Oregon State College and Portland State University. At Portland

State University, he teaches courses in human resource management, labor relations, labor negotiations and contract administration for the Division of Public Administration, Mark O. Hatfield School of Government.

Tim is an experienced keynote speaker and seminarist. He has presented more than 2,000 one- and two-day training programs on such topics as leadership, employee discipline, supervision, labor relations, performance management and other HR topics. His interest in writing about gossip evolved out of his experience resolving disputes that originated with gossip and his background studying the importance of communication in organizations.

Tim received his B.A. from Bethel College and his M.A. and Ph.D. from the University of Minnesota. He is a member of the Labor Education Research Association (LERA) and the National Academy of Arbitrators (NAA).

His primary residence is in Portland, OR, and he is blessed with a large, active family and numerous friends, who keep him busy with golf, walking, skiing, travel, and other similar pursuits.

**ELAINE PORTERFIELD,** a journalist and writer, writes for a variety of publications and media outlets. She is especially interested in health care topics, and is currently managing editor of the Washington State Medical Association's monthly magazine.

During the course of her career, Elaine has written thousands of stories that have run in newspapers, magazines and websites around the world. Her work includes stints with the *News Tribune* of Tacoma, the *Seattle Post-Intelligencer*, the Reuters News Service and *People* magazine. She's also served as a columnist for the MSN site "Moms Homeroom," writing on early learning and the brain. In addition, she has served as a newsletter editor for Comcast/Xfinity and as a travel writer with nbc.com. Her many years of work as a reporter piqued her interest in the problems of gossip as news and gave her firsthand experience in seeing the destructive side of gossip particularly as it impacts government and politics.

Elaine received her B.A. from Western Washington University in English with a minor in biology, and a master's degree from the Medill School of Journalism at Northwestern University. She has been the recipient of numerous awards for her reporting and writing, including those from the National Association of Science Writers and the National Alliance for the Mentally Ill.

She lives in Seattle and enjoys running, yoga and traveling with her family. Her current writing project is a mystery for middle grade readers.

For updates, additional information
about gossip and an interview
with the authors visit:

**UnderstandingGossip.com/resources**

To order more copies of this and
other High Tide Press publications
go to HighTidePress.com.

Quantity discounts for training
and group study.